★

SEVEN WAYS

TO CHANGE THE WORLD

D0293091

Copyright © 2008 by Jim Wallis

The author asserts the moral right
to be identified as the author of this work

A Lion Book
an imprint of
Lion Hudson plc
Wilkinson House, Jordan Hill Road,
Oxford OX2 8DR, England
www.lionhudson.com
ISBN 978 0 7459 5298 7

First HarperCollins edition 2008
First Lion edition 2008
10 9 8 7 6 5 4 3 2 1 0

Published by arrangement with HarperOne,
an imprint of HarperCollins Publishers, New York, USA

All rights reserved

Acknowledgments
Unless otherwise noted, all biblical quotations have been taken
from the New Revised Standard Version (NRSV) of the Bible

The text paper used in this book has been made from wood
independently certified as having come from sustainable forests

A catalogue record for this book is available
from the British Library

Typeset in 10.5/13 Fairfield LH
Printed and bound in Great Britian
by MPG Books, Cornwall

Praise for *Seven Ways to Change the World*

I had always been a skeptic of the church of personal peace and prosperity… of righteous people standing in a holy huddle while the world rages outside the stained glass. But I've learned that there are many people of the cloth who are also in the world – from debt cancellation to the fight against AIDS and for human rights they are on the march. Jim Wallis isn't just part of this movement – he's out front carrying a bullhorn.

Bono, lead singer, U2

T.S. Eliot once wrote that "no culture has appeared or developed except together with a religion". Jim Wallis shows in these pages how faith that shaped, can also renew, a civilization.

The Rt Revd James Jones, Bishop of Liverpool

Jim Wallis has done it again. *Seven Ways to Change the World* is heady with life stories, biblical reflection and political engagement. It is the grassroots guide to "How to change the world and why". Wallis writes at breathtaking speed taking us to the heart of the issues of the day, and inviting us to join in the task of bringing in God's kingdom. It's a book to read… and then to live.

The Rt Revd Peter B. Price, Bishop of Bath and Wells

Jim Wallis writes with a passion and enthusiasm which cannot help but infect the reader with an irresistible hope. In *Seven Ways to Change the World* he outlines a vision that would have had the great nineteenth-century evangelical reformers rising to their feet in applause. It is a vision of a new movement of social change, passionate for justice and driven by faith.

Joel Edwards, General Director, Evangelical Alliance UK

Wallis's book makes it clear that our Christian faith must interact with these questions of human suffering and injustice. Regardless of whether you land where Wallis does on particulars, if you are not asking these questions with him, you are missing out on the strategic battleground of the kingdom of God.

Gary Haugen, President of International Justice Mission

A thoughtful and stirring call to broaden our horizons and to dream, plan and work for a different reality. If you want to catch what Jim Wallis has got, read *Seven Ways to Change the World*.

Steve Chalke MBE, Founder of Oasis Global and Faithworks

The twenty-first century has been the best of times and the worst of times for religion in public life: highly visible yet highly divisive. Wallis has spent a lifetime showing that it need not be this way and argues in this book that "something is happening", the theo-political landscape is changing. *Seven Ways to Change the World* is passionate, thoughtful, biblical, personal, and, above all, hopeful. Wallis argues that "faith is coming back to life as a force for progessive social change" and outlines theological foundations, moral principles and inspiring examples that can make that change real and lasting. It is an indispensable read for those interested in the relationship between faith and politics today.

Nick Spencer, Director of Studies, Theos

Jim has sounded a clarion call once again for a revival amongst those of us who call ourselves Christlike. He hasn't called us to church however. Or to change the tune of our songs. He has called us to link, more progressively, evangelism and social action. Jim suggests that the world cannot change the justice gap unless we personally are changed – he says that "personal transformation is necessary for social movements... and social movements are necessary to transform politics". In many ways the church has not walked away from the poor and the oppressed – we can all point to our charity of choice and say we support it – but Jim's call is different and he is right. Giving is important, but personal change is the answer, especially in such a small connected world. Only when our life reflects that of personal sacrifice, of self denial, so that another can have, will we make a difference in this world.

Duncan Parker, Director of International Development (UK),
The Salvation Army

Many of the great revivals have happened on both sides of the Atlantic. From his experience in the US Jim Wallis has issued a bold challenge to Christians in the UK to experience another Great Awakening: It is time for the churches to put aside the defence of their own narrow religious interests, and embrace instead the fullness of the Gospel which calls us to an agenda of peacemaking, justice and radical love.

Jonathan Bartley, Director of Ekklesia thinktank

SEVEN WAYS
TO CHANGE THE WORLD

Reviving Faith and Politics

JIM WALLIS

LION

This book is dedicated to James Wallis Sr.,
my father, whose faith was the foundation for mine.

CONTENTS

FOREWORD BY JIMMY CARTER

In one of my most recent books, titled *Our Endangered Values*, I attempted to describe the existing relationships among religion, politics, and some of our nation's historical values. Mine was a fairly narrow focus, based primarily on my personal experiences as a Christian and as a former participant in national and international affairs. Jim Wallis came to my home in Plains and provided me with some extremely valuable advice on the emphases in my text.

It was obvious to me (and perhaps to Jim) that a much broader presentation was needed, with a special explanation of how our religious faith affects the totality of our nation's basic values, politics, and political leadership. It was also obvious that an added question needed to be answered in order to place these complex relationships into better perspective for readers: down through generations of Americans and our political leaders, what has been the history of the effect of religious faith on the shaping of political decisions?

To answer this question clearly and definitively would be possible for only a few people. I am grateful that Jim Wallis has decided to write this book, and has chosen this moment to do so. There has never been a more propitious time for the citizens of our country to comprehend this subject more clearly. It is important not only as an exercise in politics during election time (it is always election time in a democracy like ours); the crucial nature of the dissertation is that there is an almost unprecedented serious and persistent division among us – with faith and politics intertwined as never before in creating disharmony.

Public opinion polls show that, uniquely among citizens of Western democracies, we Americans exemplify a strong and undeviating commitment to our multiple religious faiths. At the same time, there has been a fairly recent violation of the time-honoured premise that, as Thomas Jefferson proclaimed, a wall should be maintained between church and state. Jim Wallis is able to give vital advice to those who would like to resolve this apparent quandary, and to do so in a way that will ease rather than exacerbate existing tensions and misunderstandings in the political and religious arenas.

What we need is a way to tap the power of the revival of faith in order to inspire and encourage the secular social reforms that are espoused in all the great religions. This is the pathway described to us in this book.

Jimmy Carter

FOREWORD BY ROWAN WILLIAMS

Jim Wallis has already begun to change the face of Christian politics in the United States, steadily pulling evangelical believers towards an agenda dominated not by issues of purely individual morality but by questions around poverty and justice and the global environment. His infectious energy as a writer and speaker has taken his message to hundreds of thousands in the States and across the world; the publication of this book in the United Kingdom should be a wake-up call to British Christians to join fully in what Jim calls a 'Justice Revival', a wave of renewed discipleship that issues in changing our world in the direction of God's kingdom.

That may be – no, it is – a task we shall never finish within human history; but God always asks us simply to start, trusting in his grace and his Spirit. Again and again in this book, we are faced with direct questions as to what we can do where we are, and we are reminded that no one is too young or too weak to join in. Inevitably, much of it is about the particular situation of the United States at present. But I hope that British readers will avoid the twofold temptation here of thinking that all the real problems belong with Them Over the Atlantic rather than us, and of imagining that what's possible by way of renewal and conversion and transforming action over there is impossible for us in Britain. Just over two hundred years ago, remember, Christian people in this country managed to change the face of the world by agitating for the abolition of the slave trade – not to mention all sorts of other great shifts in what the country took for granted about human dignity and liberty.

It can be done. This is a moving, vivid, personal summons in the name of Christ to a comprehensive conversion. I shall be doing my best to respond and to start again in being a Christian! I hope many more will respond likewise.

Rowan Williams,
Archbishop of Canterbury

PREFACE TO THE
BRITISH EDITION

I believe that the people of the UK are ready for the message of this book. My wife, Joy Carroll, is a Brit, and we frequently get across the pond. Joy was recently invited to return to London for the filming of the final two episodes of the hit comedy series, *The Vicar of Dibley*, and to be interviewed for the special television farewell to Dibley, called *The Story of Dibley*. Joy served as script consultant to the show and an informal role model, working closely with its leading character, Dawn French, and series writer, David Curtis. She thinks the funny and creative series about a female vicar in the rural English countryside gave a very human face to women priests and helped the nation's big transition to the ordination of women in the Church of England (Joy was among the first group of women to be ordained fifteen years ago). Many of the issues of social justice raised in this book are mirrored in the *Vicar of Dibley* series.

But even more central to my optimism are the relationships I have been blessed to have with some of Britain's leaders of both church and state.

I vividly remember a conversation with the then Chancellor of the Exchequer, Gordon Brown – now the Prime Minister. It was a private breakfast and we were talking about poverty, as we have for the last ten years. He said, "For the first time, we have the knowledge, the information, the technology and the resources to end extreme poverty as we know it. What we lack is the moral and political will." Then the Scotsman who is so passionate about the issue of global poverty leaned across the table at 11 Downing Street and said, "That's your job, in the churches." It felt like an altar call to the churches from a political leader who is virtually asking to be pushed by a movement to make big changes. Brown knows it's his responsibility too, and the recent speeches he has made (referred to in this book) are a virtual blueprint for a vision of globalization that is inclusive of the most vulnerable across the globe.

I am also very hopeful about the leadership of Rowan Williams, the Archbishop of Canterbury. In the run-up to the war in Iraq, Williams was especially prophetic, once quoting, "When all you have is hammers, everything looks like a nail." He is an exemplary church leader, a deeply respected theologian and scholar, a poet, and a genuine contemplative – all rare these days. What one hears in his strong words is, indeed, the authentic voice of prophetic criticism (again rare among church leaders these days).

John Sentamu, the Archbishop of York, has become known for his prophetic leadership on economic justice; Peter Price, Bishop of Bath and Wells, has been prophetically outspoken on the war in Iraq; and I recently had dinner with James Jones, the Bishop of Liverpool, who is providing the same kind of prophetic leadership on the issue of the environment and global warming in particular, leading his diocese last Lenton season in a "carbon fast". Just last month in Washington, I met again with long-time friend Joel Edwards, the leader of Evangelical Alliance in the UK and the international chairperson of the Micah Challenge, which is described in this book as the very hopeful movement from the churches of the global south focused on achieving the Millennium Development Goals, aimed at cutting extreme poverty in half by the year 2015. I have also enjoyed working with Steve Chalke, the evangelical leader who has become such a creative social entrepreneur in the UK in urban ministry and in finding solutions to such problems as education for disadvantaged youth.

All these are topics in this book, *Seven Ways to Change the World*, and these commitments are already well underway in the UK. The British people are generally much more globally aware and concerned than many Americans, and have a strong sense of "the common good" in their social life together, a central theme of this book. Your "Jubilee 2000" movement at the turn of the century around global debt relief and your recent "Make Poverty History" campaign in 2005 are discussed in this book as models for how people of faith can help catalyze social movements in society.

Both of my children are "bilingual", speaking both the English of the English and the English of the Americans, and we love both countries. In the run-up to the war in Iraq, former Prime Minister Tony Blair generously granted me and a small delegation of American church leaders a meeting with him at 10 Downing Street, where I said true friends keep their friends from making mistakes. Sadly, that didn't happen over the war in Iraq; but I am still convinced that Britain's leadership on issues of global poverty, climate change, human rights and a better path to security could significantly influence the United States' policies and offer a better kind of leadership "by example", rather than "by empire". You Brits could be the friend that we Yanks really need, and I hope you like this book.

Jim Wallis

ACKNOWLEDGMENTS

As every author knows, writing books is never just a solitary task. There are so many others involved: those who actually help you research or produce the book, those close family members and friends who are personally affected by your writing schedule and pre-occupation, those colleagues whose ideas help to shape yours, and those historical figures whose lives and work have inspired your own.

There are, as always, many people to thank for this book. First to thank is my partner and friend, Duane Shank, who again did research for this book and was my primary editor and collaborator throughout the project. Jim Rice, the editor of *Sojourners* and a long-time colleague, also did invaluable editing in the final stages. Swanee Hunt generously offered hospitality for me and my family in the mountains where I initially outlined the book. Mary Ann Richardson graciously provided a place at the beach to write during the precious days I was able to get away from Washington and other commitments. She also added wise editorial counsel, along with my old friend and former editor Roy Carlisle.

The community that is Sojourners is the continual context for my writing, speaking, and all my work; and anchors me in a perspective and vision that stay constant over the years. My co-workers are an extraordinary bunch, and are the ones who keep all our work going day after day. They all, either directly or indirectly, have a part in this book. In addition to Duane and Jim, others offered comments on parts of the manuscript and on the title, and many people here are involved with shaping the events of the book tours which we like to turn into "movement tours". They include Ryan Beiler, Joan Bisset, Jeff Carr, Robin Filmore, Larisa Friesen, Aaron Graham, Chuck Gutenson, Tim Kumfer, Chris LaTondresse, Deanna Murshed, Jack Pannell, Yonce Shelton, Sondra Shepley, Ed Spivey, Adam Taylor, and Heidi Thompson.

Key interviews and conversations also contributed to this book, including with syndicated columnists E.J. Dionne and Nicholas Kristof (must-reads for me), historian Michael Kazin, church leader and longtime friend Wes Granberg-Michaelson, author Brian McLaren (who is also my board chair), journalist and author Amy Sullivan, theologian and ethicist Glen Stassen, professor and strategist David Cortright, Rich Cizik of the National Association of Evangelicals, John Carr of the United States Catholic Conference of Bishops, David Beckmann of Bread for the World, Steve Waldman and David Kuo of Beliefnet who host the God's Politics blog, conservative leader Richard Land, rock star activist Bono, media strategist Mike McCurry, new British Prime Minister Gordon Brown, former Congressman Tony Hall, and former President Jimmy Carter, whom I also wish to thank for the foreword to this book.

Throughout this book, I name the leaders of movements past who have combined faith and social justice. Some of them, like Martin Luther King Jr., Dorothy Day, Dietrich Bonhoeffer, John Howard Yoder, and William Stringfellow, have a regular presence and influence with me. I call them my "cloud of witnesses", after the biblical phrase, and I have photos of dozens of them in my study, on the wall above the desk where I write.

Today, there are many other close colleagues who are sounding boards, collaborators, kindred spirits, and partners whom I am proud to call friends and with whom I stand shoulder to shoulder in building those same movements today; some of which represent a new generation of faith-inspired activists who now inspire me. Several of them, like Randall Balmer, Diana Butler Bass, Michael Battle, Tony Campolo, Noel Castellanos, Shane Claiborne, Chap Clark, Robert Franklin, Freddie Haynes, Obery Hendricks, Tony Jones, Alexia Kelley, Christa Mazzone, Cheryl Sanders, Barbara Brown Taylor, and Romal Tune, are now part of the "Red Letter Christians" whom I discuss in the Epilogue. Other longtime companions and key allies include Tom Allio, David Batstone, David Black, Peter Borgdorf, Steve Chalk, Tim Costello, Yvonne Delk, Ray East, Joel Edwards, Peggy Flanagan, Joel Hunter, Helene Slessarev-Jamir, Linda Lader, Rich Nathan, Mary Nelson, Glenn Palmberg, John Perkins, Sam Rodriquez, Ron Sider, Barbara Williams Skinner, Mara Vanderslice, and Sharon Watkins. And, of course, there are many other key partners around the country and across the globe who are too numerous to mention. All of them have shaped what you will read in this book.

My friends at HarperOne all have a big part in this book. My editor, Eric Brandt, is simply the best at taking what I do and making it better. My former agent and now publisher Mark Tauber and editorial director Mickey Maudlin are good friends and always very helpful to me in shaping book content and strategy. Director of Marketing Claudia Boutote, Director of Media Relations Suzanne Wickham, Associate Director of

Marketing Laina Adler, and independent publicist Kelly Hughes are so good at getting the word out. And I want to especially thank my agent, Bob Barnet, who is one of the smartest in publishing and really looks after his authors.

Last, but most important, my wife Joy, and my two sons Luke and Jack, are obviously impacted by my book writing and are amazingly supportive. Joy is always a good dialogue partner about my thinking and writing and now nine-year-old Luke is too. Both Luke and four-year-old Jack supply me with an endless supply of stories and insights that eventually make their way into my writing and speaking. I am very blessed to have a home base that literally anchors my life.

This book is dedicated to my father, who passed away while I was writing it. Jim Wallis Sr. was a man of faith who gave me the foundation for mine. He would have loved this book because it speaks of what faith can do, and that was the point of his whole life. I miss him terribly and, without the lessons he taught me, a book like this would not have been possible. This is for you, Dad. (I include the eulogy I gave at my father's funeral in the book's appendix for those readers who would like to know more about the influences that have shaped my life.)

INTRODUCTION
Something is Happening

Admittedly, religion can be a confusing subject. My then-seven-year-old son Luke came to my wife and me one day looking very concerned: "Mom, Dad, I'm worried about Max and Jonah [two of his second-grade pals on the Little League baseball team that I coach]. I don't think they believe in God or Jesus. They're vegetarians!" So Joy and I decided to take Luke to one of my book tour events in Oregon, where he would meet some godly vegetarians.

But the confusion is more serious than the misunderstandings of a little boy. After I appeared one night on Jon Stewart's *Daily Show*, I received thousands of e-mails that said things like, "I lost my faith because of television preachers, bad religious fund-raising, paedophile priests, cover-up bishops, and White House theology." Or, amazing to me, they would say, "I didn't know that Christians could care about poverty, the environment, or the war in Iraq." But when they hear that people of faith do care, and have fought for social justice, this new generation gets very excited. I meet those young people on the road all over the country, and many say to me, "I came to faith because of your book; what's next?" What's next is what this book is about.

Something is happening. Faith is being applied to social justice in ways that we might have never imagined just a few short years ago. Spiritual power is being harnessed to address the greatest social challenges that we face today.

There have been other periods in history when faith tangibly changed things. Often called "Great Awakenings", they are times when the "revival" of faith alters societies. In fact, the historians say that spiritual activity isn't called revival until it changes something, not just in people's inner lives but in society. Revivals often occur when politics is broken, when it fails to address the most significant moral issues of the day. Social movements then rise up to change politics, and the best movements usually have spiritual foundations.

What historians call the First Great Awakening took place in the 1730s and 1740s. Its leaders were preachers such as Jonathan Edwards and Gilbert Tennent, and a travelling British preacher named George

Whitefield, who had worked with John Wesley. Many credit that uprising of faith with helping to spark American independence and a new nation. That is, participating in a religious awakening helped to create a political "awakening".

The Second Great Awakening occurred between 1800 and the 1830s. Led by revivalists such as Charles Finney and Jonathan Blanchard, it embraced the clear call for the abolition of slavery that preceded the Civil War. Finney, in particular, insisted that spiritual conversion must lead to social reform. This awakening also led to the origins of Christian feminism, in leaders such as Lucy Stone and Angelina and Sarah Grimke.

The Third Great Awakening, in the latter half of the nineteenth century and the early part of the twentieth, helped usher in the progressive era, the social gospel movement, and the New Deal. This era, with its special focus on poverty, led to social reforms such as child labour law improvements, the settlement house movement, the career of social work, and youth organizations such as the YMCA. Another major focus was the temperance movement. One result was the populist presidential campaigns of William Jennings Bryan.

I regard the black church's leadership of the civil rights movement in the 1950s and 1960s as another "great awakening" of faith that changed politics. Without the participants' deep grounding in the black church, Dr. Martin Luther King Jr. and the movement would not have succeeded.

This book is not a historical treatment of any of those previous great awakenings, although it consciously draws on all of them. Rather, it is both an observation and a call regarding what may be the next one – a new great awakening – in our time. As I travel around America, I can see and feel new things happening – I find a revival of faith that is directly leading to new calls for and commitments to social justice. That rebirth and renewal of faith is being directly applied to the moral and biblical scandal of poverty around the globe and here at home, to the crises of environmental degradation and climate change that pose such a threat to God's creation, and to the multiple assaults on human life and dignity that shame our world.

Ironically, despite how the Religious Right has discredited the role of faith in politics in recent decades, faith is now coming back to life as a force for progressive social change. Though religion had come to be seen by many as the problem, faith may indeed be making a comeback as the catalyst that could provide the tipping point in finding solutions to the biggest and most significant moral and social crises of our world today.

Many of the great social issues we face feel like huge, unmovable mountains: disease pandemics that kill millions; massive inequality that imprisons half the world's people in miserable poverty; human sexual and economic trafficking; dangerous climatic changes in the earth's temperature; genocide that no one seems able to stop; so many threats to the sanctity of human life; endless violations of human dignity; and the alarming unravelling of both family and community systems.

At the same time, though, many people, especially a new generation, are discovering a key insight from the Bible: if we have faith as small as the "grain of a mustard seed", we can "move mountains". That's a good thing, because we have some real mountains to move in our world today – problems and challenges so big that they become a job for faith, a job for spiritual power applied to social change. Indeed, that's why we call it *faith*, especially needed when our problems seem overwhelming and the odds are against us. It may be that only a revival of faith can spark the necessary changes in public opinion and political will on the really big issues, and that a spiritual transformation is necessary for social change. It's about changing hearts and minds on many of the biggest moral issues of public life that fundamentally challenge who we are and what we believe. Revival is always about what God can do through us, and is now doing afresh, especially when people are adrift and society is in danger.

In addition to the great awakenings in American history, there have been many times when faith has caught fire and changed social and political circumstances in other countries around the world. This book is about the new awakening or revival that may be upon us, both in the United States and across the globe. The book doesn't claim to be starting anything but merely pointing to what is already happening and calling us to take the next steps. It is about what faith has done, can do, and might be about to do again – if we make the necessary commitments.

Such revivals of faith applied to our most significant social and public challenges also show the capacity to bring people together – even across traditional political boundaries and divisions – to find real answers and solutions. That's because faith and spirituality can take us deeper than politics can, with a moral commitment that allows us to transcend our usual ideological debates. That moral appeal can truly help us find common ground by moving to higher ground. And this is a moment filled with the opportunity for transformation – both personal and political. Indeed, they now depend on each other.

Three years ago I wrote a book called *God's Politics: Why the American Right Gets It Wrong and the Left Doesn't Get It*. The subtitle said it all. The narrow agenda of the Religious Right was in control of the public conversation about religion and politics in America, and the secular left

seemed uncomfortable even discussing "moral values". Since then, many
people have asked me what has changed. I answer: Everything.

God's Politics challenged America to "take back the faith" from the
Religious Right. And we did, as millions of Americans stood up and spoke
up for a different kind of faith. As I say to overflow crowds around the
country, "The monologue of the Religious Right is over, and a new dialogue
has now begun." And everybody cheers. In the churches, a combination of
deeper compassion and better theology has moved many far beyond the
partisan politics of the Religious Right. In politics, we are beginning to see
a levelling of the playing field between the parties on religion and "moral
values" (*Time* magazine called it a "leveling of the praying field"); and the
media are finally beginning to cover the many and diverse voices of faith.
These are all big changes in American life, and the rest of the world is
taking notice.

The hard-core Religious Right continues to get it wrong, still attempting
to restrict the language of "moral values" to just two issues – abortion and
gay marriage. But evangelicals are deserting the Religious Right in droves,
especially among a new generation of pastors and young people. The
evangelical social agenda is now much broader and deeper, engaging issues
such as poverty and economic justice, global warming, HIV/AIDS, sex
trafficking, genocide in Darfur, and the ethics of the war in Iraq. Catholics
are recovering their social teaching; mainline Protestants are asserting
their faith more aggressively; a new generation of young black, Latino, and
Asian-American pastors are coming of age for justice; Jewish renewal and
a more moderate Islam are on the rise; and a whole new denomination has
emerged – the "spiritual but not religious".

Even more amazing, the left – including the Democrats – is starting
to get it. Progressive politics is remembering its own religious history
and recovering the language of faith. Democrats are learning to connect
issues with values, engaging with the faith community, and running
more candidates who have been emboldened to come out of the closet
as believers. Many Republicans have also had it with the Religious Right.
Both sides are asking how to connect a deeper understanding of faith and
values with politics. People know now that God is neither a Republican
nor a Democrat, and we are all learning that religion is not supposed to
be in the pocket of any political party, but rather calls them all to moral
accountability.

So what's next? What comes after *God's Politics*?

Politics is still broken, and most Americans feel it. Politics has failed to
solve the big issues of our time. Whenever that happens, social movements

begin to emerge, usually around key moral issues, to challenge, move, and change politics. And, as many have noted, the best social movements usually have spiritual underpinnings. I believe that politics can be changed to deal with the many crises we face – but it probably won't be changed without the energy, commitment, and hope that powerful faith and spirituality can bring.

We have now entered the post-Religious Right era. That doesn't mean the Religious Right is dead or won't still be an influence in Republican party politics. But its "era", the peak of its influence, and its monopoly over faith and politics are now gone. Although religion has been given a negative image in the last few decades, the years ahead may be surprisingly shaped by a dynamic and more progressive faith that helps make needed social change possible. I have always been a progressive evangelical. "Progressive evangelical" has seemed to be a misnomer in recent years, but now it is becoming a movement. And I can point to a whole new generation as proof of that.

It's time to remember the spiritual revivals that led to the abolition of slave trafficking in Britain and slavery in the U.S., the centrality of the black church's leadership in the U.S. civil rights movement, the deeply Catholic roots of the Solidarity movement in Poland that led to the overthrow of communism. It's time to recall how liberation theology in Latin America helped pave the way for new democracies, how Desmond Tutu and the South African churches served to inspire victory over apartheid, how the Dalai Lama is keeping hope alive for millions of Tibetans, and, today, how the growing evangelical and Pentecostal churches of the global South (the developing or underdeveloped countries, primarily in the Southern hemisphere) are mobilizing to challenge the injustices of the global economy.

I believe that we are seeing the beginnings of a similar movement again in America. I believe we are poised on the edge of what might become another spiritual revival or awakening that will change things – big things in the world. We may be seeing the beginning of a revival for justice.

And that's what this new book is about. We've gone from a narrow religious agenda, which was used as a wedge to divide people, to a wider and deeper vision of faith and values, which could be the bridge that brings diverse people and groups together on some of the most significant issues of our time. For too long, ideological religion was a big part of our problems, but now an engaged spirituality could be a big part of our solutions.

That is the hope I'm talking about here. First, I'll describe how spiritual revival has led to dramatic social change before, and how it could do so again. Second, I'll explain the big changes in the air today regarding both religion and politics, and how we may be ripe again for genuine revival. Third, I'll lay out the important theological foundations for why and how faith is supposed to change the world, and I'll describe the fundamental "rules of engagement" for people of faith. Fourth, I'll outline what could be a new public agenda of the moral centre – different from soulless centrism – and explore the idea of the common good with its many sources, both religious and secular. Together, they may provide both a vision and a spirituality for the public engagement of faith.

After listening to real people and their problems, how do we break the political stalemates? The answer to bad religion isn't secularism or withdrawal, but better religion – both personal and public. True faith wants public engagement, but not political co-optation. Can faith be involved in politics without being usurped by it? How does prophetic politics differ from partisan politics? Why might revival be necessary to reform, and how could spiritual renewal help create a new politics for the common good? And how do we move beyond both the right and the left? Are there new options, perhaps the "conservative radical", rooted in strong tradition but radical in seeking social justice?

Then each of seven chapters will focus on one of the big commitments that relate directly to the moral issues around which the revival of faith could provide what Malcolm Gladwell called the "tipping point" for change – commitments that have the capacity to bring us together even across former dividing lines. Rather than just reciting big problems again in another laundry list of doom and dread, we will focus on seven commitments that could make the ultimate difference in resolving the great challenges we face. The key is not simply to address the issues, but rather to identify the values that are necessary for social change. Our values lead to commitments. With each commitment, the application of the energy and constituencies of faith communities could provide what is needed for real change.

Each chapter will attempt to demonstrate the theological foundations and the moral principles that undergird the political goals we seek. I will ground each of the commitments in biblical narratives, themes, and stories, emphasizing that we should arrive at our convictions and prescriptions by faith if we are "people of the book" – or by our best moral values if we are not – rather than simply out of prior political and ideological commitments that then just lead to biblical or moral proof-texting.

In each chapter, too, I will address concrete policy directions that could bridge and even transcend our bitter partisan divides and move us forward.

All the way through, I'll offer stories of real people I've met on the road, with examples of how people of faith and conscience are already making a difference.

I'll describe how the big issues affect the real lives of people outside of Washington, D.C. I'll look at the reasons for the problems people face, and how politics-as-usual has failed to solve those problems but instead remains polarized and paralyzed. Then I'll suggest how new personal commitments and spiritual renewal could change our thinking, generate new social commitments, spark social movements, and lead to real solutions.

I will point to solutions on three levels: the personal/individual response, the congregational/communal response, and the national/international political response. So the outline for the book follows this pattern: stories of people, problems, and stalemate, and then biblical stories, commitments, renewal, movement, and solutions. Finally, change comes about when real action comes out of each of our stories.

The final chapter will be especially focused on the younger (under-thirty) generation and what I think its role could be. Everywhere I go now, the crowds are not only large and diverse, but also young – half are under thirty, and half of them are under twenty-five. I'll tell some of the best stories about my relationship to this next generation and these "emerging leaders". I hope to convince them and all my readers that hope and change are really possible, that we can make a difference, that people of faith have done big things before and will do them again. I want to dare people to dream big dreams, to tell them it is okay to have ideals and work toward cultural and political transformation. Finally, in the Epilogue, we will describe the rise of the "Red Letter Christians" and how "Justice Revivals" may be coming to a city near you.

Remember, the era of the Religious Right is now past, and it's up to all of us to create a new day.

I

REVIVAL TIME
When Faith Changes Politics

Arriving in Atlanta recently for a speaking appearance, I was happy. For any preacher, Atlanta is a wonderful place to be, a place where preaching is an art form. On this occasion, I returned to a favourite place – Ebenezer Baptist Church, the home congregation of Dr. Martin Luther King Jr. The pastor, Rev. Joe Roberts, was about to retire, and he welcomed me back warmly: "You've been to the old Israel, but now you're in the new Israel" (referring to the old historic church on Auburn Avenue and the brand-new sanctuary across the street where two thousand people had gathered that evening).

I remembered. It was indeed the old place I'd been to before, on the occasion of the first annual national holiday for the birthday of Dr. Martin Luther King Jr. For their Peace and Justice service, Ebenezer had invited a young white preacher. I was excited, but very nervous. When I stepped into that historic pulpit, I froze. Dr. King had preached here, so had his father, "Daddy" King, and so had countless leaders of the civil rights movement and the leading black pastors of our time. What was a young white kid from Detroit doing in this pulpit? I was, you might say, a little tentative as I began. "Well, Martin Luther King Jr. was for justice and... p-p-peace," I stammered, "... and probably we should be too." It was something short of powerful.

But then, from the lower left side of the church, a voice boomed back at me. "Oh, help him, Lord, help him! C'mon young man, you're supposed to preach." So I started to – a little. "Aw, you're not there yet!" he bellowed. He, of course, was enacting the "call and response" tradition of the black church, which I have grown to love. The old man was the "amen corner" of Ebenezer Baptist Church, and he proceeded with a litany of "well," "yes sir," "mercy, mercy," "preach it now," and lots of "amens" until I was proclaiming, prancing, and sweating – preaching my heart out until I was thoroughly exhausted when I finally finished. Afterward, I rushed down to my amen corner, whose name was Deacon Johnson. "You just pulled that sermon out of me," I exclaimed, breathless. Standing tall, he put his hands on my shoulders and smiled at me. "Son," he said, "I've raised up many a preacher in my time."

Deacon Johnson has passed away now, Rev. Roberts told me, but I will always remember him. Just as Deacon Johnson had pulled the best out of me, I reflected that night in Atlanta, that pulpit at Ebenezer Baptist Church (and the civil rights movement rooted there) had called out the very best from the American people. The truth is that we've got some bad stuff in us as Americans, but we've got some good stuff, too. Bad religion calls forth our worst stuff, but good religion calls out our best. I smiled as I remembered how Deacon Johnson had raised me up that night, and I climbed into the Ebenezer pulpit once again. *It's time for some good religion tonight,* I said to myself.

Two of the great hungers in our world today are the hunger for spirituality and the hunger for social justice. The connection between the two is the one the world is waiting for, especially the new generation. And the first hunger will empower the second.

Those on the Religious Right did it wrong, allowing their religion to become too partisan, too narrow, and too ideological. They were used by politics and did plenty of using themselves – using both people and issues to further their own agenda. But I believe their day is over, and we have now entered the post-Religious Right era. That's not just optimism, but a claim based on serious observation, as this book will point out.

Some people believe the alternative to bad religion is secularism, but that's wrong, too. The answer to bad religion is better religion – prophetic rather than partisan, broad and deep instead of narrow, and based on values as opposed to ideology. In America, and in most of the developing world, religion is here to stay. The question is not whether faith and spiritual values will be applied to politics, but how? Can faith enter public life in ways that are respectful of democracy, pluralism, and diversity? Could spiritual renewal supply the energy that makes social justice more achievable? Is revival necessary for reform? I believe the answer to all those questions is an emphatic yes, and this book will explain why.

One learns a lot crisscrossing the country for three decades, speaking (and listening) in every part of America and to a multitude of audiences and constituencies. Because much of my speaking is also preaching, I have been with almost every religious denomination and faith community in America, and have watched the relationship between faith and politics significantly affect the issues of society – for good and ill. I've also travelled extensively overseas and been an eyewitness to many of the greatest crises the world faces today, as well as the kinds of initiatives and movements capable of changing those realities.

I have been listening, and I'd like to report that many Americans, and in particular many people of faith in America, believe we can do better with both our religion and our politics – and around the world, people are hoping that we do. Listening to people across America and throughout the world convinces me that it is time for a new kind of politics, and that a better public engagement by faith communities could help get us there. The good news is that many people are ready for both – better religion and better politics. In fact, we may be approaching a new "revival" of faith, one that opens the door for real solutions that transcend partisan politics, and leads the way to concrete victories for social justice. I am suggesting that we need nothing less than a powerful movement of faith to renew American politics – one that effectively combines personal conversion and social justice. Personal transformation is necessary for social movements, and social movements are necessary to transform politics.

For all the travels, my base has been inner-city Washington, D.C., the "other Washington" – not far from the capital city's corridors of power but very distant from the experience of the power brokers who inhabit this place. Coming back and forth has been a spiritual discipline for me. Flying away to speak or organize somewhere or journeying the few blocks to meet with the nation's political leaders – from a place where poor people struggle every day – anchors me in the realities that most of the world's people know only too well. Place yields perspective (or, as they used to say in the civil rights movement, "Your perspective is shaped by what you see when you get out of bed in the morning"), and the perspectives that shape my faith and my politics come from all the places I've been – from midwestern Middle America where I grew up, to the urban war zones I've called home for more than three decades, to the foreign capitals and shantytowns I've visited where the world is viewed entirely differently than it is by most Americans.

My favourite part of any speaking event is the question-and-answer time – which often turns into "town meetings" in cities across the nation. From those amazing public forums and the countless individual conversations around the edges of them, I feel the hunger of Americans for a new vision of our life together, and the desire to engage their faith in dealing with the urgent problems we face. I don't speak as a representative of any party; I am not an elected official or a political partisan, but rather I view the world as a person of faith who believes that real solutions must transcend partisan politics.

I am also happy to report that, despite the big problems we face, there is a lot of good news around America and across the world. Part of the good news is that many evangelical and Pentecostal Christians are leaving the Religious Right while retaining their commitment to live out their faith in the world. That significant political shift has yet to be fully recognized by the nation's media and political elites, but it could eventually provide a tipping point on many of the major issues of our time.

I also find many Catholics (especially at some of America's leading Catholic universities) who are rediscovering the depth and breadth of Catholic teaching on social justice and the transforming idea of the common good. But they are not just discovering their own church's best teachings; they are also experiencing a rebirth of faith themselves, and making it personal. This personal renewal of faith and spirituality is also occurring in some of the declining mainline Protestant churches as they discover their mission in the world. Wherever renewal is happening in the old denominations, it usually occurs around the deepening or reawakening of spirituality and even evangelism. In fact, many are learning that the social mission of the church in the world will never be accomplished without the fire and passion that comes from personal faith. The social gospel cannot be sustained without a personal experience of Jesus, who brings the good news. The leader of one of those churches, Wesley Granberg-Michaelson of the Reformed Church in America, points out that the real difference today is not between evangelical churches and liberal churches, but between churches that are settled and those that are missional.

I am especially encouraged by a new generation of black pastors who want to move beyond merely eulogizing the civil rights movement and make their own history for justice. Similarly, young Latino pastors, many of them Pentecostal, are making the critical connection between evangelism and social justice. New generations of Asian-American Christians are moving beyond the protective conservatism of their parents to a more outward-looking faith directed into their communities. Emerging immigrant churches are rapidly changing the demographics and the perspective of U.S. Christianity. These Christians are people of colour whose dynamic faith is a clear alternative to the white churches – more theologically conservative than liberal Protestantism and more socially progressive than their white-middle-class evangelical counterparts. That makes these diverse American Christians more like the rapidly growing global church. Their mixture of a strong and vibrant personal faith with a passionate commitment to social justice (including for their own congregants, who themselves are often poor) is exactly the combination that can spark revival.

Jewish renewal is under way in many synagogues, where I have found worship as lively as in any church, and where people are rediscovering their own traditions of *shalom* (peace, wholeness, and justice) and *tikkun* (to repair and heal the world). And, very thankfully, a growing number of young Muslims (including many impressive women I meet while teaching my classes at Harvard) are working toward a new kind of Islam that challenges extremists.

Then, too, there is the rapidly expanding "new denomination" of those who say they are "spiritual but not religious" and believe that political solutions will require a moral commitment. Whether or not they are drawn to religion (some are and some aren't), this new generation of young people is eager to make a difference and hungry to find that critical connection between spirituality and social justice. It's not just college students I'm talking with, but high school, middle school, and even elementary school youth who are all eagerly joining the conversation about how we can change the world. In a postmodern and, for many, a post-Christian world, young activists are searching for something to be the engine that drives their passion for justice and a solid foundation for their lives. And when they see a lived-out faith that really is committed to justice, it often becomes evangelistic for them. Almost every week young people say to me, "I've been an activist for years, but now I'm seeking the faith to sustain my life."

These are the people I regularly meet on the road. Taken together, their constituencies comprise a large and influential number of Americans, and they are mirrored in their counterparts I've met around the world. Acting together, they could create the kind of social movements that have historically made a big difference on the great moral issues of history.

Revival and Reform

Kathleen Kennedy Townsend is the eldest child of Robert Kennedy and was formerly the lieutenant governor of Maryland. In her book *Failing America's Faithful* she reflects on America's revivalist history. "Throughout history, faith has gone underground only to emerge again in Great Awakenings, readying people for spiritual exploration. There are moments in history where people are ready and able to see the connection between the rituals of prayer and worship and the larger effort of improving God's world – and I believe we are now approaching just such a time."[1]

In 2007 we commemorated the two hundredth anniversary of the ending of the slave trade by Great Britain. A popular film told the story of William

Wilberforce, the British parliamentarian who led the antislavery campaign. As *Amazing Grace: The Story of William Wilberforce* powerfully portrayed, Wilberforce was a convert in the Wesleyan revivals of eighteenth-century Britain, and his Christian faith was the central driving force behind his relentless battle against slavery. He and a group of fellow Christian parliamentarians and other laypeople known as "the Saints" were behind many social reforms that swept across England in the late eighteenth and early nineteenth centuries.

Some years ago, on a trip to England, I walked through the historic Holy Trinity Church on Clapham Common in South London. This Anglican parish was Wilberforce's home church when he wrote Britain's anti-slave-trade legislation. The rector at Holy Trinity, Rev. David Isherwood, was very proud to show me around. On the wall were pictures of typically English-looking gentlemen who had helped turn their country upside down. Finally, the rector pointed to an old, well-worn table. "This is the table upon which William Wilberforce wrote the antislavery act," he said proudly. "We now use this table every Sunday for communion." I was struck that here, in a dramatic liturgical symbol, the secular and the sacred are brought together with powerful historical force. How did we ever separate them? On this table, the slave trade was outlawed and the body and blood of Christ was celebrated each week. What became of religion that believed its duty was to change its society on behalf of justice?

William Wilberforce and his group of friends profoundly changed the political and social climate of their time. Wilberforce was a convert in a revival that shook his society. His life and his vocation as a member of Parliament were dramatically and forever altered by his newfound faith, and Wilberforce became a force for moral politics. His mentor, John Newton, who worked in the slave trade before he became a minister, became well known for writing the beloved hymn "Amazing Grace". Later, Newton also used his influence as a religious leader in the battle against slavery. We can read his immortal words "Amazing grace, how sweet the sound, that saved a wretch like me" not only as a testimony of private guilt, individual salvation, and personal piety, but also as a clear and public turning away from the social sin of trafficking in human flesh. Newton wasn't just suffering from existential angst; he really was a wretch – a slave trader – and had his life transformed by Jesus Christ! Newton's conversion eventually produced a social and political transformation as well as a personal one. And that is the key to real revival.

The same became true of Wilberforce, who first heard Newton speak when he was young but regarded his real conversion as confirmed following a series of conversations with Newton in 1785–86. At the conclusion of their conversations, Newton said, "The Lord has raised you up for the good of the church and the good of the nation." Two years later Wilberforce introduced his first anti-slave-trade motion in Parliament. It was defeated, and it would be defeated nine more times before it passed in 1807. It was a historic and moral victory, but Wilberforce wouldn't be satisfied until slavery was abolished altogether. A new Wilberforce biography notes that "probably the last letter" John Wesley ever wrote encouraged Wilberforce: "Oh, be not weary in well-doing. Go on, in the name of God and in the power of His might."[2] Wilberforce continued working tirelessly toward that goal, year after year. Finally, in 1833, the House of Commons passed a bill abolishing slavery altogether; Wilberforce died three days later, his work finally done.

Similarly, in the nineteenth century, American religious revivalism was linked directly with the abolition of slavery and other movements for social reform. As historian Michael Kazin says, "From the Second Great Awakening in the 1820s to the 1920s, there was a period where social movements were infused with the evangelical spirit."[3] Christians helped lead the abolitionist struggle, efforts to end child labour, projects to aid working people and establish unions, and even the battle to obtain voting rights for women. Here were evangelical Christians fighting for social justice, precisely because of what God had done for them – an activity with which evangelicals have not been associated in more recent times.

Nineteenth-century American evangelist Charles Finney didn't shy away from identifying the gospel with the antislavery cause. He was a revivalist and also an abolitionist. For him, the two were closely connected. Finney, who has been called the father of American evangelism, directly linked revival and reform and popularized the altar call. Why? To sign up his converts for the antislavery campaign! They would commit their lives to Christ and then enlist for God's purposes in the world. That's the way it always is for revival – faith becomes life-changing, but rather than remaining restricted to personal issues and the inner life alone, it explodes into the world with a powerful force. For Finney, taking a weak or wrong position on social justice was a "hindrance to revival".

William Jennings Bryan (1860–1925), another seminal figure almost forgotten in modern political discussion, shows that progressive evangelicalism is nothing new, as he linked personal faith to political populism. Bryan is described in a new biography, A Godly Hero, as the most influential American political figure of his time who was not a U.S. president. Bryan's biographer, Michael Kazin, writes, "For many of his correspondents, Bryan was not merely a favourite politician. They believed him to be a godly

hero who preached that the duty of a true Christian was to transform a nation
and world plagued by the arrogance of wealth and the pain of inequality."
A "radically progressive interpretation of the gospels" drove Bryan's political
career, which included "three campaigns for the White House, his work for
a dazzling variety of causes both secular and religious, and thirty continuous
years of theatrical preaching throughout the nation and the world". Bryan's
"creed", says Kazin, "married democracy and pietism in a romantic gospel
that borrowed equally from Jefferson and Jesus".[4]

In a conversation I had with Kazin, he noted that very few biographers
of Bryan were "really able to explain how Bryan could be a conservative
in religion and a liberal, even radical, in politics, without seeing any
contradiction between the two – because the wisdom about that is that
there was this great schism between people who were fundamentalists
theologically and people who were liberal politically. Bryan didn't see any
difference between his religion and his politics. He thought they were
quite consistent."[5]

Martin Luther King Jr.'s personal faith journey and the spiritual power
of the black churches were absolutely central to the civil rights movement.
Arising clearly out of the black church tradition of America and the
Ebenezer congregation his father led, the bright young Martin Jr. was
steeped in the intellectual and liberal social gospel tradition during his
seminary and postgraduate years. But as the freedom struggle intensified,
the faith of Martin Luther King Jr. became much more personal. His
theological liberalism was not an adequate foundation for what he would
ultimately face. My experience is that the more deeply one moves into
the struggle for social justice, the more important personal faith becomes.
There is, indeed, a genuine tradition of theological liberalism that leads
to a social gospel, but there's also an evangelical tradition in which Jesus
brings one to social justice.

At the height of the Montgomery bus boycott, King received dozens of
death threats by phone and mail. One evening in January 1956, the young
minister had a pivotal experience, which would later be referred to as his
"kitchen table conversion". Stewart Burns recounts King's epiphany in *To
the Mountaintop*:

Around midnight, as he struggled to sleep, the phone rang one more time.
"Listen, n*****," an ugly voice crackled over the wire, "we're tired of you
and your mess now. If you aren't out of this town in three days, we're going to
blow your brains out and blow up your house." He paced the bedroom floor
in angry fear, then walked across the hall to the kitchen and heated some

coffee. He tried to find solace in what philosophy and theology had taught him about the meaning of evil. Could there be good without evil? Could there be redemption without sin? No answer came to shake his despair. Nothing relieved the fear in his gut. He was ready to give up.

"I got to the point that I couldn't take it any longer," he recalled in a sermon the summer before his death. "I was weak. Something said to me you can't call on Daddy now," as he had in past troubles. "You can't even call on Mama now. You've got to call on that something in that person that your daddy used to tell you about. That power that can make a way out of no way." He had to call on the Holy Spirit's power to help him through. The church had been so much his home all of his young life that he had never stepped outside of it far enough, or boldly enough, to forge his own relationship with God, with Jesus, with the Spirit – not that of his father or mother or Ebenezer Baptist in Atlanta.

He discovered at this midnight hour that "religion had to become real to me" – not merely the hand-me-down family business – "and I had to know God for myself. With my head in my hands, I bowed down over that cup of coffee. Oh, yes, I prayed a prayer. I prayed out loud that night. The words I spoke to God that midnight are still vivid in my memory. Lord, I'm down here trying to do what's right. I think the cause that we represent is right. But Lord, I must confess that I'm weak now. I'm faltering. I'm losing my courage. I am afraid. The people are looking to me for leadership. I can't let the people see me like this because if they see me weak and losing my courage, they will begin to get weak. I am at the end of my powers. I have nothing left. I've come to the point where I can't face it alone."

"At that moment," he continued, "I experienced the presence of the Divine as I had never experienced Him before. I could hear an inner voice saying to me, Martin Luther, stand up for righteousness, stand up for justice, stand up for the truth. And lo, I will be with you, even until the end of the world. I heard the voice of Jesus saying still to fight on. He promised never to leave me, never to leave me alone. No, never alone. No, never alone. He promised never to leave me, never to leave me alone."[6]

That experience and the deep personal faith that continued to sustain him shaped Martin Luther King's political commitments and public leadership. For faith to keep him going, it had to get "real", it had to get personal. Likewise, the social change we need today will not come about just through "education", through selecting the right "issues", through finding the right "policy ideas". As important as education, issues, and policy ideas are, we will need something deeper. We will need societal transformation for real social change, and that never comes about without personal transformation as well. Faith can provide the fire, the passion, the strength, the perseverance, and the hope necessary for social movements to win, and to change politics. Without that, it's just a debate over issues and ideas. And when the going gets tough or even risky and dangerous, many people will give up (or go back to watching television) – unless they have learned to tap the deep resources of faith.

Can we imagine the success of freedom in South Africa without Archbishop Desmond Tutu and the South African churches, or what the "spiritual formation" of twenty-seven years in prison did to shape Nelson Mandela, arguably the greatest political leader of the twentieth century? Desmond Tutu used to talk about a letter he received from a small group of cloistered religious women in a convent somewhere in the rural United States. They told the archbishop that they had covenanted together to pray for him every day during their early morning prayers at 4:00 a.m. For Tutu, this knowledge – that no matter what he would face on any given day, the day had begun with those faithful women praying to God, specifically for him – became a real source of strength. I had the blessing of being present for the inauguration of Nelson Mandela as president of the new South Africa. The occasion showed me again how much history really can be transformed – from seemingly hopeless oppression to the kind of justice that brings hope to all. And that's precisely what faith can do. Faith reminds us that change is always possible.

Two days before Mandela's inauguration, I was at the famous FNB stadium in Soweto for what was billed as a "National Service of Thanksgiving". For forty-six years the people of South Africa had lived under the most brutal forms of racial oppression in the system of apartheid, Mandela told the crowd. "Nothing I can say can fully describe the misery of our people as a result of that oppression, but the day we have been fighting for and waiting for has come. We are saying, Let us forget the past, let us hold hands, it is time now to begin anew. The time has come for men and women, African, coloured, Indian, white, Afrikaans and English-speaking, to say we are one country, we are one people." That rally in Soweto took place because Mandela wanted to thank the South African communities of faith, in particular, for keeping the hope of change alive.

For the next several days, Mandela set the tone. He invited his former jailers to be special guests at his inauguration, and he invited his opponents into the new government. His inaugural address was a "rainbow covenant" of promises to his people. "We enter into a covenant that we shall build the society in which all South Africans, both black and white, will be able to walk tall, without any fear in their hearts, assured of their inalienable right to human dignity – a rainbow nation at peace with itself and the world." Then in a ringing appeal for reconciliation, he proclaimed, "The time for healing of the wounds has come. The moment to bridge the chasms that divide us has come. The time to build is upon us."[7] His faith, and that of so many others, had led to a new South Africa. These are the things that God would want, I heard many of my South African friends say. And everyone believed, on that day, that God was smiling.

The list goes on and on. The stubborn faith of Archbishop Karol Józef Wojtyla, who became Pope John Paul II, was ultimately too much for the communist regime in his native Poland, and Catholic foundations were absolutely central to Lech Walesa's Solidarity union movement that brought down the Soviet-backed government. The "base communities" of Latin America, studying the Gospels with the lens of "liberation theology", became the schools and breeding grounds for resistance to military dictatorship, and those communal experiments in democracy helped set the stage for the new and fledgling democracies that would eventually replace junta after junta throughout the continent.

Archbishop Oscar Romero of El Salvador was one of the best known among all the Latin American church leaders, and he was martyred for his faithful leadership. In his last sermon before he was assassinated, Romero said:

> Let no one be offended because we use the divine words read at our Mass to shed light on the social, political, and economic situation of our people. Not to do so would be unchristian. Christ desires to unite himself with humanity, so that the light he brings from God might become life for nations and individuals. I know many are shocked by this preaching and want to accuse us of forsaking the gospel for politics. But I reject this accusation... Each week I go about the country listening to the cries of the people, their pain from so much crime, and the ignominy of so much violence. Each week I ask the Lord to give me the right words to console, to denounce, to call for repentance. And even though I may be a voice crying in the desert, I know that the church is making the effort to fulfill its mission.[8]

The Philippines' strongman Ferdinand Marcos seemed invulnerable until the "People Power" movement brought him down, with the critical support of Catholic Archbishop Cardinal Jaime Sin of Manila and the vital networks of the church's priests, religious women, and lay leaders who joined the people in the streets.

In India, Gandhi, a spiritual leader as much as a political one, led the movement for independence from Great Britain. A person of deep faith who drew from many traditions, Gandhi would sometimes halt the political progress of the movement to engage the nation in periods of fasting and prayer so that the people might be better prepared for freedom. Dietrich Bonhoeffer, the young German pastor whom Hitler executed, became the spiritual heart and soul of the Confessing Church resistance to the Third Reich, which they believed had committed religious offences and not just political ones.

The revival of faith often precedes social resistance and reform, and is usually necessary for either to occur. Wesley, Newton, Wilberforce, Finney, Bryan, King, Rosa Parks, Fannie Lou Hamer, John Paul II, Walesa, Romero, Tutu, Mandela, Gandhi, Bonhoeffer, Dorothy Day, Sojourner Truth, and the countless others who make up the "cloud of witnesses" (as the writer of the New Testament book of Hebrews put it) are a testimony to the power of conversion, the persistence of faith, and the achievement of social justice. At home, in my upstairs office, I have all their pictures on the wall over my desk as a regular reminder of what is indeed possible "by faith".

The Revival of Justice

Stories of faith and courage such as those just mentioned provide an enduring testament to hope – even against seemingly insurmountable odds. I believe we may be on the verge of such a revival again, a renewal of faith and spirituality that could be applied to some of the biggest moral issues of our time and make the most significant difference in resolving them. That is the thesis of this book.

The Religious Right is over, but the revival may be just beginning – a revival of justice. Some will question these assertions, but I believe them to be true. Mark Twain was once asked if he believed in infant baptism and replied, "Believe in it – Hell, I've seen it!" That's how I feel about the prospects for spiritual revival and social justice today – I don't just believe it, I'm seeing it across the country and around the world.

I have often said that I am a nineteenth-century American evangelical born in the wrong century. But now a new generation of evangelical students and pastors is coming of age. Their concerns are the slavery of poverty, the sexual trafficking of God's children, environmental "creation care", human rights and the image of God in genocidal places such as Darfur, and how the Prince of Peace might view our endless wars and conflicts. Whether they know it or not, these young activists are really nineteenth-century American evangelicals (or eighteenth-century British evangelicals) for the twenty-first century. As I said in the Introduction, I am a progressive evangelical. During the years dominated by the Religious Right, a "progressive evangelical" was thought to be a misnomer – but now it's becoming a movement.

Recently I was preaching at an evangelical Christian college in the American Midwest. I called for a new generation of Martin Luther Kings and William Wilberforces. Afterward, two young women were waiting to talk to me at the end of a long line of students. When they finally got their turn to speak, they looked me straight in the eye and said, "We are going to be the next Martin Luther King Jr. and William Wilberforce, and we just wanted to tell you that." I told them I was glad to meet them now before they became famous! But they were serious, and so was I. Stories from earlier centuries can inform a new generation of Christians in the struggle to reunite faith and social justice for our time.

Across the nation and around the world, I'm hearing a new hope for that kind of movement. From a new day in South Africa to the tearing down of the Berlin Wall, from the success of peace plans in violence-torn urban neighbourhoods in America to models that actually work to solve the problems of poverty in unlikely places, and to the nascent signs of democracy in places where oppression ruled a few short years ago, I've seen too much not to be hopeful, or naïve, about the challenges we face.

My purpose in this book is to explore the prospects for a revival of faith that changes politics. As I speak and listen to large and diverse audiences in every part of America, I find a deep hunger, especially among members of the younger generation, for something worth committing one's life to. As I said at the outset of this chapter, the two great hungers of our time are the hunger for spirituality and the hunger for social justice – and the connection between the two has great power to motivate people to action. The world is especially waiting for a new social and political agenda drawn not from bickering partisan loyalties, blatant ideological bias, or corrupting special interests, but rather from our deepest moral values.

We will explore what that agenda might look like by addressing the issues that pose the most fundamental threats to our moral integrity and social survival: the world's dangerous levels of inequality; the perils of climate change and environmental degradation; the worst assaults against human life and dignity; the forces that undermine family and community; and the escalation of violent global conflicts over culture, religion, and power. And we will propose the fundamental commitments that can change those big issues.

This will clearly be a book about politics, but it's about much more than politics. It will also be a book about theology, moral philosophy, and spirituality – because politics can be shaped by all three. Principles rooted in religion are critical to any discussion of moral values, among them the idea of the common good, which also has secular roots. Religious communities must resist partisan politics but must hold up the dignity of life, the principles of human rights, the real problem of evil, the dangers of violence, the protection of the environment, the value of family and community, the foundations of social justice, and much more. I'll write about these topics from the point of view of a public theologian, revival preacher, and faith-based social activist.

On many of the critical issues of the day, I firmly believe that there is common ground to be found. And I believe that the prospect of real social change can be animated by the testimony and action of faith. But I will also suggest that political appeals, even if rooted in religious convictions, be argued on moral grounds rather than as sectarian religious demands – so that the people (citizens), whether religious or not, may have the capacity to hear and respond. I will demonstrate how religion must be disciplined by democracy and contribute to a better and more moral public discourse. Religious convictions must therefore be translated into moral arguments, which must win the political debate if they are to be implemented. Religious people don't get to win just because they are religious (in a nation that is often claimed to be a Judeo-Christian country). They, like any other citizens, have to convince their fellow citizens that what they propose is best for the common good – for all of us and not just for the religious. Clearly, part of the work to be done includes teaching religious people how to make their appeals in moral language and secular people not to fear that such appeals will lead to theocracy.

The politicizing of religion by the Religious Right has caused much reaction, even the rejection of faith by many. But in many faith communities, the religious partisans have lost much of their control of the political agenda. The Religious Right had many legitimate concerns but failed to pursue them in ways that were both effective and consistent with the gospel. If its strategy was wrong, what is a better way? What will be the social and political agenda for people of faith now? What will be the impact of faith and faith communities on the critical issues of the day? What's next?

I strongly believe that faith matters and that it can make a difference, not only in our personal lives but also in our world. Remember, church historians tell us that spiritual activity isn't called revival until it has changed something in a society. In other words, spiritual renewal does not necessarily become spiritual revival without some decidedly social consequences. The time is ripe for the kind of spiritual revival that leads to clear social consequences. When politics can't resolve problems, the role of social movements – movements with spiritual foundations – becomes more and more important. This book will focus on how movements change politics, and how spiritual renewal changes movements.

So many people are fed up with both parties, deeply alienated by the corruption and hypocrisy that now dominate politics, yet are ready for serious public engagement on the issues that stir their deepest values and convictions. A common-good agenda, rooted in the moral centre, could unite diverse people on the really big issues. I believe it is indeed possible to "find common ground by moving to higher ground" and actually make some progress on the most important questions of our time. It is my hope that this book might also provide some moral accountability in the political context and be a fruitful catalyst for broad public conversation about the state of our nation and the state of our values.

That hope, though, still depends upon spiritual revival. In January 2007 while in Davos, Switzerland, at the World Economic Forum, I had an epiphany. It was during a session on "Promises to Africa" about whether and how the world would fulfill the commitments it had already made to the African continent in aid, debt cancellation, and making trade not only freer but fairer. Everyone agreed that the world had fallen far short of fulfilling the promises made, but those gathered looked forward to making more progress at the next G8 meeting scheduled for that summer in Germany. Then British Prime Minister Tony Blair, who was on the panel, was lauded for the singular leadership he had offered at the previous G8, and he argued strenuously for finally dealing with how unjust the global rules of trade are for the poorest countries and peoples.

One of the German representatives on the panel raised the issue of public opinion. He said the German public didn't care much about the issues of global justice and pointed his finger at Bono, another panelist. "We need the celebrities to come!" he exclaimed. Bono smiled back at him and gave him a salute, as if to accept his marching orders. The German was right: until we can move public opinion on the big issues, we are unlikely to change them. But if we are dependent only on "celebrities" to do that, we are in serious trouble. Bono, in particular, is much more than a celebrity; he is a serious activist, a committed Christian, and a friend – who happens to be one of the most popular rock stars in the world. Nobody in the world has done more than him to awaken the public conscience to global poverty and disease.

But in a conversation later that night, Bono agreed that celebrities alone won't be enough to change public opinion; that we need nothing less than a revival of faith, worldwide – a lived-out faith that demands action from governments on the most fundamental issues of justice. He told me how excited he was to hear about the ways evangelical Christians in America were changing, and when I told him about plans for "justice revivals" across the country and eventually around the world, his face lit up. "Justice revivals!" he repeated back to me, and he immediately quoted from Jesus in Luke 4: "The Spirit of the Lord is upon me, because he has anointed me to bring good news to the poor. He has sent me to proclaim release to the captives and recovery of sight to the blind, to let the oppressed go free, to proclaim the year of the Lord's favour." He knew it by heart and said, "That's what you have to preach!" Indeed. We must go back to Jesus, who was quoting Isaiah. If the great mountains of greed, injustice, and indifference are to be moved, they will most likely be pushed aside by the mustard seeds of faith.

2

CHANGES IN THE AIR
The New Agenda

One day in Washington I received a visitor who told me he was a pastor at a church with five thousand members that had planted more than two hundred new churches. He told me, "I am conservative on Jesus, conservative on the Bible, conservative on the resurrection, but I am becoming... a liberal [he almost whispered] on poverty and social justice. I'm a Southern Baptist from Texas, and I am not supposed to think these things... Are there other people like me?" he asked with utter sincerity. I assured him he was in good and growing company.

Change is definitely in the air. Dramatic new developments in the churches and in the larger religious community, especially among evangelicals, could be setting the stage for the kind of revival we've just discussed. Moreover, all indicators show that Americans are hungry for a new kind of politics.

Our political context has become a bitter partisan wasteland, bereft of real solutions. Most people that I talk to are extremely weary of the kind of politics now practised (by both sides) in Washington, D.C. Attacking the other side, exaggerating our differences, never listening to the concerns of political opponents, and, finally, winning power by any means necessary are all current practices that prevent us from finding answers to our most vexing problems. While the contest for power has always been a Washington staple, in past years many politicians at least talked to one another, even liked one another, and sometimes cooperated on important issues. That seems mostly lost now, and the political and media veterans in the nation's capital agree that things have gotten much worse. For too long we have been captive to a politics of blame and fear, while America is eager for a politics of solutions and hope. My conversations across the country tell me that America is ready for that new kind of politics.

When I listen to people of faith, I sense a similar discomfort about religion being made into a partisan commodity, too often used and abused for political purposes. Religious communities believe it is indeed part of their mission to address societal issues on the basis of their own values of compassion and justice. But they want to practise prophetic, not partisan, politics and to hold all sides accountable. I believe faith communities should be the ultimate swing vote, always examining issues and candidates on the basis of their own religious convictions. The faith community should be in nobody's political pocket and, indeed, will often be required to demonstrate public and political leadership in vital matters that secular politics tends to ignore. I believe it is time to offer that prophetic religious leadership, and that America's faith communities are ready for that role.

I find a real hunger in my country for a new kind of public discourse that can address the big issues facing the nation. Many Americans sense that most of our pressing problems have an essentially moral character. It is the role of the faith community to constantly remind us of that. As Dr. Martin Luther King Jr. once said, "The church must be reminded that it is not the master or the servant of the state, but rather the conscience of the state." But religion has no monopoly on morality. Today, we need a new morally centred discourse on politics that welcomes each of us to the table. It's time for a new public discussion on the values of politics – a discussion we all need and for which we are all needed.

Name any of the big issues today: impoverishment in the midst of wealth; the threat of climate change; disease pandemics around the world; genocide and violations of human rights; the threats of terrorism and endless war in response; the breakdown of families and communities; the persistent divisions of race, class, and gender; and the multiple threats to human life and dignity. Politics seems helpless to resolve any of them. Because the competitions of rights and interests have replaced any notion of the common good, politics isn't working anymore. Real solutions will require not only our best thinking, creativity, and dialogue; they will also challenge our basic values and call us to moral transformation and spiritual renewal. Again, a revival of faith could provide the engine of transformation.

We will discuss in chapter 4 how a restoration of the common good in our public life is essential, but it will take the help of spiritual revival to get us there. It isn't just the agenda and content of politics that have failed, but also the process. There will be no change without social movement, and no movement without personal and social transformation.

God's Politics turned out to be the right book at the right time, just after the election of 2004. The discussion it created helped open up a new conversation about faith, values, and politics in America. I wrote it partly to challenge the political right and its highly partisan religionists, who had dominated the national discourse on this topic for many years. At the same time, I also wanted to critique the political left's silence on the connection between religion and public life, and its badly mistaken unwillingness to join the conversation about moral values, too often preferring a purely secular approach to politics.

The left had clearly lost its way, even forgetting its own history on the subjects of religion and values (remember the civil rights movement led by the black churches?), and the right had made the discussion both too narrow and too partisan, turning religion and moral values into divisive wedge issues that, it turns out, alienated many people. The surprising success of *God's Politics* – a book on religion and politics with a progressive perspective – simply revealed what was already there. It revealed that millions of Americans who are also people of faith and/or who care deeply about moral values simply don't feel represented either by the Religious Right or the secular left and are looking for a better alternative.

In the past three years, I have been able to speak directly to hundreds of thousands of people, reach millions more through media coverage, and have many conversations with America's political leaders on both sides of the aisle. As a result, I have come to three clear conclusions. First, when it comes to faith and politics, the monologue of the Religious Right is indeed over and a new dialogue has begun. Second, now is the time for movements seeking social justice and peace to recover or find their faith and values and, indeed, to rediscover the social power of spiritual revival. Third, the evangelistic call of our time is to a personal faith that includes a passionate commitment to justice.

Let's look at the profound changes taking place among pastors and among students – all pointing to the possibility of a spiritual revival that could change politics for the better.

The Pastors

One of the most encouraging signs today is that a new generation of evangelical pastors, even some in the "megachurches", are discovering the countercultural character of the message of Jesus and his kingdom of God. Moving away from the consumer ethics of suburban "seekers" who want comfortable church campuses that supply multiple services and one-stop shopping for affluent professional families, these pastor-teachers are beginning to articulate the kingdom as a new order that challenges American Christians' easy wealth and mindless nationalism, and instead calls their members to sacrificial service on behalf of a broken humanity.

The opening line of Rick Warren's best-selling book *The Purpose Driven Life* confronts Christian narcissism directly: "It's not about you." I first met Warren when we were both speaking at the World Economic Forum in Davos, Switzerland, and all we talked about for three days was poverty and disease in Africa. Warren ran into controversy when he invited Barack Obama to speak to a conference on AIDS at his Saddleback Church in Southern California, because the senator's views on abortion and homosexuality were not acceptable to his conservative critics. But Kay Warren, Rick's wife, had a reply:

> Twenty-five years into the AIDS pandemic, being HIV-positive still carries stigma and shame. But God cares for the sick and so must we. ... It's not a sin to be sick. The Bible tells us Jesus was repeatedly "filled with compassion" as he encountered broken bodies and broken minds. While polite society vigorously avoided contact with those they considered diseased outcasts, Jesus responded in a radical way: He cared, he touched, he healed... We live in a broken, sinful world. We all make mistakes, but at the same time God cares passionately about everyone he has made. You never find Jesus asking people how they got sick, not once does he ask that. When sick people came to him, he simply said, "How can I help you?" And that's where we're trying to go. That needs to be the first question out of our mouths.[1]

Kay Warren seems to understand that the kingdom of God is a revolution of love, not of retribution.

I've also got to know Bill Hybels, founder of the Willow Creek Association with eleven thousand growing churches, who now pushes his huge network on issues of race and poverty. At a conference on Christians and race at which we both spoke, I was moved by how candid this very successful pastor was as a "white man who still doesn't get it but is trying to". Both the black and the white pastors in attendance were deeply impressed by Bill's honest and humble heart. Hybels invited Bono to address his annual leadership conference, which is downloaded by satellite to more than seventy thousand conservative evangelical pastors and lay leaders. When Bono quoted the fourth chapter of Luke, many in the crowd wept. Cally Parkinson, who runs the Willow Creek media relations department, was leaving the event when she overheard one pastor say to another, "I went in there wondering if Bono was a Christian, and I came out wondering if I was."[2] Bill Hybels seems to understand the kingdom's revolution of reconciliation and justice.

Greg Boyd, a Minnesota pastor, lost one thousand members of his congregation when he began preaching a series of sermons against Christian nationalism in America. He still leads the Woodland Hills Church in St. Paul, and his best-selling book *The Myth of the Christian Nation* created controversy and landed him on the front page of *The New York Times*. Rob Bell, pastor of Mars Hill Bible Church in Grandville, Michigan, leads a megachurch of postmodern young worshippers and records popular videos on key gospel themes that challenge the values of the culture as well as the established church. His bestselling book *Velvet Elvis* is for people who, as he puts it, "are fascinated with Jesus, but can't do the standard Christian package". I've met another megachurch pastor named Bob Roberts Jr. who has been on a pilgrimage with his large congregation. They became involved in service projects not just close to home but in far-flung places such as Afghanistan. Their involvement has given these Christians a global perspective. They no longer think like the conservative Texans all around their church, but more like the body of Christ in a broken world. His latest book, *Glocalization: How Followers of Jesus Engage the New Flat World,* says it all: Bob Roberts is now a pastor who walks the talk. His stories of travels around the world are captivating and his commitment to serving Christ by serving others is inspiring.

One of my personal favourites among young Christians is Shane Claiborne, a dynamic teacher and leader who has helped foster a network of intentional Christian communities in some of the poorest places in America, where earnest young disciples seek to follow in the steps of Jesus in what *Christianity Today* has called "the New Monasticism". Like the early Sojourners community, these communal experiments have become schools for discipleship that will help form the next generation.

Shane is a good example of the old adage, "Be careful what you pray for." Evangelicals like to pray that Christian young people will learn to love Jesus and follow in his steps. Well, that's exactly what this young Christian activist is talking about in his book *The Irresistible Revolution*. But the places that following Jesus has led Shane Claiborne to are not exactly the comfortable suburban environs that many evangelical Christians inhabit today. His journey of discipleship has taken him away from the conformist cultural habits of most middle-class believers. Worst of all, his notions of fidelity to the gospel seem to counter directly the political loyalties that many on the Religious Right have made into an almost-doctrinal litmus test of faith. For several years now, Shane and The Simple Way community have been experimenting with the gospel in the streets of Philadelphia and Calcutta, in the intensity of Christian community, and even in the war zones of Iraq.

As Shane puts it in his book, "We narrowed our vision to this: love God, love people, and follow Jesus." He describes their life in one of Philadelphia's poorest neighbourhoods:

> We hang out with kids and help them with homework in our living room, and jump in open fire hydrants on hot summer days. We share food with folks who need it, and eat the beans and rice our neighbor Ms. Sunshine makes for us. Folks drop in all day to say hi, have a safe place to cry, or get some water or a blanket. Sometimes we turn people away, or play Rock, Paper, Scissors to see who answers the door on tired days. We run a community store out of our house. We call it the Gathering, and neighbors can come in and fill a grocery bag with clothes for a dollar or find a couch, a bed, or a refrigerator. Sometimes people donate beautiful things for us to share with our neighbors; other times they donate their used toothbrushes. We reclaim abandoned lots and make gardens amid the concrete wreckage around us. We plant flowers inside old TV screens and computer monitors on our roof. We see our friends waste away from drug addiction, and on a good day, someone is set free. We see police scare people, and on a good day, we find an officer who will play wiffleball with his billy club. We rehab abandoned houses. And we mourn the two people who died in this property (where I am now writing). We try to make ugly things beautiful and to make murals. Instead of violence, we learn imagination and sharing. We share life with our neighbors and try to take care of each other. We hang out on the streets. We get fined for distributing food. We go to jail for sleeping under the stars. We win in court. We have friends in prison and on death row. We stand in the way of state-sanctioned execution and of the prison industrial complex.[3]

Shane Claiborne's disaffection from America's cultural and patriotic Christianity came not from going "secular" or "liberal" but by plunging deeper into what the earliest Christians called The Way, the way of Jesus, the way of the kingdom, and the way of the cross. He is the first to admit that what he and his spiritual cohorts are doing seems quite "radical", even "crazy", and maybe "insane". But he also has come to question the sanity of the consumer culture, the distorted priorities of the global economy, and the methodology of the warfare state, while at the same time rediscovering the biblical reversal of our social logic – that the foolishness of God has always seemed a little nuts to the world.

Visiting Shane's community, I was reminded of another young Christian community three decades ago, in the process of founding a new magazine and movement. In the Sojourners community we were also young evangelicals who found that neither our churches nor our society was measuring up to the way of Jesus – not even close. Our battle then was against a private piety that limited religion to purely personal matters, and accepted the economic, political, and military realities of the time. We desperately wanted to see our faith "go public" and offer a prophetic vision with the power to change both our personal lives and our political directions. I remember working on the draft of a new and very hopeful manifesto back in 1973. Called the "Chicago Declaration of Evangelical Social Concern", it was signed by leaders from both an older and a younger generation of evangelicals and was destined, we hoped, to really change things.

But then came the Religious Right, with evangelical faith going public but not in the ways we had hoped. Christian concerns were reduced to only a few "moral issues", most having to do with sex and the dominance of Christian language in the public square, and pacts were soon made with the economic and political agenda of America's far right. After thirty years, much of America became convinced that God was a Republican, and the enduring image of Christianity became the televangelist preacher.

All that is changing now, however, and I can feel a new momentum and movement. Many who have felt left out of the "faith and politics" conversation are now beginning to make their voices heard. A fresh dialogue about how to apply faith to social justice is springing up across the land.

A new convergence, across the theological spectrum, is occurring on issues such as overcoming poverty, both in the forgotten places of our own country that Hurricane Katrina has revealed and in the destitution and disease of the global economy to which the world is awakening. Christians are naming the environment as "God's creation" and insisting upon its care. Church leaders and evangelical seminary professors are challenging the theology of war and the religion of empire that emanate from the highest places of political power.

The greatest sign of hope, though, is the emergence of a new generation of Christians eager and ready to take their faith into the world. The Christianity of private piety, affluent conformity, and "God Bless [only] America" has compromised the witness of the church while putting a new generation of Christians to sleep. Defining faith by the things you won't do doesn't create a compelling style of life. And young people are hungry for an agenda worthy of their commitment, their energy, and their gifts.

This new generation of believers is waking up and catching fire with the gospel again. Theirs is an emerging Christianity that could change the face of American religion and politics. Their vision cannot easily be put into categories of liberal and conservative, left and right, but rather has the capacity to challenge the categories themselves. I've met these new Christians across the country and have worked with an extraordinary group of them at Sojourners. Their faith is intended to change this world, not just prepare them for the next. God is again doing something new.

The revival of faith always creates new communities, new forms of worship, new music, new models of service, and new calls for justice. It almost always originates outside the established church structures, but eventually begins to infuse new life even into them. That has been our experience at Sojourners, and with what I see happening in new communities such as The Simple Way and many others, it seems to be happening all over again.

What's very clear in all these new pastors' voices is how completely they have rejected the Religious Right. In a powerful talk at an event that Sojourners cohosted before the 2006 election in the key swing state of Ohio, Pastor Rich Nathan of the Vineyard Church of Columbus, the second largest congregation in that state, said:

> I've spent my entire adult life inside the evangelical world. For those of you who are not familiar with what an "evangelical" is, we are people who take seriously what can be called "classical Christianity". We really believe the historic creeds of the church – the Apostles, Nicene, and Caledonian Creeds. Like all classical Christians, we believe that God is a Trinity – Father, Son, and Holy Spirit. We evangelicals believe that Jesus Christ is God come in the flesh. That he was literally born of a virgin. That he suffered under Pontius Pilate. That he was crucified, died, and buried and rose bodily from the dead. We evangelicals believe that Christ ascended into heaven and that he is one day going to come back to judge the living and the dead. So we believe what classical Christians have always believed and taught throughout the 2,000 years of church history. And as children of the Reformation, we also believe that the Bible is our final authority for faith and practice.

All that affirmation of Christian orthodoxy is what the crowd probably expected. What came next they didn't.

> But as I travel around the country and interact with a wide variety of evangelical leaders, I have discovered a changing landscape. I believe we are going to see an entirely new trajectory for evangelical political involvement over the next decade. I am grateful that there is a broadening of the list of people who are now considered spokespersons for the evangelical movement. There are

lots of us evangelicals who have found ourselves increasingly uncomfortable with the media's selection of a few people of decidedly conservative politics who are regularly called our spokespeople. Whenever I hear this handful of people talk, I think: This person doesn't speak for me. When did anti-gun control through an expansive read of the Second Amendment become a Christian issue? Don't you hate it when someone's views are 180° out of sync with yours and yet they are called your spokesperson? You say, "When did I vote for them?" I am so grateful that there is a broadening of the evangelical agenda that expands beyond abortion and gay marriage. There are many evangelicals coming out in opposition to global warming. There are more evangelicals speaking out about global poverty and the relief of Third World debt and AIDS. And I'm proud of the fact that evangelicals are taking the lead on some of the world's most pressing issues.[4]

A changing landscape indeed.

The Students

Perhaps even more exciting to me is what's happening among young Christians today, many of whom are students at evangelical Christian colleges, Catholic universities, and secular schools where they are members of vital Christian student groups. They are the future, which is feeling very bright to me.

I meet young evangelical and Catholic students who come out by the thousands almost every week to hear a different vision of how their faith can make a difference in the world, and poverty is usually at the top of their priority list. Children dying in Africa are of deeper concern to most of them than anti-gay-marriage amendments. I marched with hundreds of them (and my own two young sons) to the U.S. Capitol in the spring of 2006 carrying signs that read POVERTY IS NOT A FAMILY VALUE and MAKE POVERTY HISTORY.

I've been to more than fifty campuses over the past two years. My visit to Bethel University is a good example of those visits. Bethel is a conservative evangelical school in Minnesota, the heartland of the American Midwest. It has long been regarded as a safe and secure place for conservative Republican politics, and even as fertile recruitment ground for the Religious Right. In the elections of 2000 and 2004, most Bethel students would certainly have voted for George W. Bush. But the wind is changing at Bethel. My visit there was a dramatic demonstration of a sea change that will be significant for both faith and politics in America.

I started my day at Bethel by speaking in chapel and asking the students to "clear up the confusion" in this nation about what it means to follow Jesus. I challenged the term that has come to be associated with schools like theirs – conservative evangelical – and asked if they were really evangelicals, or just conservatives. I asked them if they wanted to be true evangelicals, defined by the root meaning of the word *evangel,* which literally means "good news". The word was used by Jesus in his opening statement in Nazareth, recorded in Luke 4, where he defined his own mission by saying, "The Spirit of the Lord is upon me, because he has anointed me to bring good news ['the evangel'] to the poor." Therefore, I told the young audience, any gospel that isn't good news to the poor simply isn't the gospel of Jesus Christ.

It was clear from the response in chapel that day that the new generation of evangelical Christians wants to be, like Jesus, good news to the poor. Because of that, their agenda is now much broader and deeper. I learned that Bethel students still believe that the sanctity of life and healthy family values are indeed very important and that we need a deeper moral discussion of both. But they also care deeply about poverty, global warming, sex trafficking and human rights, genocide in Darfur, and the ethics of the war in Iraq. And they are eager for an agenda that will call forth their best gifts, energies, and the commitment of their lives. They have found those two thousand verses in the Bible that speak of God's concern for the poor and vulnerable. For them, environmental concern is "creation care". They want a "consistent ethic of life" that addresses all the places where human life and dignity are threatened – not just one or two.

That doesn't mean that their votes, which conservative Republicans have taken for granted, will now automatically go to liberal Democrats. Instead, they are eager to challenge the selective moralities of both left and right and respond to a moral agenda for politics that will hold both sides accountable. In the future, a candidate (from either party) who speaks the language of moral politics and lifts up the issues of social justice about which the Bible talks so much could attract the attention of this new generation.

In the evening, the students came back, along with many others, for a forum on just how faith should relate to politics in our time. I was joined by a local pastor, Rev. Greg Boyd, whom I mentioned earlier. The two of us agreed that fidelity to Jesus Christ comes before politics, and we found that we shared a deep appreciation of John Howard Yoder's classic book *The Politics of Jesus,* with its "understanding of Jesus and his ministry of which it might be said that such a Jesus would be of direct significance for social ethics" and "the case for considering Jesus, when thus understood, to be not only relevant but also normative for a contemporary Christian social ethic."[5] Greg shared his cynicism for politics in general and his dislike of how some on the Religious Right have made politics a divisive issue in churches. He doesn't want to see the same thing on the left either, and I agreed. Together we had a very good dialogue about both the opportunities and the dangers of political engagement for Christians.

The people we lifted up as having done it right included Dr. Martin Luther King Jr., William Wilberforce, Mohandas Gandhi, and Dietrich Bonhoeffer. But this was one of those nights when the speakers and the messages were less important than the crowd who came to hear. Every place to sit or stand in Benson Great Hall was filled by young evangelicals eager to discuss how they should engage the world. Numerous faculty members said they couldn't remember a bigger event in Bethel's history, and it was certainly a dramatic demonstration of how things are changing in the evangelical world – especially among younger evangelicals. This evangelical crowd was larger than the one that turned out a couple of weeks later for a James Dobson "moral values" rally in the Twin Cities, which was clearly designed to mobilize more Republican votes.

Almost every week, I find the same thing happening at Christian colleges across the nation. CNN was at Bethel to capture the event, and afterward spoke to a roundtable of evangelical students. For me it was a day filled with hope and the possibility of a new faith-inspired generation that might truly shake up politics – just the way people of faith and conscience are supposed to.

In conversation after conversation with these younger evangelical pastors and students, I have come to the same startling observation. The Religious Right is being replaced with Jesus.

Sea Change

Another change of great significance is how the Religious Right and their allies in the Republican Party are losing control of their ability to define exactly what the "moral values" issues really are. The signs of a major political shift and realignment began soon after the 2004 election. Evangelical activism to protect God's creation became publicly visible in a new way. This included Christian concern over global warming in particular – which was resisted unsuccessfully by the old Religious Right, and which offered a potential tipping point on the climate-change issue. A host of other issues were soon part of a broadened and deepened evangelical agenda –

most connected to poverty, human rights, and social justice. Even American military and foreign policy has begun to come under critique by Christian scholars (including evangelicals), who have focused on the ethics of war and the dubious morality of the U.S. response to terrorism. Slowly, even the media are reporting on the widening evangelical concern about human life and dignity.

In October 2004 the National Association of Evangelicals adopted a significant document meant to be a guide to evangelical social engagement. Called "For the Health of the Nation", it offered a more comprehensive approach than single-issue political voting, addressing all the above-named issues. The previous evangelical commitments on abortion and family values remained, but even those contentious issues are provoking a deeper and healthier dialogue than in times past. This widening of the evangelical social agenda signals a fundamental sea change in the religious community's relation to politics – and a clear indication that the Religious Right has lost control of the discussion. John Green, the highly respected religious researcher at the University of Akron's Bliss Institute, has found that while 22 per cent of the electorate consists of white evangelicals, only half of them are solidly committed to the Religious Right. The other half are more "centrist" and "modernist" evangelicals whose votes are very much in play and could be drawn to a candidate sharing their broad range of values. A clear political fact began to emerge: the future of American politics could be decisively shaped by what moderate evangelicals and Catholics decide to do.

Since the election of 2004, there has begun to be a levelling of the political playing field when it comes to religion and politics. Democrats have done some soul-searching (and some political maths) and are again becoming a party more friendly to faith (partly by rediscovering some of their own history). And the Republican right's diminished political influence and control has also become good news to the moderate Republican tradition, which desperately needs to be recovered.

Democratic senator Barack Obama offered the most thoughtful and balanced perspective on the connection between faith and politics that Washington, D.C., had seen for many years when he spoke to a Sojourners conference in June 2006. It was perhaps the most important speech on the subject of religion and public life since John F. Kennedy's famous address in Houston during the 1960 presidential election campaign. Senator Obama described his own personal journey of faith and answered the question of whether faith should address public issues with a resounding yes, but he went on to say that the crucial question is how religion and politics connect.

The contributions of religion to our public life are indeed essential, he said, but they must be offered in ways that are consistent with our traditions of democracy and pluralism – which is both possible and necessary. It was indeed significant that a Democrat gave such a penetrating analysis of the subject, and it constituted a fundamental challenge to his own party's reluctance in recent times to address the topic. Senator Obama said:

> If we truly hope to speak to people where they're at – to communicate our hopes and values in a way that's relevant to their own – we cannot abandon the field of religious discourse. Because when we ignore the debate about what it means to be a good Christian or Muslim or Jew; when we discuss religion only in the negative sense of where or how it should not be practiced, rather than in the positive sense of what it tells us about our obligations towards one another; when we shy away from religious venues and religious broadcasts because we assume that we will be unwelcome – others will fill the vacuum, those with the most insular views of faith, or those who cynically use religion to justify partisan ends… More fundamentally, the discomfort of some progressives with any hint of religion has often prevented us from effectively addressing issues in moral terms. Some of the problem here is rhetorical – if we scrub language of all religious content, we forfeit the imagery and terminology through which millions of Americans understand both their personal morality and social justice. Imagine Lincoln's Second Inaugural Address without reference to 'the judgments of the Lord', or King's 'I Have a Dream' speech without reference to 'all of God's children'. Their summoning of a higher truth helped inspire what had seemed impossible and move the nation to embrace a common destiny.[6]

The watershed 2006 midterm elections marked a turning point for the Religious Right's hold on evangelical voters. Many analysts commented on the significant shifts among religious voters in the midterm elections, in what Steve Waldman of Beliefnet described as the "smaller God gap" between Republicans and Democrats. Moderate Christians and some conservative Christians – especially evangelicals and Catholics – wanted a broader moral agenda. National exit polls showed that 6 per cent more Catholics and 5 per cent more white evangelicals had supported Democratic candidates in House races than in the 2004 elections. Eight per cent fewer evangelicals voted for Republicans in 2006 than voted for President Bush in 2004. Many of those polled expressed concern about poverty, the war in Iraq, strengthening working families, and protecting the environment as important moral values. Where Democratic candidates engaged in specific outreach to faith communities – as Republicans have done systematically for years – in states such as Ohio, Pennsylvania, and Michigan, the changes in voting patterns were double and triple the national turnaround.

Again, though, it would be a mistake to see these shifts in purely partisan terms, or for Democrats to believe that they have locked up these religious voters. Rather, the changes are much more the result of growing social compassion and deeper theological reflection – prompting a political reconsideration among many, and leading to a fresh questioning of how their faith should shape their politics on the issues that arise directly from religious conviction.

A late-2006 exit poll conducted by Zogby International showed why these shifts have occurred. Iraq was considered the "moral issue that most affected [my] vote" by 45.8 per cent of voters, almost six times as many voters as named abortion and almost five times as many as named same-sex marriage. Iraq was the top moral issue among Catholics, born-again Christians, and frequent church attendees. Poverty and economic justice topped the list of "most urgent moral problem[s] in American culture". When Catholics were asked to name the most important value guiding their vote, 67 per cent chose "a commitment to the common good – the good of all not just the few", while 22 per cent chose "opposing policies such as legal abortion, gay marriage, and embryonic stem cell research".[7]

When Focus on the Family's James Dobson said the moral values voters stayed home, he was simply wrong, and the data showed it. They just didn't think his moral values were the only – or most important – ones. Several anti-gay-marriage amendments did pass, but by smaller margins than similar initiatives had passed in 2004. As a headline in the *Columbus (Ohio) Dispatch* said, "Faithful voted on values: war, scandals and social justice all swayed religious voters." And on those issues, the 2006 election results led to three conclusions.

First, the American people voted to correct the disastrous mistake of the Bush administration's war in Iraq – and this was the central motivating moral issue of the election. The electoral results called for a new national debate on Iraq, leading the U.S. Catholic bishops to reiterate their call for "a responsible transition". The continuing violence and death in Iraq had reached intolerable levels. As of Election Day, 2,836 Americans and hundreds of thousands of Iraqis had died in this disastrous war. The people spoke, and there was a mandate to change the course of U.S. policy in Iraq. Even the president acknowledged this with his announcement of the resignation of Defense Secretary Donald Rumsfeld the day after the election. The new Democratic Congress now had no choice but to seek alternatives to the administration's course in Iraq. And with specially commissioned reports quickly following the election, a national debate about how to end the war finally began, and even the Bush administration's postelection escalation of the war had to be phrased as a change in course. But even fewer Americans supported that direction, including 60 per cent of America's evangelicals who were now firmly opposed to the war.

Second, the American people voted to reject the economic unfairness of Republican leadership, and "economic justice" topped the list of urgent moral problems for most Americans – despite decades of conservative media rhetoric that continually blamed the poor for their problems and relentlessly told us that the best way to help working families is to make the rich richer. Voters recognized that while the economy is in good shape for some, there are still too many people left out, especially working families – families with parents working full time, playing by the rules, and still raising their children in poverty.

It is significant that in all six states where an initiative to raise the minimum wage was on the ballot, it passed – in five cases, by overwhelming margins. In each of these minimum wage campaigns, people of faith and many congregations were vitally involved, which suggested that people of faith consider fair wages for workers a biblical issue and a family-values issue. Work needs to work, and if you work hard and full time in America you shouldn't be poor. The new Democratic leaders pledged to pass a minimum wage increase in the first one hundred hours of the new Congress, and they did so. In his postelection press conference, President Bush said this was "an area where I believe we can... find common ground". Three senators appeared with four religious leaders at a January 2007 press conference celebrating a successful vote in the U.S. Senate on minimum wage, and the contribution that religious communities had brought to this victory was clear to all.

Finally, the 2006 exit polls told us that Americans are tired of the culture of corruption that now plagues Washington. While ready to hold both parties accountable for better ethics, they primarily blamed the party in power for the moral abuse of the political process. Three Republican members of Congress had been indicted because of financial and political scandals. One was already in prison. Others, from both parties, are under investigation. Congress has refused to resolve the scandal of pork-barrel spending (patronage) and the ability of special-interest money to determine policy decisions. When a party has been in power too long, just staying in power becomes more important than truth-telling, which was unfortunately also true when Democrats controlled both houses of Congress. According to the Associated Press, more than 40 per cent of evangelical voters said that corruption and scandal were extremely important in their vote. The voters' message was that we need political leaders, of both parties, who believe in the importance of integrity, humility, honesty, and commitment to the common good – and are willing to challenge their own party's desire for power at the expense of moral principle.

The election results did not mean that secular people (among whom I count many close allies) didn't or shouldn't share in the progressive victory, or that religious and secular people shouldn't build important coalitions around key issues (they must). But the results did suggest that the Religious Right (religious fundamentalists) had suffered a major defeat and no longer controlled the political agenda for people of faith. Moreover, those on the left who have too often disdained the role of religion in politics, the participation of the faith community, and even the moral values conversation itself (people I would call secular fundamentalists) also lost some of their control of the process. Democrats were far friendlier to faith than they had been in the recent past and the results were clear – and cause for both religious and secular progressives to celebrate. The election saw victories for many Democrats who speak openly about their faith and how it informs their political views. In Ohio, former Methodist minister Ted Strickland defeated the Religious Right's favourite candidate, Kenneth Blackwell, for governor; Bob Casey, a devout Catholic and a pro-life Democrat, was elected senator over conservative Republican Rick Santorum in Pennsylvania; and also in Ohio, Democrat Sherrod Brown defeated Republican Senator Mike DeWine with a distinctively populist and faith-friendly campaign. Both religious and secular fundamentalists have had real power in their respective constituencies – and both groups lost influence in the 2006 election.

In No Party's Pocket

Significant shifts in evangelicals' thinking on the moral issues that matter to them politically have been occurring for some time now, and I see evidence of it every week that I am on the road. Democrats don't automatically benefit from that, but any candidate who speaks a moral language of politics could. Richard Cizik, of the National Association of Evangelicals, told the online magazine Salon.com after the 2006 election, "Look. To be biblically consistent you have to be politically inconsistent. Evangelicals have to follow their Lord first, and not simply bend to the whim of a political party for the advantages that come with it... We need as evangelicals to take stock of where we are as a country – not just ecclesiastically and theologically and otherwise, but politically too. And right now is as good a time as any to take serious stock."[8] In the upcoming election year of 2008, many moderate evangelicals and Catholics will be, as they say in politics, "up for grabs". But as we say in churches, people are carefully thinking and praying as never before, and are no longer in any party's pocket.

The shift away from the Religious Right is not necessarily a shift to the left. And that is exactly the point that must now be understood. I find more and more people who are tired of the Religious Right, but that doesn't mean they now simply long for a religious left. In fact, it is the typical right-left divide on almost every political issue that makes them weary. Rather, like most Americans, they are searching for a new political agenda that doesn't fit the standard right-left battles of American politics and is more consistent with their deeply held values. That new agenda would be good news for the majority of Americans who are alienated by the political extremes of right and left and hungry for a new moral centre for our public life.

What would such a new political agenda look like, one that moves us beyond the colour-coded cultural divisions of "red" and "blue" that the political class and media pundits continually impose upon the country? If many Americans are actually closer to "purple", as is often suggested, what might be a compelling vision that could evoke their convictions, reflect their values, summon their commitments, and change America? What would a broader and deeper moral politics or values politics begin to look like? That is a subject we will soon take up. But first, what are the rules of engagement for Christians? What are the principles that must guide our social and political witness in the world?

After a long lunch conversation with Pastor Rich Nathan, whom I quoted above, he showed me around his huge church complex in Columbus, Ohio. Surrounded by low-income housing and the poor families who inhabit it, the church was about to open a new community centre that would offer medical and legal services, computer and technology skill sharing, job training, after-school youth and tutoring efforts, and programmes on nutrition, athletics, arts, family support, and, of course, spiritual formation.

Pastor Rich, as everyone calls him, asked me some probing questions about the role of the church and the role of the government in meeting human needs, and I could see that he was clearly searching for new answers that didn't fit into old political categories. I told him he had three choices. The first would be to say that such social programmes should be the work of individuals and churches, but not of the government, as many conservatives contend. Their church could feel some pride in meeting the needs of those immediately around them, but the tacit support of his congregation for conservative political policies that continually cut back basic social services for low-income families and children would lead to disaster for those unable to find their way to islands of hope like his centre. Another option would be to leave social action to government agencies, as some liberals would prefer. The church could just stick to a gospel of private salvation and not get involved with social justice.

Or they could adopt a third way. They could lead by example in providing needed services in effective ways that help free people from the prison of poverty. And through the love and sacrifice of their members at the centre, they could prophetically challenge the social institutions and political leaders of their community, state, and nation to do more – much more – to respond to the needs of those Jesus called "the least of these". Immediately he knew the choice he wanted to make. Since then, their mayor, their member of Congress, and several county officials have visited the centre and been reminded of their own responsibilities. I've learned that those who are most directly involved with the poor have the most credibility in telling their elected officials that "budgets are moral documents" reflecting the values and priorities of a family, church, organization, city, state, or nation. They tell us what is most important and valued to those making the budget.

Rich was looking for those principles of engagement for Christians in the world, and to them we will now turn.

3

HOW TO CHANGE
THE WORLD, AND WHY
Rules of Engagement

M y first encounter with the question of faith and politics was a particularly painful one. It happened when a church elder from my small evangelical Christian congregation took me aside one day. I was just a teenager, but I was increasingly troubled by the racial segregation and hostility in my hometown of Detroit in the 1960s, and by the racial separation even in the churches. My forays into the inner city became a spiritual journey for me, putting me into relationship with new realities and friends that my protected white middle-class culture had tried to keep me from ever encountering. But once you cross over to the "other side", it is almost impossible ever to go back.

Perhaps sensing my agitation and impatience with the stance of my home church toward the racial polarities tearing our city apart, the church elder tried to counsel me. "You have to understand, Jim, that racism has nothing to do with Christianity," he said. "That's political, and our faith is personal." I think that was the night that I left my childhood church and faith, at least in my head and my heart – and within a few years I was gone altogether from religion. I came back to faith as a young adult (that's another story) with the conviction that God is personal, but never private, and I have spent the rest of my life exploring the public meaning of personal faith.

Many Christians do want to engage the world with their faith but wonder how to do so. They worry about being faithful to the gospel, and about not compromising the church's witness in the world, becoming tainted with partisan politics, or replacing faith with ideology. All these are valid concerns. I believe our faith calls us to transform the world, but how we do so is very important. That is the topic of this chapter.

Let's start with a foundational principle. Faith is not just for the next life, the hereafter; it is precisely intended to transform this world in the here and now – otherwise, most of the Bible makes no sense at all.

Faith should be both personal and public, and never just private. What are the compelling reasons to take faith into the public arena, and what are the dangers in doing so? Why must we engage in a witness to the world, and how do we keep that witness from becoming compromised and used for narrowly partisan or ideological agendas? I've spent the last three decades asking these questions as a Christian, but often in relationship to other faith traditions as well. What was (and what is) the nature of Jesus' mission, which he called the kingdom of God? Is it for the world at all, or only to take believers out of the world to get us ready for heaven, or perhaps just to form countercultural communities in the world that we merely invite other people to join? Does the kingdom of God have any witness to the world, beyond the believer and the community of faith? Is the kingdom of God political – and if so, how?

For the World

New Testament scholar N. T. Wright gets us right to the heart of the matter:

> For generations the church has been polarized between those who see the main task being the saving of souls for heaven and the nurturing of those souls through the valley of this dark world, on the one hand, and on the other hand those who see the task of improving the lot of human beings and the world, rescuing the poor from their misery. The longer that I've gone on as a New Testament scholar and wrestled with what the early Christians were actually talking about, the more it's been borne in on me that that distinction is one that we modern Westerners bring to the text rather than finding in the text. Because the great emphasis in the New Testament is that the gospel is not how to escape the world; the gospel is that the crucified and risen Jesus is the Lord of the world. And that his death and Resurrection transform the world, and that transformation can happen to you. You, in turn, can be part of the transforming work. That draws together what we traditionally called evangelism, bringing people to the point where they come to know God in Christ for themselves, with working for God's kingdom on earth as it is in heaven. That has always been at the heart of the Lord's Prayer, and how we've managed for years to say the Lord's Prayer without realizing that Jesus really meant it is very curious. Our Western culture since the 18th century has made a virtue of separating out religion from real life, or faith from politics. When I lecture about this, people will pop up and say, "Surely Jesus said my

kingdom is not of this world." And the answer is no, what Jesus said in John 18 is, "My kingdom is not from this world." That's *ek tou kosmoutoutou*. It's quite clear in the text that Jesus' kingdom doesn't start with this world. It isn't a worldly kingdom, but it is for this world. It's from somewhere else, but it's for this world.[1]

Wright, an evangelical theologian and Bishop of Durham in the Church of England, describes why after years of writing about Jesus, his recent book, *Simply Christian,* is full of topics such as poverty, the environment, and human rights, which he sees as the logical next step in his vocation as a New Testament scholar: "Thirty years ago I would have said those were secondary issues. There's an old evangelical saying, 'If he's not Lord of all, he's not Lord at all.' That was always applied personally and pietistically. I want to say exactly the same thing but apply it to the world. We're talking about Jesus as the Lord of the world – not the Lord of people's private spiritual interiority only, but of what they do with their money, with their homes, with the wealth of nations, and with the planet."

I remember an event in Washington, D.C., at which Wright was the guest speaker. The lunch seminar was sponsored by a conservative policy group in town and hosted by one of its senior staff who, like Wright, is a conservative evangelical. The session was held right before the start of the war with Iraq. When Wright was asked about the impending U.S. military action, he surprised his right-leaning hosts and most of the attendees by coming out clearly against it.

Wright understands that the real political questions for Christians are always questions of worship: who or what is finally "lord" for us, where does the ultimate authority lie, what is God like, and therefore how are we to live in the world? Wright says, "The key to mission is always worship. You can only be reflecting the love of God into the world if you are worshipping the true God who creates the world out of overflowing self-giving love. The more you look at that God and celebrate that love, the more you have to be reflecting that overflowing self-giving love into the world."[2] What a radical political alternative that is – a kingdom defined by the power of love, definitely not from the world, but emphatically for the world. Dorothy Day, the founder of the Catholic Worker movement who was always in the midst of service to the poor of New York City and resistance to the violence of the state, used to remind her followers, "Love is the measure."

I cannot count the number of times I've been faced with mistranslations or misunderstandings of Jesus' words that Wright refers to, "My kingdom is not of this world." That statement has been used to justify every manner of Christian withdrawal from the world of politics and, often transparently, a Christian acceptance of the political status quo. Of course, Jesus' kingdom is not "of" this world, in the sense of being "from" this world, as Wright says. Jesus' kingdom is not like the other kingdoms of the world, and that's the point. It's a different kind of kingdom from the worldly kingdoms based on money, power, violence, and sex. The kingdom of God, which Jesus came to inaugurate, is meant to create an alternative reality in this world and, ultimately, to transform the kingdoms of this world. Inaugurated by Jesus, but not yet brought to its final fulfilment, it is always a kingdom that is "already" but "not yet".

I remember being told as a boy by an elder in my church that Jesus' Sermon on the Mount was for a different "dispensation" – for heaven and not for this world. I was very puzzled; why would we need teachings such as "blessed are the peacemakers" or "love your enemies" in heaven? Don't we need that right here and right now in this world? I wondered as a young Christian. I didn't think that violence would be a big problem in heaven, but it certainly was on this earth, and Jesus seemed to be offering us some very radical alternatives in response to it. I soon realized that the Christians I knew thought Jesus' teachings were too radical and somehow had to be put aside, or at least postponed, especially since those Christians supported every war their government ever fought.

The Politics of Jesus

Some of the best guidance I have ever found to the "politics of Jesus" comes from the writings of John Howard Yoder, a public theologian who taught at Notre Dame and at the Associated Mennonite Biblical Seminaries in Elkhart, Indiana. His book *The Politics of Jesus* is still the one I most recommend to young Christians. In this classic work, Yoder makes four dramatic assertions:

1. "[T]he ministry and the claims of Jesus are best understood as presenting to [people] not the avoidance of political options, but one particular social-political-ethical option."

2. "That Christ is Lord, a proclamation to which only individuals can respond, is nonetheless a social, political, structural fact which constitutes a challenge to the Powers."

3. "The cross of Calvary was… the political, legally to be expected result of a moral clash with the powers ruling his society."

4. "If God is the kind of God-active-in-history of whom the Bible speaks, then concern for the course of history is itself not an illegitimate or an irrelevant concern. No mystical or existentialistic or spiritualistic depreciation of preoccupation with the course of events is justified for the Christian."[3]

I first met John Howard Yoder when he came to see us in the early years of the Sojourners community. His visits helped us to take our life as a community seriously – as a political sign to the world and as an agency for transformation in society. Yoder was very concerned about politics and a faithful Christian witness in relationship to it. He helped us to understand that Jesus and his kingdom have revolutionary implications for this world – not just a comforting word of reassurance for the next one, not merely a call to a countercultural parallel existence (which was often the temptation for those of his own Mennonite heritage).

The *Politics of Jesus,* and the work of other biblical theologians,[4] suggests that Jesus indeed confronted concrete political options in his day – options that correspond to most of our own. There were the Sadducees (the Jewish religious officials who collaborated with the Roman rulers), the Pharisees (the other establishment religious leaders who practised a strict piety and upheld the requirements of Hebrew law), the Essenes (monastic communities that withdrew from mainstream society into the wilderness in order to live out a faithful, alternative, and highly ascetic existence), and the Zealots (who politically opposed the hated Roman occupiers and sought to organize revolutionary violence against them).

Yoder and others point out that Jesus had deep relationships among the Essenes (the communities from which his predecessor John the Baptist may have come) and real political sympathy for the Zealots (even though he rejected their violent methodology), but he had no attraction for the establishment collaborators and the pietists, who were his constant adversaries. In the end, Jesus clearly rejected all the main political options of his time and inaugurated one that was completely new – called the kingdom of God, which brings a different kind of revolution, one of both love and justice.

For anyone wanting to understand better the Christian witness to the world and to politics in particular, I would recommend everything that Yoder wrote. One of the most cogent pieces of writing on the subject of

Christian engagement with politics is Yoder's *The Christian Witness to the State,* an academic monograph published in 1964 that should be required reading for those who wrestle with the proper role of government and the church's relationship to it. "It is possible," he wrote, "for the Christian or the Christian church to address to the social order at large or to the state criticisms and suggestions concerning the way in which the state fulfills its responsibility for the maintenance of order."[5]

With the declining influence of the Religious Right, we are now in a new day in regard to faith and politics. But if the Religious Right was the wrong way to engage politics, what is a better way to do it? If neither secularism nor withdrawal is the answer, what is the way forward? If faith belongs in politics, as I believe it does, how can it avoid being usurped by politics? In our rejection of the Religious Right's discredited effort to "politicize" the gospel, how can we resist the church's natural temptation to withdraw from politics altogether? Instead, how can faith communities learn the principles of faithful political witness and involvement on the basis of the kingdom of God?

Rules of Engagement

So what are the "rules of engagement" for Christians? Here are seven basic principles for Christian political involvement in the world.' (These lessons can also be applied to other faith traditions, with important translations and real differences duly noted.)

1. God hates injustice.

God hates injustice, and so should we if we are God's children. The injustice of this world cries out to heaven, and God gets angry over it. When we do, too, it is a sign of the image of God in us. The prophet Amos actually uses the word *hate* to describe God's response to social celebrations, religious sacrifice, and empty worship in the face of oppression. "I hate, I despise your festivals, and I take no delight in your solemn assemblies. Even though you offer me your burnt offerings and grain offerings, I will not accept them... Take away from me the noise of your songs; I will not listen to the melody of your harps. But let justice roll down like waters, and righteousness like an ever-flowing stream" (Amos 5:21–24).

Justice matters to the biblical prophets, who become especially incensed when the poor and the innocent are manipulated, exploited, or abused by the rich and powerful. And Jesus reserves his strongest words of judgment

for those who fail to "feed the hungry, give drink to the thirsty, welcome
the stranger, clothe the naked, care for the sick, and visit the prisoners".
He says that as we have done, or not done, to "the least of these", we have
done, or not done, to him. In chapter 25 of Matthew's Gospel, and in the
world's most desperate places, God takes on "the distressing disguise of the
poor", in the words of Mother Teresa and Dorothy Day.

As Martin Luther King Jr. put it, "A minister cannot preach the glories
of heaven while ignoring social conditions in his own community that
cause [people] an earthly hell."[7] When young people today are appalled
upon learning that young women and children are being "trafficked" in
modern sexual and economic slavery, or that death has become a social
disease in this world because of grotesquely unequal access to health care
and life-saving drugs, or that their favourite shoes and outfits were made in
oppressive sweatshops, or that the equivalent of the Asian tsunami death
toll happens in Africa every month, or that class and race and gender still
determine one's share of life even in America – when they learn of these
things and are appalled, it shows that God is still alive in them. When
young people have to leave the church to pursue social justice, as I did as a
teenager, it is a tragedy. But when their passion for justice can re-energize
the life of the church, it is a blessing.

The Bible names three categories of persons who need protection, who
are always in need of justice. First, there is the "widow and the orphan",
a regular concern of the prophets. The "widow and the orphan" stand for
all those excluded from economic opportunities and social justice – often
because of the actions of the strong and powerful. Even today, women
and children are usually the greatest victims of injustice and poverty.
Second, there is the "stranger", representing those who are outside the
majority culture because they are members of minority groups – usually
racial minorities. Accepting the equality of "the other" in the majority
community is still the core issue in regard to racism and the explosive
subject of immigration around the world. Third, there is the "enemy",
often the most vulnerable of all. Nations, especially superpowers, seem
to need enemies to rally their citizens and protect their power – the
infidels, the communists, the terrorists, and so on. Jesus doesn't say that
our enemies are not real, but only that we love them anyway. Loving our
enemies doesn't mean submitting to them or accepting their agendas, but
it does mean treating them as human beings who possess the image of
God. (As one bumper sticker put it, WHO WOULD JESUS TORTURE?) How
many churches since 9/11 have preached on Jesus' commands to live as
peacemakers and to love our enemies?

German theologian Dietrich Bonhoeffer was executed by Hitler's Third Reich for resisting its power and trying to protect its victims. The choice between power and the weak was central to what he preached. "Christianity stands or falls with its revolutionary protest against violence, arbitrariness, and pride of power and with its plea for the weak," Bonhoeffer wrote. "Christians are doing too little to make these points clear rather than too much. Christendom adjusts itself far too easily to the worship of power. Christians should give more offence, shock the world far more, than they are doing now. Christians should take a stronger stand in favour of the weak rather than considering first the possible right of the strong."[8]

2. The kingdom of God is a new order.

Jesus proclaimed in the Gospel of Matthew, "Repent, for the kingdom of heaven is at hand." The word he used was *metanoia*, which in the Greek literally means transformation, from the root of the word *metamorphosis*. He is saying that a whole new order is about to enter history and, if you want to be part of it, you will need a change so fundamental that the Gospel of John would later refer to it as a new birth. Being born again was not meant to be just a private religious experience that is hard to communicate to others, but rather the prerequisite for joining a new and very public movement – the Jesus and kingdom of God movement. It is an invitation to a whole new form and way of living, a transformation as radical as a caterpillar becoming a butterfly. It is far more than a call to a new inner life, or a rescue operation for heaven. It is an announcement of a new order of life that is intended to change everything about the world, and us with it.

In Matthew 5, 6, and 7, Jesus offers his Sermon on the Mount, which serves as the manifesto of his new order, the Magna Carta of the new age, the constitution of the kingdom. It utterly reverses the logic of this world, all its earthly kingdoms, and all its political options. In the kingdom of God, those who will be "blessed" or "happy" will be the poor, the poor in spirit, those who mourn, the meek, those who hunger and thirst for righteousness (better translated as "justice"), the merciful, the pure in heart, and the peacemakers. Those who live like this will be the essential "salt" to preserve the world, the "light" to show the way, and, often, those who will be persecuted for doing right.

Jacques Ellul, a French sociologist and theologian who became a resistance leader during the Nazi occupation, writes these extraordinary words in his classic book *The Presence of the Kingdom*:

Now the situation of the Christian in the world is a revolutionary situation. His share in the preservation of the world is to be an inexhaustible revolutionary force in the world... The fact that Christians, as human beings, at certain periods in history lose sight of the revolutionary character of their religion, does not mean that the Holy Spirit has ceased to work, and that the position of the Christian, to the extent in which he confesses his faith in the world, has ceased to be revolutionary. In consequence of the claims which God is always making on the world the Christian finds himself, by that very fact, involved in a state of permanent revolution.[9]

In other words, the Christian presence in the world is a perpetually revolutionary posture. This is not, however, another call to violent insurrection; it is much deeper and more "revolutionary" than that. The kingdom is an "upside-down kingdom", as Donald Kraybill has called it.[10] The kingdom of God literally brings a great reversal to the values, assumptions, and norms of the world as we have known them. This is why Christianity in defence of the established order – "Christendom", "Christian civilization", "Christian nation", "Christian empire", and the rest – has never made sense.

The kingdom's great reversal is seen clearly in Mary's song of worship, the Magnificat (Luke 1:46–55), in which she offers praise to God for what he will do through her. This young, unmarried peasant girl, from an oppressed race in an occupied country, was chosen to bear the new king for the new kingdom. From the start, Mary gets it: "He has scattered the proud in the thoughts of their hearts. He has brought down the powerful from their thrones, and lifted up the lowly; he has filled the hungry with good things, and sent the rich away empty." These are not the sweet musings of a modest faith-based social-services provider, but rather the proclamation of a spiritual and social revolution.

In all my growing-up years in our evangelical church, I never heard a sermon on the Sermon on the Mount. For the early church, it was the foundational teaching for instructing new converts in how to live "the way" of Christ, but it seemed to have no relevance to us as middle-class American Christians. We would never have thought our faith to be "revolutionary". But after leaving the church and reading all the revolutionaries, I encountered the Sermon of the Mount afresh, as more revolutionary than anything I had found in Karl Marx, Che Guevara, or Ho Chi Minh. This kingdom promised to change everything – personally, spiritually, economically, culturally, and politically – beginning with our lives and extending into the world. I signed up.

Jacques Ellul helped me understand what I had signed up for:

> The actual events of our world only acquire their value in the light of
> the coming Kingdom of God... Now in this matter the Christian has
> no right to keep this truth to himself; by his action and by his thought
> it is his duty to bring this "coming event" into the life of this present
> world. He has to carry into the actual world of the present day elements
> which belong to the eschaton. In so doing he fulfills a prophetic function,
> and as historians have observed, the prophets of Israel always had a
> political part to play, which, in connection with their civilization, was
> genuinely revolutionary... This then is the revolutionary situation: to be
> revolutionary is to judge the world by its present state, by actual facts, in
> the name of a truth which does not yet exist (but which is coming) – and
> it is to do so, because we believe this truth to be more genuine and more
> real than the reality which surrounds us.[11]

The kingdom of God is a new order.

3. The church is an alternative community.

Mohandas Gandhi, an admirer of Jesus but not a Christian, got it right when
he said, "You must be the change you want to see in the world." Jesus' call
was not just to a new order but also to a new community. The community
would be a pilot project for the new order, a demonstration of what is coming,
and an invitation to a new communal reality. In his essay "The Kingdom
as Social Ethic", Yoder writes, "The alternative community discharges a
modelling mission. The church is called to be now what the world is called
to be ultimately."[12] That's the starting point for faithful political witness –
the life of the church itself, which is meant to be an alternative community
living a new way of life, visibly demonstrating the values of Jesus and the
kingdom of God. That necessarily will create a countercultural community
living by different values from the surrounding society and providing a real
evangelistic model of the healthier and more human way of life that the
gospel offers. The church must therefore offer an alternative view of the
world, an alternative narrative of cultural values, an alternative model for
human existence, and an alternative vision for politics. This suggests that
the church will usually be more faithful as a "prophetic minority" than as the
dominant religion.

To live by alternative values is itself a political act. For the early
Christians, and for us, to say that "Jesus is Lord" is a profoundly political

statement. It means that nobody else is Lord, including Caesar and the Roman Empire, our own political rulers, and the totalitarian claims of any state or empire. The early Christians were actually accused of "atheism" because they rejected the gods of the Roman world. One wonders whether our churches today would be so accused for rejecting the modern gods of our consumer culture and market economy, or the political patriotism of the American superpower.

The problem comes when the church is so conformed to the values of the world that it offers no real alternative to the ruling societal values and has virtually nothing to say to the world's cultural norms or political ethics. It's when the church becomes a mere thermometer that takes the temperature of the world and adjusts accordingly, instead of a thermostat that actually changes the social temperature.

The central founding text for our early community of seminarians was Romans 12:1–2: "I appeal to you therefore, brothers and sisters, by the mercies of God, to present your bodies as a living sacrifice, holy and acceptable to God, which is your spiritual worship. Do not be conformed to this world, but be transformed by the renewing of your minds, so that you may discern what is the will of God – what is good and acceptable, and perfect." That became our social and political guide. Such an alternative community doesn't need to conform to "political realism" to be effective. Rather, as Yoder writes:

> There is an alternative narrative... the believing community has a longer sense of history past and future than do their oppressors, or than majorities unaware of alternatives to their own world. They also see the same facts differently. They do not assume that the only way to read national and political history is from the perspective of the winners... A minority group with no immediate chance of contributing to the way things go may still by its dissent maintain the wider community's awareness of some issues in such a way that ideas which are unrealistic for the present come to be credible later... The acceptance of the role of prophetic minority means to reject majority status and acceptance and is, at the same time, the key to the community's ultimate political impact... Another way a minority can be the conscience of society is to continue to voice the claims of unrepresented peoples and causes, when they do not yet have the ear or the heart of the majority. A minority can do for a society what the conscience does for an individual.[13]

Majorities normally don't change things; creative minorities do, and the majority just goes along in the end. As anthropologist Margaret Mead famously said, "Never doubt that a small group of thoughtful, committed citizens can change the world. Indeed, it is the only thing that ever has."

Faithfulness comes before effectiveness. It is easier to understand obedience than to calculate success. Even the best-intended political actions often have quite unintended consequences. Therefore, it is always a better course to pursue what we know to be right. "What would Jesus do?" is still a good question. Martin Luther King Jr. even said that those being faithful to their convictions are more crucial to a society than those who conform to the culture in order to be more "effective". King wrote:

> But there are some things in our social system to which I am proud to be maladjusted and to which I suggest that you too ought to be maladjusted. I never intend to adjust myself to the viciousness of mob-rule. I never intend to adjust myself to the evils of segregation and the crippling effects of discrimination. I never intend to adjust myself to the tragic inequalities of an economic system which takes necessities from the masses to give luxuries to the classes. I never intend to become adjusted to the madness of militarism and the self-defeating method of physical violence. I call upon you to be maladjusted... The world is in desperate need of such maladjustment. Through such maladjustment we will be able to emerge from the bleak and desolate midnight of man's inhumanity to man into the bright and glittering daybreak of freedom and justice.[14]

King believed the key to social change was in the hands of maladjusted nonconformists, who would play the crucial prophetic role in any society. He concluded, "This hour in history needs a dedicated circle of transformed nonconformists. The saving of our world from pending doom will come not from the actions of a conforming majority but from the creative maladjustment of a transformed minority."[15] King's maladjusted nonconformists are a critical metaphor for the church.

4. The kingdom of God transforms the world by addressing the specifics of injustice.

Even though the community of faith is meant to be countercultural, its role in the world is transformational. In his classic work *Christ and Culture,* H. Richard Niebuhr suggests that we have to choose between the two, but we do not. Christ is both "against culture" and the "transformer of culture".

Because the kingdom is not born of worldly kingdoms, biblical politics resists ideology and the notion of ideal societies, and instead focuses on specific issues and reforms. If our starting point is the kingdom of God, we should reject allegedly utopian or perfect societies, which are impossible creations for sinful people in a fallen world. "Ideology" is the political name and "idol" is the religious name for humanly constructed and supposedly ideal societies that aim at perfection or close to it. Clearly, some of the worst oppressions in history have been perpetrated by ideological regimes pretending to be creating perfect societies. In fact, the subordination of persons to great causes and ideological visions is often the great justification for atrocities.

For Christians, people are always more important than causes. That's why human rights, in the face of regimes that regularly violate those rights in the name of ideology and the state, have often been so important to communities of faith. Rather than seeking to construct perfect social orders, which are impossible, we should instead seek concrete reforms of the actual social situations and circumstances in which the church finds itself. We should challenge societies and states not with unreachable utopian dreams but with specific demands that make justice and peace more possible. Yoder puts it well:

> The Christian speaks not of how to describe, and then to seek to create, the ideal society, but of how the state can best fulfill its responsibilities in a fallen world. The Christian witness will therefore always express itself in terms of specific criticisms, addressed to given injustices in a particular time and place, and specific suggestions for improvements to remedy the identified abuse. This does not mean that if the criticisms were heard and the suggestions put into practice, the Christian would be satisfied; rather, a new and more demanding set of criticisms and suggestions would follow. There is no level of attainment to which a state could rise, beyond which the Christian critique would have nothing more to ask; such an ideal level would be none other than the kingdom of God... The kingdom of God is the touchstone of the Christian's political reality, and all other realities are evaluated by the kingdom.[16]

That is hardly a formula for political withdrawal, or a retreat to private poverty or exemplary sectarian communities. To reject the false and dangerous claims of ideological visions and regimes does not exempt us from political engagement, but rather invites us to the very social participation that societies and states need – evaluating them by a specific set of standards outside of themselves. Not to engage is to accept the status quo. As Yoder puts it:

> [M]any like to think that God and his Spirit are in one world and [people] and their politics in another. Some religious people believe that about God, and some politicians believe it about politics, but both are mistaken... The choice or the tension which the Bible is concerned with is not between politics and something else which is not politics, but between right politics and wrong politics... A related misunderstanding is the notion that it might be possible for Christians to avoid or withdraw from the political realm simply and entirely... It is possible to avoid having an outspoken political witness or to avoid criticizing existing structures, but then that silence is also a positive political action, accepting things as they are.[17]

The kingdom is the vision, but concrete political priorities and policies bring us closer to it or farther away from it. Martin Luther King Jr. had a dream – a vision he called the "beloved community", one completely consistent with the kingdom of God. But he fought for specific goals, such as the civil rights law in 1964 and the voting rights act in 1965. Similar reforms in American society have been motivated by faith-inspired visions, including the movement to abolish slavery, the establishment of women's suffrage and workers' rights, and child labour law reform.

In South Africa, Archbishop Desmond Tutu spoke of a nonracial "rainbow nation", but the starting place was the first South African election held on the principle of one person, one vote. Tutu supported the African National Congress, the political movement that led the anti-apartheid struggle. But when the ANC won and became the establishment, Desmond Tutu became its prophetic critic. I witnessed a debate between the ANC and Archbishop Tutu's policy people about whether the South African government should continue as the continent's leading arms supplier, a legacy of the white regime. The ANC said yes, somebody had to supply weapons for Africa's conflicts, and why let the Americans and French do it? Tutu said no, arguing for a new kind of country on the African continent. Tutu then preached the kingdom value of forgiveness and established a Truth and Reconciliation Commission that offered the new nation some very crucial healing through truth-telling about the great abuses of the former system of apartheid. Tutu remained prophetic, from regime to regime.

Similarly, and from a different religious tradition, the Buddhists in Vietnam challenged the U.S. imperial war against their country, but then protested the abuses of the communist government that took over after the war. Like many prophetic religious minorities, the Buddhists were persecuted by both sides. Jews have often played a similar role. In the tradition Rabbi Abraham Joshua Heschel articulates in his classic book *The Prophets,* the Jewish community has often stood up for justice in the societies in which it resides as a minority – even to the point of voting against its own economic self-interest.

It is impossible not to be involved in politics – our action or inaction will move us closer to or farther from the kingdom of God. Yoder affirms that and talks as well about the concept of vocation:

> The choice is not between God and politics, nor between the Spirit and "men", but between the politics of men (and women) in their (our) rebelliousness and the politics of men (and women) under the teaching and empowerment of God's Spirit. The difference is not one of realms but of paths; not of levels but of options... There is no special realm of "politics" which Christians, or the church, can avoid and leave to its own resources, or leave to be run by its own rules. True, there are varieties of gifts and divisions of labor in the social order as in the church. It is not the personal gift of everyone to be a leader or a militant in the area of social righteousness, any more than everyone should be an apostle... But that is said about the member, not the body... To ask whether, as a believing people, we should be "involved" is hardly ever the right question. The question is on which side to be involved, which issues to give priority to, and what methods to use.[18]

And that is the issue. What are the issues that we decide to embrace, what will our priorities be, and what options and methods will we employ?

5. The church is the conscience of the state, holding it accountable for upholding justice and restraining its violence.

There is a biblical role for the state, just as there is for the church, and they are not the same. According to Romans 13, the state is supposed to protect the innocent and punish the guilty, and to uphold the rule of law; 1 Timothy 2 adds the function of keeping the "peace". When the state fulfills its role properly, it allows the church to do its work in the world. The church must become "bilingual" in speaking the evangelistic message of the kingdom of God to all that will hear while also speaking to the state about its role and responsibilities. Justice, equity, and fairness become concerns for the Christian community and standards to which the government is held to account.

One could say that people of faith should endorse a "limited" view of government. This is not the old conservative proposal for small government, sometimes cynically argued in order to reduce the public sector's ability to counter the power of the wealthy and ensure more fairness and balance in a society. But neither is it an argument for big government that usurps more and more control in a society and puts in jeopardy both individual rights and countervailing powers to the state. Clearly, the answer to the endless left–right debate is neither small government nor big government, but rather effective, smart, and good government.

All three sectors of a society need to be functioning well for its health and well-being – the private (market) sector, the public sector, and the civil society (nongovernmental and nonprofit organizations, of which faith communities are a part). It is indeed like a three-legged stool. When one leg is too long (or too powerful) and the others too short (or too weak), the stool loses its balance and is in danger of falling over. Each sector has crucial roles to play, and each should do what only it can do and not replace what the others can do better. A society works when each sector does its share and does what it does best.

After Hurricane Katrina struck, religious communities were the first on the scene to give practical assistance to the people of New Orleans and the Gulf Coast, and they did so far better and faster than every level of government. The religious communities showed both more compassion and greater effectiveness than many governmental agencies, which were exposed for their incompetence. Many pointed out these facts to bolster their arguments against the role of government generally. But while churches can bring relief, they can't rebuild levees. And if you could add up the complete budgets of all our religious congregations and put the total amount at the service of poverty relief, it would still fall far short of the need – both at home and around the world. Churches cannot provide health care for forty-seven million Americans who don't have it, or ensure enough affordable housing to working families, or provide social security for the elderly or a social safety net for children. Only governments, often working with the civil society, can do that. Nor can the churches provide jobs with a living family income for parents with dependent children. Only the private sector and the labour movement can assure adequate and fair employment, with justice in the workplace. And contrary to the antigovernment rhetoric of the Religious Right, many religious and charitable groups helped prompt the New Deal by calling for the government to take a more active role in relieving poverty and ensuring fairness in American society.

To maintain order and security for its citizens and to uphold the rule of law, the state is allowed the use of force, but only within clear boundaries. Nowhere in the Bible is the state given a blanket authorization to use violence, without regard for any standards or accountabilities. Indeed, the Hebrew scripture's admonition of "eye for eye, tooth for tooth" (Exodus 21:24) was designed as a restraint on violence, not an expansion of it. The purpose of restraining and limiting violence that we find in the Hebrew scriptures (the Old Testament, to Christians) comes to fruition in the nonviolence of Jesus, the one who fulfills the prophecy of Isaiah's suffering servant. Nonviolence becomes the methodology of the kingdom of God. Jesus tells his followers to put away their swords, and his disciples in the first three centuries did just that by refusing to serve in the military. After Constantine and the state establishment of Christianity, Christians began to join in the state's police forces and armies. Augustine soon intervened to guide that involvement with strict criteria for a "just war", to which few of our modern wars would conform.

It is painfully clear that Jesus calls us to nonviolence and not to "just wars". Jesus said the peacemakers, not the war-makers, are the ones who will be blessed. It is also quite evident that when he commanded us to love our enemies, he really meant it. But, admittedly, no nation-state is going to behave that way; it's hard enough for those who call themselves disciples of Christ. So Augustine, Aquinas, and others came along to give the state some criteria or benchmarks for deciding whether wars were just. Since governments are not about to live by the ethics of Jesus, that's probably a good thing. At least, in the intention of the just-war theory, the violence of the state would be restrained by some very rigorous criteria. Paul suggested the same in Romans 13 – that the state has an ordering role, but not a blank cheque.

By the classic criteria, the U.S. war in Iraq was not a "just war". During the run-up to the war, a majority of church bodies and their leaders around the world said just that. Pope John Paul II was quite agitated about the buildup toward war against Iraq and, had he been a younger, healthier man, might actually have intervened to prevent the unjust war. Cardinal Ratzinger (now Pope Benedict XVI) also spoke strongly against war. Even most evangelical Christians around the globe were against the American war in Iraq, and continue to be – a fact that the U.S. media also missed. There were others, such as the Southern Baptists in the United States, who supported their president's war, but on an international scale they were clearly the exceptions.

Augustine said that Christians should go to war only as the very last resort and only with great reluctance and many tears. That reluctance stands as a critique of the attitudes of many contemporary American churches who, despite being followers of the Prince of Peace, are often the easiest to convince that our country should go to war.

Again, Dr. King reminds us that violence is most often counter-productive, usually serving to make worse the conditions it purports to solve. King put the contemporary choice before us most clearly. "It is no longer a choice," he said, "between violence and nonviolence. It is either nonviolence or nonexistence..."[19]

Jesus calls for nonviolence and tells us to love our enemies, but nations can still be held to the requirements and ethics of the "just" uses of force. Although it is unrealistic to expect nation-states not to use force to protect their citizens and uphold the law, we can insist that governments seek to resolve conflicts with the least violence possible. Yoder writes, "A realistic Christian social critique will always require the highest attainable aim. We do not ask of the government that it be nonresistant [nonviolent]; we do, however, ask that it take the most just and least violent action possible."[20] The Pentagon cannot be expected to be faithful to the teachings of Jesus, but the church should be.

One can accept the state's use of force in maintaining the rule of law and protecting the innocent, for example, without condoning capital punishment. One could also accept the state's role in protecting national security and defending the nation without condoning the weapons and tactics of modern warfare. The use of force suggested in Romans 13 is closer to what we would today call the "policing" function of the state than it is to the preemptive wars of a superpower. N. T. Wright and others are asking how Romans 13 might be applied to the urgent need for more effective institutions of international law and peacekeeping enforcement, as opposed to the limitless character of modern warfare. We will say more about this in chapter 10.

The church's life and work is not meant to replace the necessary (and biblical) role of government but to offer an example of compassion and justice. And the church's prophetic witness should hold the state, not just the religious community, accountable. We should lead by example, offering prophetic witness and, when necessary, even resistance. I have Martin Luther King Jr. on one of my shoulders and Dorothy Day on the other – both whispering in my ears. And they don't always say the same things. Dorothy called for resistance to the powers that be. I have a quote from her hanging above my desk that says, "Most of our problems stem from our acceptance of this filthy, rotten system." (Dorothy wasn't always poetic or understated.) Martin Luther King Jr. called for radical reform of the structures of injustice, believing that "the arc of the universe is long, but it bends toward justice".[21] Like both of them, I have been arrested many times for nonviolent civil disobedience (twenty-two times to be exact), which is a way both to resist and to change the structures of injustice. As Gandhi demonstrated, one uses different tactics and methods for different purposes and times – education, advocacy, testimony, preaching and speaking out, marching and demonstrations, relationships with political leaders, mobilizing mass constituencies, using the media, symbolic protests, pragmatic organizing, prayer, worship, and civil disobedience. Prayerful and strategic discernment is always employed to determine when and how various methods are used. But it is essential to be specific about what you want to change and how you want to hold the state accountable to justice.

6. Take a global perspective.

Nationalism doesn't go well with the kingdom of God. The church is the international body of Christ, and "God Bless America" is not found in the Bible. Christian faith is growing most rapidly and impressively in the developing world and the poorest places on earth – among people who feel no loyalty to America and mostly see the United States in two ways: as the world's wealthiest nation on top of a global economy that is not very friendly to them, and as the last remaining superpower whose geopolitical interests are often not compatible with their own. American Christians often have a difficult time with those realities, but they now shape the perspective of global Christianity. Most of the world's Christians, including most evangelicals internationally, did not support the American war in Iraq and do not support U.S. foreign policy generally.

It is absolutely extraordinary what happens to ordinary American Christians who travel overseas, especially for reasons of mission: their perspective changes dramatically. One of the reasons that many younger Christians are more critical of American values and policies than an older generation is that they have seen more of the world on mission trips; they have talked with their spiritual counterparts around the globe and heard alternative views on international issues. To take a global perspective on politics, to value other countries' interests as much as our own, and, perhaps most critically, to count all the world's children equally as important as our own – all will significantly alter our political views.

Here's an insight that is fundamental, and yet profoundly obvious: we are to be Christians first and citizens of our country second – not the other way around. As obvious as that is, the notion would revolutionize faith and politics in America if the church would ever grasp its primary international identity. American churches may be the only places on earth where national flags are displayed in many sanctuaries – American flags on one side and Christian "flags" on the other. In the United Kingdom, even with its state church, there are no flags in the sanctuaries. Why should our views on political subjects be determined by what is expected from us according to our sociology – race, class, and nation – rather than our theology? Shouldn't our identity as kingdom people and members of the global community of the church come first? In too many American churches, sociology consistently trumps theology. To turn that around would transform American religion – and politics.

The gospel especially doesn't coexist well with empire, and that includes American empire. The book of Revelation is filled with apocalyptic images of the ultimate confrontation between the lamb of God and the beast of Babylon, interpreted by most biblical scholars (and likely the book's readers at the time) as a metaphor for the Christian confrontation with the Roman Empire. And of course John, the author of the text, was writing in exile from Rome, on the island of Patmos. The universal claims and ambitions of empire are always in competition with those of the kingdom of God. Global empires run into conflict with those whose allegiance is to another global community: the body of Christ.

Today, because of the international identity of the church, which knows no national boundaries, the body of Christ could play a crucial role in the current context of "globalization". While globalization has a powerful economic driving force, it shows no comparable ethics. Globalizing, we are told, is inevitable in every sector, but we are offered no moral guidelines for how it should happen. Are there any rules and, if so, what are they? Who benefits and who suffers? Who determines that? Globalization has an irresistible logic, but no sustaining moral ethic. Here is where the church, an international community of faith that has known globalization for two thousand years, could play a leadership role. By providing exemplary leadership in how the church itself behaves globally, it could offer critical prophetic leadership to help establish values and rules of globalization that would protect the vulnerable populations on the planet. The church and other religious communities could help establish the "rules for the global neighbourhood", the title of a session I was part of at the World Economic Forum in 2007.

One example of that leadership is the emerging movement in the churches of the global South called the Micah Challenge, which works at achieving the United Nations' "Millennium Development Goals" to cut global poverty in half by 2015. The goals have been agreed to by 189 nations, but implementation is far behind schedule. The moral force of the church's leadership and witness, along with its growing constituency in the global South, could help achieve these critical goals. Perhaps an alternative global community could model the ethics that globalization so desperately needs.

7. Seek the common good.

For Christians, a commitment to the kingdom mandates that we seek the "common good" of the societies in which we live. And that is true for other faith traditions as well. There are various references in the Bible to the common good within the church – for example, the description of the common purse in Acts and Paul's admonitions in 1 Corinthians 12. But there are also references to the broader society. The prophet Jeremiah's letter to the exiles in Babylon urged that they "seek the welfare of the city where I have sent you into exile, and pray to the Lord on its behalf, for in its welfare you will find your welfare" (Jeremiah 29:7). The NIV translates the phrase as "seek the peace and prosperity" of the city. The Hebrew word used is *shalom,* which is often translated simply as "peace". But *shalom* has a deeper and richer meaning – it connotes completeness, soundness, welfare, health, safety, peace, and right relationships.

Another example is found in the prophet Nehemiah. After the exiles return from Babylon to the destroyed city of Jerusalem, Nehemiah gathers them: "Then I said to them, 'You see the trouble we are in, how Jerusalem lies in ruins with its gates burned. Come, let us rebuild the wall of Jerusalem, so that we may no longer suffer disgrace.' I told them that the hand of my God had been gracious upon me, and also the words that the king had spoken to me. Then they said, 'Let us start building!' So they committed themselves to *the common good*" (Nehemiah 2:17–18; emphasis added).

Jeremiah suggests that we learn to seek the welfare – the common good – of the places where we have been placed. Nehemiah gives everybody a job to do and gets them building again – building for the common good. Wouldn't it be wonderful to hear an evening news report on the work of Congress that day that paraphrased what happened in Jerusalem after the people heard the call from Nehemiah: "So they committed themselves to the common good"!

Catholic social teaching is rich with the idea of the common good, as are Protestant traditions with their idea of the "public good". Black church history is filled with a faith that cared for the whole community when nobody else did, and held neighbourhoods together like spiritual glue. As we have seen, evangelical revivals led to social reforms and transformed both American and British society. Jewish concepts of *shalom* and *tikkun* are all about the common good, and the concept is rooted deep in the history and theology of Islam. We also find the concept of the common good in the American and constitutional tradition, which welcomes secular citizens to the conversation as well. "We the people" created our government – "to promote the general welfare."

How we define politics is very important. Politics embraces not only legislative and electoral activism, but also how a community/society organizes itself, how it makes decisions, and what decisions it makes. The Greek word *polis* (from which we get the word *politics*) refers to the people, the public square, and the search for the common good. It means a discourse about values, right and wrong, and the ways of sustaining or restoring the healthy social and moral fabric of a society. So politics is about putting forth new ideas, solving problems, resolving conflicts, finding common ground, and, above all, making sure no one is left behind. It requires an informed and involved citizenry that believes what it thinks and does can make a difference. Such citizens believe that their real political involvement has more to do with the time, energy, gifts, and resources they put into rebuilding their own local communities than it does with pulling a lever on the first Tuesday of November.

The U.S. Catholic bishops offer four principles that should guide our faithful political engagement.

1. As an institution, we are called to be political but not partisan. The church cannot be a chaplain for any one party or cheerleader for any candidate. Our cause is the protection of the weak and vulnerable and defence of human life and dignity, not a particular party or candidate.

2. The church is called to be principled but not ideological. We cannot compromise our basic values or teaching, but we should be open to different ways to advance them.

3. We are called to be clear but also civil. A church that advocates justice and charity must practise these virtues in public life. We should be clear about our principles and priorities, without impugning motives or name-calling.

4. The church is called to be engaged but not used. We welcome dialogue
with political leaders and candidates, seeking to engage and persuade
public officials. But we must be sure that events and photo ops are not
substitutes for work on policies that reflect our values.[22]

Individuals are called to Christ, to join the new order of the kingdom
of God, to enter into an alternative community living by its new values, to
engage the world around critical and specific issues of injustice, to hold
the state accountable and limit its use of force, to always maintain a global
perspective, and to seek the common good of the place where we find
ourselves.

We now turn to the question of the agenda for that common-good
politics.

4

THE MORAL CENTRE

Politics for the Common Good

L et me start with two jokes, one religious and one political.
First the religious joke:
Two senators – one a Republican and the other a Democrat –
were eating together in the Senate Dining Room. The Republican senator
said, "You Democrats know nothing about religion!" "That's not true,"
insisted the Democratic senator. "We know a lot about religion." So the
Republican issued a challenge, "I'll bet twenty bucks you can't recite the
Lord's Prayer!" The Democrat said that was easy, and began, "Now I lay
me down to sleep, I pray the Lord my soul to keep." The Republican then
reached for his wallet and replied, "Darn, I didn't think you could do it!"

Now the political joke:
A man was drowning in the Potomac River, about one hundred feet
offshore. The Republicans ran down to the river, saw his predicament,
threw him fifty feet of rope, and yelled out to him, "The rest is up to you."
The Democrats then heard about the drowning man and the Republicans'
failure to rescue him. When they reached the riverbank, they saw that
the poor guy was about to go under, still about a hundred feet offshore.
So the Democrats threw him two hundred feet of rope – and let go of
their end.

The first joke was told to me by Richard Land, president of the Southern
Baptist Convention's Ethics & Religious Liberty Commission, and I told
him the second one back. We laughed hard at both of them. The two of us
are often placed on opposite sides of the political spectrum, but we liked
the jokes – one suggesting that the idea of religion belonging to only one
party is silly, and the other that both ideological sides are failing to solve
many of our deepest problems.

The truth is that the political categories of left and right simply don't fit
religion, and it is a big mistake to try to fit religion into them. Moreover,
the left/right framework doesn't work anymore in secular society either; it
has both polarized and paralyzed us, and it doesn't result in solutions.

The politicians in Washington, D.C. – on both sides of the aisle – have a habit of taking a problem and doing two things with it. First, they try to make people afraid of the problem, and second, they try to blame it on the other side. Then they take a poll to see whose spin won. The election is just the final poll. It's the politics of blame and the politics of fear. But people around the country are tiring of that. Many are now searching for a politics of solutions and a politics of hope.

The media are no better than the politicians. I've been in countless pre-interviews before television appearances, and I've learned that they are really auditions to see if the talking heads are going to have enough conflict to make for good television. I once went on CNN to debate the war in Iraq. When my opponent came on the screen, we greeted each other as friends, even though we disagreed about the war. I could see the disappointment in the face of the show's host. (*Oh no,* he must have thought, *they're probably going to be nice to each other!*) We were indeed, and had a cordial, civil, but informative discussion on whether or not Iraq was a just war.

One Sunday morning, when Richard Land and I were on *Meet the Press* along with Jerry Falwell and Al Sharpton, the shrill religious and political invective between the two of them was even too much for Tim Russert to control. The next day a story in the Memphis *Commercial Appeal* reported that Land and I had tried to take the conversation to a higher level but, "according to people who watched the show, Land and Wallis were like dorky hall monitors caught in a gang fight between the Bloods and the Crips, or rather in this case between the Neocons and the Libs".[1]

In such a combative political and media climate, nobody gets around to finding solutions to the problem being discussed. Rather, it's the political battle to gain advantage, or the media sensationalism, that turns public forums into gladiator rings and news-show hosts into celebrities.

Politics is truly broken and needs to be fixed. The good news is that people around the country are ready for something different. How do we move from a politics of blame and fear to a politics of solutions and hope? How can we move from left versus right to right and wrong? Could there be a new consensus around the values of the common good? I think so. It's been encouraging to work with some conservative Christian leaders, such as Richard Land, Samuel Rodriguez, Bishop Harry Jackson, and Joel Hunter, on a number of common concerns that cut across traditional left/right lines.

The Moral Centre

People I meet across the country are yearning for a moral centre to our public life and political discourse, with a fundamental emphasis on the common good. This is not just another argument for more centrist politics, so much in vogue these days. The mushy political middle isn't the answer, and a vague and compromising centrism that merely splits the difference on whatever the current political spectrum happens to be at the moment isn't particularly attractive.

Rather, the people I hear from around the nation and around the world want to understand better the moral choices and challenges that lie beneath our political debates. They don't want to just go "left" or "right", but deeper. Seeking to find the moral ground on which a new political consensus can be built and better decisions made is much more appealing than a weak and soulless centrism. More and more people want to see a common-good politics replace the politics of individual gain and special interests.

The moral centre also appeals to the "centre" of people's lives, which current political options often do not. What are the real and practical issues that affect people's daily experience and relate to what is actually going on in their everyday decisions, challenges, and choices? What is at the centre of people's lives and what appeals to their most basic moral concerns and values? It's time to create a new political language, from a moral centre, that focuses on the common good.

I believe values will and should be the focus of America's political future, but that "moral values" will no longer be reduced to a small number of hot-button social issues, too often used as wedges for partisan purposes – to divide and conquer for political gain. Moral politics, like the values that come from faith, would best be used not as a wedge to divide but as a bridge to unite us on the truly important issues in our public life. The moral-values discussion is now wider and deeper than it was in the past, and it is now extending to how we treat or respond to the poor, the environment, human rights abuses, pandemic diseases that wipe out millions of people, issues of war and peace, the crucial matters of family and community, and a consistent ethic of life. All of these issues go beyond the selective moralities of left and right.

The common good as a political agenda could offer a clear and compelling vision for America's future, and for the international community as well. Common ground can be found on many of our most critical issues.

In the late Senator Paul Wellstone's *Conscience of a Liberal*, he ends the introduction by saying: "Now is the time for progressives to thrust forward new ideas and new leaders. People yearn for a 'politics of the centre' – not 'the centre' so widely discussed by politicians and pundits in Washington but rather a politics that speaks to the centre of people's lives: affordable child care, good education for children, health security, living-wage jobs that will support families, respect for the environment and human rights, and clean elections and clean campaigns." Wellstone hoped to provide "insights into how we can reclaim the politics of compassion, how government can be a force for good, and how we can improve the lives of our children, our communities, and our nation for generations to come".[2]

At the same time, I am heartened by those seeking to forge a broader, deeper, and more compassionate conservative agenda that focuses on many of these same fundamental issues. Michael Gerson, former speechwriter and policy adviser to George W. Bush, well represents the "compassionate conservative" agenda so much talked about in the early days of the Bush administration but then sadly forgotten. Gerson writes: "Many evangelicals have begun elbowing against the narrowness of the religious right, becoming more globally focused and more likely to consider themselves 'pro-life and pro-poor'. ... [I]n reacting against the harsh tone of some on the religious right, many have been led back to the text of the Bible itself. Throughout the prophetic tradition of the Hebrew Scriptures and the teachings of the New Testament, social arrangements are judged by their effect on the weak." He cites race and poverty as an example:

> Hurricane Katrina revealed a kind of persistent poverty that leaves many Americans with no connection to, or stake in, the American economy. It also revealed a political class in Washington, in both parties, that seems to view this as an unfortunate fact of life, rather than a scandal that must eventually be addressed. A new faith-based agenda should include policies that provide help for overwhelmed pastors and neighborhood activists who are salvaging discarded lives; encourage mentors for abandoned children; and promote wealth-building to overcome the economic legacy of slavery and segregation.[3]

Indeed, convergences between those from the right and left sides of the political spectrum will become more and more possible as people from both sides focus on a broadly conceived moral-values agenda. Those from both sides signed on to join "Evangelicals for Darfur" and placed full-page ads in ten newspapers across the country (including *The New York Times, The Washington Post,* and *USA Today*) aimed at persuading President Bush to take decisive action to end the genocide in Darfur, and saying, "While we often disagree on matters of politics, we are united in the belief that your leadership can make the critical difference in Darfur. We join together now to urge you, in the words of Proverbs 24:11–12, to 'rescue those being led away to death'." Conservative Christian radio stations ran many radio spots on Darfur for free. Similar coalitions of politically conservative and progressive religious leaders are forming around comprehensive immigration reform and even around opposition to the death penalty. Concern for the environment and climate change also draws the religious community across political lines, as do global poverty and HIV/AIDS. The moral centre and the common good defy ideological categorization.

The Common Good

Preaching in Columbus, Ohio, the week before the 2006 election, I said, "On Tuesday, you won't be able to vote for the kingdom of God. It is not on the ballot. But there will be electoral choices that significantly impact the common good. And they are important." By making the war in Iraq and growing economic inequality two of the top issues, the voters helped put the common good on the agenda. But after the nation had voted, many in the religious community vowed to be at the doorstep of the newly elected and empowered politicians, to hold them accountable on the issues that arise from our deepest convictions.

Let's look at what we mean by the common good. In the preceding chapter we pointed to the biblical basis for seeking the common good. Jeremiah told the Jews to "seek the welfare of the city" that they were in, even as exiles. And, upon their return, Nehemiah famously told the children of Israel to rebuild the city of Jerusalem, and the biblical story says they "committed themselves to the common good". The early Christians held a "common purse", and Paul speaks of Christians using their gifts for the common good.

The concept is, of course, central to Catholic social teaching, and it can be seen in both the social gospel tradition of liberal Protestantism and the social revival tradition of evangelicalism. It is at the heart of the history of the black churches, and it can be found in both Jewish and Muslim traditions as well. And, obviously, the common good and the "general welfare" are foundational to the American constitutional tradition and thus accessible for both religious and secular citizens.

Here are some of those sources for the idea of the common good.

First, let's go a bit deeper into Catholic social teaching. In *Faithful Citizenship*, a helpful pamphlet published for the 2004 election, the U.S. Catholic bishops wrote, "Politics in this election year and beyond should be about an old idea with new power – the common good. The central question should not be, 'Are you better off than you were four years ago?' It should be, 'How can "we" – all of us, especially the weak and vulnerable – be better off in the years ahead? How can we protect and promote human life and dignity? How can we pursue greater justice and peace?'"

The bishops offered the simple but powerful metaphor of the "table" and asked:

> Who has a place at the table of life? Where is the place at the table for a million of our nation's children who are destroyed every year before they are born? How can we secure a place at the table for the hungry and those who lack health care in our own land and around the world? Where is the place at the table for those in our world who lack the freedom to practice their faith or stand up for what they believe? How do we ensure that families in our inner cities and rural communities, in barrios in Latin America and villages in Africa and Asia, have a place at the table – enough to eat, decent work and wages, education for their children, adequate health care and housing, and most of all, hope for the future?... A table is also a place where important decisions are made in our communities, nation, and world. How can the poorest people on Earth and those who are vulnerable in our land, including immigrants and those who suffer discrimination, have a real place at the tables where policies and priorities are set?[4]

I am an evangelical Christian, but I am also a convert to Catholic social teaching with its long and rich history. It suggests that the good of each individual is necessarily and vitally connected to the common good. The common good is understood as "the sum total of social conditions which allow people, either as groups or as individuals, to reach their fulfilment more fully and more easily".[5]

Catholic social teaching suggests that the common good consists of three essential elements: (1) respect for and promotion of the fundamental rights of the person, (2) social well-being and the development of the spiritual and temporal goods of society, and (3) the peace and security of the society and of its members. The common good should "make accessible to each what is needed to lead a truly human life: food, clothing, health, work, education and culture, suitable information, the right to establish a family, and so on". With that understanding, the role of the state is "to defend and promote the common good of civil society, its citizens, and intermediate bodies". I especially like this commentary on the common good: "The order of things must be subordinate to the order of persons, and not the other way around... This order is founded on truth, built up in justice, and animated by love." And finally, "The common good of the whole human family calls for an organization of society on the international level to provide for the needs of all."[6]

The notion of the common good has a long history, going back more than two thousand years and finding its roots in Plato, Aristotle, and Cicero. Catholic ethicist John Rawls defines the common good as "certain general conditions that are... equally to everyone's advantage". An essay titled "The Common Good" concludes:

> The common good, then, consists primarily of having the social systems, institutions, and environments on which we all depend work in a manner that benefits all people. Examples of particular common goods or parts of the common good include an accessible and affordable public health care system, an effective system of public safety and security, peace among the nations of the world, a just legal and political system, an unpolluted natural environment, and a flourishing economic system. Because such systems, institutions, and environments have such a powerful impact on the well-being of members of a society, it is no surprise that virtually every social problem in one way or another is linked to how well these systems and institutions are functioning.[7]

Conservative evangelicals such as Michael Gerson are also using the language of the common good. Gerson writes, "[F]or many, including me, Roman Catholic social thought provided a more sophisticated model of social engagement than a fractured Protestantism had produced. Evangelicals began to talk of subsidiarity (the imperative to respect and strengthen value-shaping institutions of community and family) and solidarity with the poor, and the pursuit of the common good, in ways that were not allergic to government."[8]

The idea of seeking the common good is central to the black churches. Dr. Robert Franklin, president of Morehouse College in Atlanta, writes in his book *Crisis in the Village* that "our shared, common ground must become the basis for collective action on behalf of the larger public good. Indeed, whatever common ground we can find or claim in this troubled time is a high moral achievement."[9]

That idea also can be traced back to the African concept of *ubuntu*, which Archbishop Desmond Tutu describes as:

> ... a concept that we have in our Bantu languages at home. Ubuntu is the essence of being a person. It means that we are people through other people. We cannot be fully human alone. We are made for interdependence, we are made for family. When you have ubuntu, you embrace others. You are generous, compassionate. If the world had more ubuntu, we would not have war. We would not have this huge gap between the rich and the poor. You are rich so that you can make up what is lacking for others. You are powerful so that you can help the weak, just as a mother or father helps their children. This is God's dream.[10]

Tutu notes:

> It embraces hospitality, caring about others, being able to go the extra mile for the sake of others. We believe that a person is a person through another person, that my humanity is caught up, bound up, inextricably, with yours. When I dehumanize you, I inexorably dehumanize myself. The solitary human being is a contradiction in terms and therefore you seek to work for the common good because your humanity comes into its own in belonging.[11]

The common good was the power behind Martin Luther King Jr.'s call for a Beloved Community. "This idea, beyond any other, was the fulcrum of all that Jim Lawson was teaching us," writes civil rights leader and member of Congress John Lewis. "It was at the center as well of everything Dr. King was working toward. As both men understood it, and as we were taught to believe in our workshops, the Beloved Community was nothing less than the Christian concept of the kingdom of God on earth. According to this concept, all human existence throughout history, from ancient Eastern and Western societies up through the present day, has strived toward community, toward coming together. That movement is as inexorable, as irresistible, as the flow of a river toward the sea."

It means, says Lewis, that "We must not turn away from one another. We must not retreat into separate tribes of like-minded, like-looking people who worship the same god, wear the same clothes, read the same books, and eat the same food as one another. This is the way of exclusion, not inclusion. We cannot afford to keep going this way. If we are to survive as a society, as a nation, we must turn toward one another and reach out in every way we can."

Lewis concludes:

> I believe the power and the endurance of Martin Luther King Jr.'s vision
> and leadership was the fact that it extended to all people, regardless of class
> or race. Most of the American people, black and white alike, understood
> and believed his message of brotherhood and justice, a message that cut
> across all lines of wealth, or color, or gender, or age. They understood it and
> they felt it when he spoke of the Beloved Community. Consider those two
> words. "Beloved" – not hateful, not violent, not uncaring, not unkind. And
> "Community" – not separated, not polarized, not adversarial. People are
> dying to embrace those feelings, if only they could trust, if only they could
> dare to believe, both in one another and in their leaders.[12]

As Dr. King powerfully described it in his last book, "We have inherited
a large house, a great 'world house,' in which we have to live together... a
family unduly separated in ideas, culture, and interest, who, because we
can never again live apart, must learn somehow to live with each other in
peace... All inhabitants of the globe are now neighbors."[13]

Related to the common good are the Jewish concepts of *shalom* and
tikkun. The Hebrew word for peace is *shalom* but it means far more than
our usual understanding of the term. It includes wholeness, completeness,
balance, healing, well-being, tranquillity, prosperity, security, and, of course,
justice. The pursuit of peace, in this wider and deeper definition, is the
responsibility of persons, structures, and groups – a Jewish common good.
And *tikkun* means "to heal and repair the world". It is a command to fix
the common good when it is broken. Both *shalom* and *tikkun* are activist
concepts aimed at overcoming injustice, conflict, strife, and violence. The
Shalom Center in Philadelphia describes the varieties of peacemakers in the
Jewish tradition as including "skillful mediators like Aaron, compassionate
teachers like Hillel, people who disobeyed unjust laws like Shifrah and Puah
and resisters during the Holocaust, organizers like Rose Schneiderman,
thinkers and activists like [Martin] Buber and [Abraham Joshua] Heschel,
writers like Elie Wiesel, our personal family peacemakers".[14]

We also find the concept of the common good in Islam. Islamic scholar
Reza Aslan writes that the idea is based in the Bedouin tribal ethic:

> The strictures of Bedouin life naturally prevented the social and economic
> hierarchies that were so prevalent in sedentary societies like Mecca. The
> only way to survive in a community in which movement was the norm and
> material accumulation impractical was to maintain a strong sense of tribal

solidarity by evenly sharing all available resources. The tribal ethic was therefore founded on the principle that every member had an essential function in maintaining the stability of the tribe, which was only as strong as its weakest members.[15]

At the beginning of the revelation of the Qur'an, Aslan says, theology was not the main thing on Muhammed's mind: "At this point in his ministry, Muhammed had a far more urgent message. That message... dealt almost exclusively with the demise of the tribal ethic in Mecca. In the strongest terms, Muhammed decried the mistreatment and exploitation of the weak and unprotected. He called for an end to false contracts and the practice of usury that had made slaves of the poor. He spoke of the rights of the underprivileged and the oppressed, and made the astonishing claim that it was the duty of the rich and powerful to take care of them. 'Do not oppress the orphan,' the Qur'an commands, 'and do not drive away the beggar.' (93:9–10)... Muhammed was not yet establishing a new religion; he was calling for sweeping social reform. He was not yet preaching monotheism; he was demanding social justice."[16]

My friend Imam Feisal Abdul Rauf of the Cordoba Initiative explained further:

Islamic Law, known as the Sharia... is said to have one over-arching objective: the "good" (called "maslaha") of humankind in this life and the next. This concept of maslaha can be accurately translated into English as the "common good". The six sub-objectives of Islamic Law that flow out of the meta-objective of maslaha are the protection and furtherance of: life, religion, intellect, honor, family, and property. Thus all Islamic law is to further these major "objectives" or "aspects of the common good"; they describe the common good... we might even call them the "sub-common good," to turn a phrase.[17]

The common good also has secular roots, beginning with the Preamble to the U.S. Constitution: "We the People of the United States, in Order to form a more perfect Union, establish Justice, insure domestic Tranquility, provide for the common defense, promote the general Welfare, and secure the Blessings of Liberty to ourselves and our Posterity, do ordain and establish this Constitution for the United States of America."

At a 2006 conference titled "Securing the Common Good", the Center for American Progress summarized the concept and its contemporary relevance:

The common good, as both a philosophical ideal and approach to governing, has a rich history in the civic strands of American thought and in the values and principles of the U.S. Constitution. It is also a powerful theme in the social teachings of many major faith traditions. In both the civic and faith realms, a commitment to the common good means pursuing policies and community actions that benefit all individuals and balance self-interest with the needs of the entire society. It recognizes that government – while not the only tool – is essential for helping people pursue their dreams, and that the business, labor, faith, and NGO communities play a critical role as well. The common good approach to politics represents a clear break with the radical individualism, corruption, and greed that define contemporary American life. It marks the end of a politics that leaves people to rise and fall on their own.[18]

One of the speakers at the conference was former President Bill Clinton, who traced the idea back to the founding fathers. "In the context of late 1991, I defined the common good as a new covenant for equal opportunity, shared responsibility, an inclusive community, and an aggressive approach to try to create those values throughout the world at the end of the Cold War," Clinton said. "It was what I thought America should do to advance the common good – really just a restatement of what our founders pledged their lives, their fortunes, their sacred honor to do. form a more perfect union."[19]

On the progressive left, the common-good idea is also being rediscovered as a more compelling overarching moral agenda than the "identity politics" and the politics of "rights" that have dominated the liberal agenda in recent decades. After Aristotle, Augustine, and Thomas Aquinas, we are now hearing from people such as Michael Tomasky of *The American Prospect* magazine:

In terms of political philosophy, this idea of citizens sacrificing for and participating in the creation of a common good has a name: civic republicanism. It's the idea, which comes to us from sources such as Rousseau's social contract and some of James Madison's contributions to the Federalist Papers, that for a republic to thrive, leaders must create and nourish a civic sphere in which citizens are encouraged to think broadly about what will sustain that republic and to work together to achieve common goals... Against this small-r republican tradition that posits sacrifice for larger, universalist purposes is another tradition that has propelled American liberalism, that indeed is what the philosophers call liberalism proper: from

Locke and Mill up to John Rawls in our time, a greater emphasis on the individual (and, later, the group), on tolerance, on rights, and on social justice. In theory, it is not inevitable that these two traditions must clash. But in the 1960s, it was inevitable that they did.[20]

The idea of the common good is a direct challenge to the rampant individualism that shapes our society in every way. The common good begins with respect for the individual, but places each person in the context of all his or her social relations. John Carr, secretary of the Office of Social Development and World Peace of the U.S. Conference of Catholic Bishops, analyzes the current problem well. He says we are confronted today with two kinds of individualism, one from the right and one from the left. From the right, we face a "market individualism" that evaluates everything and everyone by their economic worth. From the left, we face a "lifestyle individualism" that values personal freedom above all social responsibilities. Carr writes:

> I find so much of politics shaped by different kinds of rampant individualism. For many Democrats and those on the cultural left, a kind of lifestyle individualism elevates personal identity and autonomy above all else, making "choice" an ultimate criteria for public life. For many Republicans and some on the economic right, a kind of free-market individualism dominates, insisting the market solves all problems and winners and losers are simply inevitable. Both these directions neglect a sense of the common good and have very little room for a priority for the poor and vulnerable.[21]

Clearly, the common good challenges both of these individualisms, the ethics of both the right and the left. No wonder the common good has few advocates on Capitol Hill, as lobbyists and special interests too often dominate the debate. Yet, I believe, the country is hungry for just such a vision and ethic, if a political leader had the courage to offer it. E. J. Dionne – my favourite syndicated columnist and a devout Catholic – described the common good in a recent conversation, reflecting on the relationship between personal freedom and social responsibility:

> Even if you are deeply libertarian – and I think every American has a strong and healthy streak of libertarianism in him or her – you must recognize that individual liberty requires collective work so it can survive and be vindicated. The oldest line in the world [is] that "if your liberty is threatened, my liberty can be threatened too". I think we've lost sight of the social basis

for liberty. Therefore, even libertarians ought to be communitarian. Even libertarians ought to have a sense of the common good. Only certain kinds of societies can be really effective in remaining free societies. When societies become radically unequal, freedom can be threatened, not just because you undermine the freedom to act of those at the bottom of the heap, but also because the society can become very unstable.

Then Dionne applied a common-good vision to the family:

Some of this comes out in arguments about the family – and this has absolutely nothing to do with gay-rights issues. Conservatives argue, quite rightly, that on the whole kids are better off in intact families when they are raised by two parents. All the evidence says that conservatives are right about that. Liberals resisted this for a while. I think they resist it less now. But then the question becomes, Okay, you're for the family, what do you do about it? If we have a whole bunch of young men who've grown up in broken families, in violent neighborhoods, and end up in prison, how is that going to help strengthen the family? There is a moral basis for a healthy family, but there's also an economic basis for the healthy family. The job of progressives is not to argue with conservatives about whether family is important or not. They should agree with them on that. They should argue with them about whether conservative policies strengthen or undermine the family. I think that's a metaphor for how you think about the common good.

Finally, Dionne tied the idea of the common good to his own family, and the all-important political question of taxes:

I try to think about this a lot in terms of "Well, I have my own political views, but how is politics good for my kids?" One way to look at it – and not irrationally – is to say, "If my taxes are cut, I can leave my kids more money, I can spend more money on their education, I can do all these kinds of things." But the other question is, What kind of a society will my kids be happy in and will they prosper in? I really think that they will be happier in a society with a strong sense of the common good, where we do actually care about each other, where we're not broken down into different hostile groups, where we're not in gated communities radically separated from one another. So the question is, How do you not only look at your kids' self-interest in narrow terms, but how do you look to their long-term well-being in broader terms?[22]

New Directions

Could the concept of the common good help us create a new political narrative that could achieve some consensus on critical issues? I think it could.

Who is left out or left behind is always a religious and moral question. In the Hebrew scriptures, the health of a society was measured by how it cared for its weakest and most vulnerable, and prosperity was to be shared by all. Jesus proclaimed a gospel that was "good news to the poor". A commitment to "the least of these" is central to my personal faith and compels my public actions as an evangelical Christian. Almost two years after the television images of Katrina were seared into our minds, thiry-seven million Americans still live in poverty, left out and left behind. Globally, thirty thousand children die needlessly every day from hunger and disease, and the images of Africa haunt the world and inspire new commitments from rock stars, megachurch pastors, and a new wave of young people.

Here at home, too many people are still poor despite having jobs and working hard, which mocks the American dream. In the world's richest country, needless poverty shouldn't be tolerated any longer. Too many people are still trapped in a polarized debate about poverty. Liberals champion necessary and effective government programmes, but often then disregard cultural and family issues that reinforce the vicious cycle of poverty. Conservatives advance a pro-family agenda, but then often disregard realities that dramatically affect families, such as low wages, lack of health care, lack of child care, and little access to affordable housing. It is time to lift up practical policies and effective practices that "make work work" for low-income working families and challenge the increasing wealth gap between rich and poor. And that's exactly what we will be discussing in chapter 5.

We must find a new moral and political will to overcome poverty that combines personal and social responsibility, makes a primary commitment to support strong families, focuses on reversing cultural breakdown, and operates with a more honest assessment of both the individual decisions and social systems that trap people in poverty. Answering the call to lift people out of poverty will require moral commitment and bipartisan political leadership. I have spoken with leaders from both parties about creating a real antipoverty agenda in Congress, including issues of both personal and social responsibility. We need a grand alliance between liberals and conservatives to produce new and effective strategies to confront both the cultural and the economic causes of impoverishment and to help the poor escape the prison of poverty.

Around the world, what the United Nations describes as "extreme poverty" and Bono calls "stupid poverty" simply is not morally acceptable when we really could end it, if we had the moral and political will. The global challenge will not be met until we commit ourselves to three critical goals: more focused and effective aid by the wealthy countries, with transparency and good governance from the poorest countries; the cancellation and redirection of resources that already impoverished nations must now use to service their crippling debt burden; and, most critically, a dramatic move from free trade to trade justice – allowing the poorest nations of the world to earn their way out of poverty by reversing the systematic tilt of globalization's rules and practices in favour of the already wealthy nations. An economist once wrote that the average European cow is subsidized at a higher level than that at which half the world's people are forced to live – two dollars per day. As long as the richest farmers in the world's wealthiest nations receive such lucrative agricultural subsidies, the cotton farmers of West Africa will never be able to sell their goods at a high enough price to enable them to support their families. At root, it is indeed a moral question we must confront: are other people's children as important as our own? The challenge of equality and diversity will be the focus of chapter 7.

Our earth and the fragile atmosphere that surrounds it are God's good creation. Yet, our environment is in jeopardy as global warming continues unchecked and our air and water are polluted. Good stewardship of our resources is a religious and moral question. Global warming and environmental protection are becoming moral imperatives for a new generation that speaks of "creation care". Energy conservation and less dependence on fossil fuels are commitments that could dramatically change our future, from the renewal of our lifestyles to the moral redemption of our foreign policies. We'll discuss all of these in chapter 6. This is such a big issue in American life and politics that, eventually, some smart political leaders will run on this agenda – and win.

Strong families are foundational to the well-being of any society. A culture that promotes healthy families is necessary to raise our children with strong values, and the breakdown of family and community in our society must be addressed. But we need serious solutions, not merely the scapegoating of others. Neither political party has yet to offer a genuinely comprehensive pro-family agenda, and it's about time we had one. We'll offer one in chapter 9.

And wouldn't coming together to find common ground that dramatically reduces the number of abortions be better than both the left and the right using it as an issue to divide us? Some new initiatives in Congress aimed at abortion reduction, sponsored by both Democrats and Republicans, hold out that very promise. And does the sanctity of life apply to only one issue or must it be addressed to all the questions concerning the protection and dignity of life "from womb to tomb"? We'll look at these questions in chapter 8.

Rev. Joel Hunter, senior pastor of the Northland Church in Longwood, Florida, had been chosen in 2006 to be president of the Christian Coalition. But he resigned before taking office, saying that the Coalition leadership opposed his plans to increase the range of issues they were involved in. "I wanted to expand the issues from only moral ones – such as opposing abortion and redefining marriage – to include compassion issues such as poverty, justice, and creation care," Hunter said in a statement. "We need to care as much for the vulnerable outside the womb as inside the womb."[23]

In Iraq, the cost and consequences of a disastrous war are also moral issues that our country must address. As leaders in both political parties have recognized, the only moral and practical course now is to change U.S. policy, starting with an open, honest, and full national debate about one question: how to extricate U.S. forces from Iraq with the least possible damage to everyone involved – to Americans, Iraqis, their Middle Eastern neighbours, and a world longing for security. There are deeper questions as well, including how to confront the real threats of terrorism without resorting to endless and counterproductive war-making; how to address the root causes of the anger and despair that so easily recruit for horrendous violence; and in particular, how to resolve the intransigent Israeli/Palestinian conflict that breeds such deep resentment. The moral challenge to us, in confronting the threats of terrorism, is not to become monsters ourselves as we seek to defeat other monsters. Theologically and practically, how do we take the problem of evil seriously without falling into evil ourselves, and without forgetting the moral connection between ends and means? We will address these crucial and complicated issues in chapter 10.

Across the political spectrum, the desire for integrity in our government is growing. Corruption in government – the way that money and power distort our political decision making and even our electoral processes – violates our basic principles. In a political culture with seemingly never-ending scandals, our values should lead us to insist on both electoral and lobbying reform and an end to pork-barrel spending, earmarks, and the influence of special interests on policy decisions. We must restore trust in our government and reclaim the integrity of our democratic system. This will entail placing the public interest over narrow private or special interests. The hunger for integrity, both personal and public, and the need for a new style of leadership will be the subject of chapter 11.

The politics we have become used to cannot change these realities, and it continues to be paralyzed by them. We need a new politics of values that could rise to the occasion, summon the best in the American people, and unite us to solve the moral issues of our time. Americans are much less concerned about what is liberal or conservative, Democratic or Republican, than about what is right and what works.

All the great social reform movements of our past – abolishing slavery, establishing civil rights, extending voting rights, protecting workers, creating safety nets for our most vulnerable citizens – have required a moral definition of politics and popular social movements that had spiritual foundations. We have done this before and we can do it again.

The path of partisan division is well worn, but the road of compassionate priorities and social justice will lead us to a new America. That is an America that reflects all our best values. Building that new America will require greater moral leadership from both Democrats and Republicans, from our religious communities, and from each and every one of us.

The Conservative Radical

We are on the brink of a new kind of "prophetic politics" that would be a "fourth option" in our public life – beyond liberal, conservative, and libertarian. It could also create new initiatives that cut through the vicious culture wars that destroy our political process and make talk-show hosts rich. War is not the answer to the deep challenges our culture faces, but what could bring about some peace? Maybe by listening to the other side, instead of just trying to defeat and destroy it, we might learn some things. Maybe there are insights from all sides that we need right now, but perhaps we ultimately need to transcend our contemporary political options if we hope to make real progress. E. J. Dionne comments on how we might learn to talk to each other politically:

> I know my sense of what politics should be like was shaped by the fact that I grew up in a politically diverse family, so I argued with people whom I didn't hate. Indeed, I argued with people I actually loved. It created a different sense of what "argument" was… Dr. King's commitment [was] not to destroy or defeat adversaries, but to convert them. It's a very interesting notion. For

King it wasn't "convert" in the sense that "I have higher wisdom". It was
to change people's way of looking at things... Christopher Lasch said, "In
authentic argument you have to be willing to put your views at risk." You
really have to enter imaginatively into the ideas of your opponent. If you at
least begin in that spirit – and being all sinners we'll always fail sometimes –
you can have a different kind of approach that doesn't look like the "I'm right
and you're an idiot" kind of politics that is dominant.[24]

Conservatives have been right about the importance of culture and
values and the necessity of personal responsibility; but they have been
morally compromised by favouring the rich over the poor and middle classes
and by conforming to American nationalism and militarism. Liberals have
been right to talk about social responsibility and the need for government
to ensure fairness and opportunity and a more level playing field; but
they have mostly failed to affirm the importance of fundamental moral
values in our national life, which could be done without compromising
their values of democracy and pluralism. Libertarians are right about the
importance of freedom and liberty and the need to protect civil liberties
from the encroachments of government, especially at a time when national
security and the "war on terror" are regularly used as arguments for taking
away individual rights that form the core of the American ideal and that
past generations have fought so hard for. But they are wrong when their
political philosophy degenerates into merely "leave me alone" and "not in
my backyard" politics – when the libertarians forget that our individual
rights exist as part of a social fabric whose health and vitality serve to
protect and give broader social meaning to our freedom.

As the limitations of the current political options have become more
apparent and as their ideological rigidity blocks social cooperation and
political solutions, I have become ever more convinced of the need for
another way. And one seems to be emerging. We see a new kind of politics
growing around the country. It is socially "conservative" or traditional
on matters of personal behavior and responsibility, rooted in strong moral
values that include the sanctity of human life, and deeply committed to
the crucial bonds of family. At the same time, it is also strongly populist
with regard to economic fairness and justice, quite communitarian in its
sense of social responsibility, deeply committed to environmental care, and
increasingly antiwar in its stance toward foreign policy. At the heart of this
new (and very old) option is the integral link between personal ethics and
social justice, and the refusal to separate the two.

Not surprisingly, such commitments flow naturally from the religious values of many Americans – integrity, fidelity, compassion, generosity, and a perspective that is more global and not merely national. Even among members of Congress, we now see some newly elected officials who don't fit the old moulds. Socially conservative, economically populist, and antiwar are no longer mutually exclusive commitments.

It is possible to be committed to the sacredness of life without isolating those who are making desperate choices. Although abortion is always a moral tragedy, the strategy of prevention, giving practical support for low-income women, and offering concrete alternatives may be a better response than condemnation and criminalization. It is possible to be strongly for marriage and family without being against gay rights. We see marriages with real commitment to equality and mutuality between men and women, and are discovering that parenting is the ultimate test of family values.

It is possible to call for personal responsibility and social responsibility at the same time. It is possible to preserve the environment and turn back the threats against our fragile planet while also promoting the economic growth that can lift people out of poverty. It is possible to love one's country while admitting its mistakes, holding it to higher standards, and insisting that God's blessings are not bestowed on one nation alone. It is possible to take the reality of evil and the existence of enemies very seriously, yet to see the "logs in our own eye" and prefer the skills of conflict resolution and the requirements of justice over the habit of war. All these things are indeed possible, and could unite the best instincts of principled conservatism and progressive liberalism while balancing the values of both freedom and community. As E. J. Dionne puts it:

> You can chase the center, or you can try to create one. Our task is to create a new political center that is moderate in tone and understands that people are tugged by tradition – and that that's not automatically a bad thing – but that has a problem-solving orientation that's fundamentally egalitarian. I don't think those two things are at odds. Indeed, one of the reasons I have all my life been drawn to the power of religion is because religious traditions tend to reflect the popular moral sense.
>
> An awful lot of people who say they are conservative are also people who, if you ask them specific questions, would say that they don't like a society dominated by greed. They don't like a society dominated by selfishness. They don't like a society in which the only thing you think about is yourself. A lot of those instincts on the part of very conservative people, on many specific questions, will tug them in a progressive direction.

Progressives, for a while, lost track of how to have a conversation with those folks. Or they ended up looking down their noses at those folks. For me that was always wrong, partly because I've known people like that all my life. Some of them are far more generous in the way they lead their own lives than a lot of people who are liberal.[25]

Perhaps it is time to move beyond the old exclusive categories of liberalism and conservatism. Maybe what we need is a new paradigm altogether – we might call it *the conservative radical*. To be conservative means to be rooted – in a tradition, in faith, in core values. To be radical also means to be rooted (*radical* comes from the Latin word *radix,* meaning "root"), which gives one a consistent perspective on the world. So these two – radical and conservative – may not be contradictory but in fact deeply complementary.

What we need most are people rooted in "conservative" values and commitments but willing to be "radical" enough to apply those very values in the real world. If we are to preserve the values (a conservative goal) of equality and justice, for example, they require radical application to the needs of a broken world (a liberal goal). Dorothy Day of the Catholic Worker movement was a conservative radical – applying the values of her faith to life. It has been said that "she loved the truth enough to live it". So were Mother Teresa, Martin Luther King Jr., and Dietrich Bonhoeffer – they were all rooted in conservative traditions that made them radicals in the world.

Ultimately, we are known and judged by what we say yes to and what we say no to. We say yes to the conservative values that root us, and then say a radical no when those values require it. A conservative radical doesn't fall neatly into any of our modern political categories and options but could help transform them all. And that might lead us to some real solutions, and perhaps even bring a measure of peace to a political culture that is still at war.

What follows now are seven "commitments" that could change our polarized and paralyzed debate and perhaps move us forward. We have to find common ground by moving to higher ground. And we have to break the political impasses and public apathy that prevent us from finding solutions to some of the biggest moral issues of our time. These commitments, if made by individuals, congregations, and communities, and finally by our political leaders, might help us reach a "tipping point" on those great issues and break through to some real answers. And in the process, we might even experience some healing of our broken political process.

5

INCLUSION AND OPPORTUNITY
The Welcome Table

To meet and to come to know the poorest of God's children does change us and could, ultimately, change the facts of poverty. That's what happened to Bono on an early visit to Africa. He tells the story.

> Before I had kids, in Ethiopia in this camp/feeding station where I was working with Ali, a man came up to me with his boy, beautiful boy, proud of his son and begged me to take his son home and through the translator, he just repeated over and over, you take him with you. If he stays here he will surely die. The rules of camp are that you can't take people home, you can't adopt… But somewhere I did take them home. And I'm working for that boy now. And I have kids of my own now and I have to remind myself that this feeling I have for my kids, these Africans have for their children…[1]

I am a father of young children, too, and I simply can't imagine what it would be like to decide to give your son away in order to save his life. The incident cut right to Bono's heart, as it does to mine every time I tell the story.

A parable of the kingdom:

> On one occasion when Jesus was going to the house of a leader of the Pharisees to eat a meal on the sabbath, they were watching him closely… He said also to the one who had invited him, "When you give a luncheon or a dinner, do not invite your friends or your brothers or your relatives or rich neighbours, in case they may invite you in return, and you would be repaid. But when you give a banquet, invite the poor, the crippled, the lame, and the blind. And you will be blessed, because they cannot repay you, for you will be repaid at the resurrection of the righteous" (Luke 14:1, 12–14).

This gospel story from Luke tells us what God is like, and what God wants us to be like. Unlike the way the political issue of poverty is often discussed – debating the causes of poverty, blaming the poor for their condition, or trying to do things to or for them that might improve their plight – God wants us to bring them in. God wants us to bring them to the table, invite them into relationship, get to know who they are and what's going on in their lives (that's what you do with dinner guests), and so lay the foundations for a new community in which everyone gets changed.

One of the most famous African American spirituals, "The Welcome Table", is based on this gospel story. The words go like this:

We're gonna sit at the welcome table,
We're gonna sit at the welcome table one of these days,
Hallelujah!...
All God's children around that table...
No more fightin or grabbin at that table...
I'm gonna walk the streets of glory...
I'm gonna get my civil rights...
We're gonna sit at the welcome table one of these days.

The "welcome table" is an excellent image and metaphor for both the spiritual transformation and the political strategy needed to overcome poverty. It changes us and our approach to poor people. It helps us to understand who poor people really are, what they need, and how the rest of us (including our values and our systems) need to change. Poor people no longer remain at arm's length in their ghettoized isolation when we join together at the welcome table, when they are invited to join us in our own communities, where together we find solutions to our common problems.

Most of the biblical insights about overcoming poverty seem to have to do with inclusion, bringing people into the community and incorporating their needs into the common life. In the scriptural examples, poverty is resolved by bringing people into relationship and community: welcoming the poor to the banquet table; instructing landowners to leave produce at the edges of the fields for "gleaning"; Jesus' example of the Good Samaritan's giving of his time and treasure to the one in need; the sharing and distributing of goods in the new economy of the early church; Paul's missionary collections for the poorest churches.

Another biblical theme is the insistence upon justice, exemplified by the Jubilee tradition in ancient Israel, a periodic economic levelling during which land was returned, debts forgiven, and slaves set free (Leviticus 25). The Hebrew prophets seem especially hard on those who deliberately exploit and abuse the poor and vulnerable through selfish greed or corruption of the law. The God of the Bible is not merely a God of charity but a God of justice who holds kings, rulers, judges, and employers accountable for how they treat widows, orphans, and workers over matters of land, labour, and capital. All this is rooted in the call to right relationships, which is at the heart of the biblical notion of justice itself. So re-establishing a right relationship to the poor is the beginning of ending poverty. We all learn the meaning of right relationships when we sit together at the welcome table.

Millions of American Christians are discovering God's concern for his poorest children, and their biblical rediscovery could well change the political issue of poverty in the United States and around the world. That movement is paralleled in other faith traditions. Moreover, millions of people who aren't religious are being drawn to the issue as a fundamental spiritual and moral imperative. For some, poverty is becoming a focal point of faith; for others, a magnet drawing them to faith itself. The power of this growing constituency could indeed provide a tipping point on the issues of global and domestic poverty.

On the way to church one Sunday morning, I was reading a *New York Times* column by Nicholas Kristof to my wife, Joy, as she drove. It began:

> Cast your eyes to the right and meet Hidaya Abatemam, whom I met last month in a remote area of southern Ethiopia. She is six years old and weighs 17 pounds.
>
> Hidaya was starved nearly to death and may well have suffered permanent mental impairment, helping to trap her and her children – if she lives that long – in another generation of poverty.
>
> Yet maybe the more interesting question is not why Hidaya is starving but why the world continues to allow 30,000 children like her to die each day of poverty.
>
> Ultimately what is killing girls like her isn't precisely malnutrition or malaria, but indifference. And that, in turn, arises from our insularity, our inexperience in traveling or living in poor countries, so that we have difficulty empathizing with people like Hidaya.
>
> I often hear comments from readers like, "It's tragic over there, but we've got our own problems that we have to solve first." Nobody who has held the hand of a starving African child could be that dismissive.[2]

From the backseat of the car, my eight-year-old son, Luke, who had been listening, was incredulous, "Seventeen pounds and six years old! How could that happen?" he exclaimed. We explained, as we had before to him, that thirty thousand children around the world die each day from lack of clean drinking water, from diseases that none of his friends would ever get, and simply from not having enough to eat. Four-year-old Jack was now listening, too, as his older brother asked, "Don't people know about this? Why don't they do something? We have to, it's really sad."

The Three Obstacles

So why don't we do something? When it comes to finally doing something about poverty – actually seeing results in bettering the lives of poor people around the world and in our own country, even looking forward to ending poverty as we know it – I believe we have at least three major obstacles.

The first obstacle is the low priority of poverty on our national and international political agendas. Poor people are just not on the list of top issues. There are about three pharmaceutical industry lobbyists for every member of Congress, but very few advocates for poor children on Capitol Hill. Politicians prefer to talk about issues that affect the middle classes because they know where the votes are, and they know that low-income people have the lowest voter turnout of any group in society (and don't make many political donations either!). Just getting by from day to day is about all that most poor parents and their kids can accomplish, plus they don't often see that election outcomes have very much effect on the quality of their lives.

The second obstacle is the debate over strategy that we quickly get into – about the causes and solutions of poverty – even when some event again brings the existence of so many poor people to public attention (as Hurricane Katrina did). Poor people are not just trapped in poverty, but also in the debate about poverty. Both liberals and conservatives spend more time blaming each other for the problems of poverty than finding practical solutions to them. And the bitter debate, finally, just makes people turn away and believe that nothing can be done.

The third obstacle is perhaps the foundation of the first two. It is the lack of relationship with the poor. The vast majority of people in the richest half of the world's population or in the top two-thirds of U.S. society have almost no relationship to the people at the bottom. Lack of relationship leads to lack of understanding, empathy, and urgency and creates stereotypes, myths, excuses, and passivity.

Change begins with a new relationship to the poor.

I remember being in London just before the 2006 G8 annual meeting in Glen Eagles, Scotland. A trans-Atlantic summit of church leaders from the United States and the United Kingdom had been arranged to help move the G8 agenda on increased aid for Africa, on further debt cancellation for the most impoverished countries, and on the critical issues of "trade justice". Trade justice – for example, removing unfair agricultural subsidies, such as subsidized cotton production in developed countries, that undercut the market and have destroyed the livelihood of many African farmers – would allow the world's poor countries to earn their own way out of poverty. Rules of trade still benefit the wealthy nations over the poorest ones when pharmaceutical patent protections prohibit developing countries from importing desperately needed generic medicines.

In our daylong meeting at Lambeth Palace, cohosted by Archbishop of Canterbury Rowan Williams, there was a very dramatic moment when Daleep Mukarji, head of the British church agency Christian Aid, began to snap his fingers. "Thirty thousand children dying every day comes to about one every three seconds," he said, "and that's about this long." As he solemnly snapped his fingers every three seconds, the room got very quiet and the sound of each death pierced the silence. Try it sometime yourself. Go into a quiet room, take a deep breath, and then begin snapping your fingers every three seconds. Then say a prayer.

In the column referred to earlier, Nicholas Kristof went on to announce an opportunity his paper was providing for university students to travel with him on his journalist trips to places where children like Hidaya live, and to encourage young people to go there on their own – to learn more about the world than they ever would in their classrooms. In an earlier conversation, Kristof told me his own story and talked about why he goes to the forgotten and invisible places of the world to write his columns.

Over time as a foreign correspondent, I became interested in public health issues. It seemed to me that that was a place where we in journalism and also the political system utterly failed the people. When you looked at the numbers of people who were dying from diarrhea caused by bad water or malaria because they didn't have mosquito nets – that's something that has demanded more attention.

Since it was always happening, it never seemed newsworthy. Politicians didn't even know or think about it. To make these stories resonate with American audiences, I tried to find individuals who Americans could care about.

I always feel a little bit in danger of treading beyond the boundaries of objective journalism and into some kind of advocacy. People will call me and say, "You're such a great crusader." I always flinch at that. "Crusader" to a journalist has this connotation of being more into the cause than into some sort of objective truth. But you really can't just forget about these people that you meet when it's so easy to make a difference.[3]

I don't believe the facts of global poverty will change us until they become personal for us. Literally half of God's children on this earth, three billion people, live on less than two dollars a day. And more than one billion people live on less than one dollar per day. The U.N. calls that extreme poverty. Gordon Brown, the prime minister of Britain, once said that we now have "the knowledge, information, technology, and resources to end extreme poverty; the only thing we lack is the moral and political will". One of the principal reasons we lack the will is that the vast majority of those of us in the more affluent half of the world simply don't know anybody in the poorest half. It's easy to pass over statistics; it's much harder to forget your friends.

Michael Sandel, a professor of politics at Harvard University, has a provocative and revealing metaphor for our isolation from one another. He starts talking about baseball and how everyone used to experience the game in the same way – you all got hot or rained on and ate the same bad hot dogs. But then came the skyboxes, and some of us now stayed dry and watched our favourite players run around the field from air-conditioned comfort looking through glass windows while dining on fine cuisine. It's ruined baseball, says Sandel. But even worse, we now see the "skyboxification" of America, as he puts it. "And that includes us," Sandel challenged an affluent and mostly liberal audience who had come together at a high-powered social retreat to discuss great ideas. Those who live their lives in skyboxes cannot possibly understand how most of the world's people are forced to live. Personal transformation, understanding, and effective strategies will never be found on the inside of a skybox.

In the early days of the Sojourners community, I was part of a household in a five-bedroom house (with one bathroom) with a single mother and nine children under the age of fourteen, along with six other people. That taught me much more about "urban welfare families" than I had learned studying sociology in college. It also turned that mom and her kids from statistics into friends. Little Leon used to wait for me to come home from work, daring me to drop my briefcase and give him a hug with a tough-kid challenge, "I bet you can't pick me up!" His gruff voice and stern face would turn to giddy and joyful laughter as I picked him up and lifted him over my head. The prophet Isaiah said that the fast God chooses is to "bring the homeless poor into your house", and after doing that I understood why – so we could understand each other at the welcome table.

Meeting refugee families in the corrugated metal shacks of South African shantytowns, or sleeping in hammocks that drop magically from the ceiling at night to accommodate an extraordinary number of people in one-room huts in rural Philippine villages, taught me more about those one billion people who live in extreme poverty than all the U.N. reports I had read. When a six-year-old curls up on your lap and falls asleep while looking up at the star-filled sky with his own dreams, you really don't want him to become one of those thirty thousand finger snaps.

At Washington, D.C.'s National Prayer Breakfast in 2006, there was an unlikely preacher. "If you're wondering what I'm doing here at a prayer breakfast," he said, "well, so am I. I'm certainly not here as a man of the cloth, unless that cloth is leather." But then Bono, the Irish rock star from U2, began to preach:

> The one thing we can all agree, all faiths and ideologies, is that God is with the vulnerable and poor. God is in the slums, in the cardboard boxes where the poor play house. God is in the silence of a mother who has infected her child with a virus that will end both their lives. God is in the cries heard under the rubble of war. God is in the debris of wasted opportunity and lives, and God is with us if we are with them.
>
> From charity to justice, the good news is yet to come. There is much more to do. There's a gigantic chasm between the scale of the emergency and the scale of the response. And finally, it's not about charity after all, is it? It's about justice. Let me repeat that: It's not about charity, it's about justice.
>
> And that's too bad. Because you're good at charity. Americans, like the Irish, are good at it. We like to give, and we give a lot, even those who can't afford it. But justice is a higher standard.
>
> Africa makes a fool of our idea of justice; it makes a farce of our idea of equality. It mocks our pieties, it doubts our concern, it questions our commitment. Sixty-five hundred Africans are still dying every day of a preventable, treatable disease, for lack of drugs we can buy at any drug store. This is not about charity, this is about justice and equality.[4]

I said to Bono afterward that his sermon was the most religious I had ever heard him get. "I got carried away," said Bono. It's time for all of us to get carried away. In his extraordinary address, Bono said that "God is with us, if we are with them." Notice he didn't say if we are "for" them, but rather "with" them. Being "for" the poor simply isn't enough, especially from a place of affluent comfort. It simply doesn't change us enough, give us enough passion, create enough energy, or make inaction on poverty unacceptable. It doesn't get personal; and until it does, we won't change the facts of poverty.

It's not just the poor around the world, so far from us, that we have not seen or known, but even some of God's poorest children who live much closer to home. Hurricane Katrina began to open our eyes.

What the Waters Revealed

Hurricane Katrina destroyed entire cities, the lives of more than a thousand people, the homes of hundreds of thousands, and the confidence of millions in their government's commitment and ability to protect them. Much of New Orleans was emptied of its people, and broad areas of the Gulf Coast were devastated. More than one million Americans were displaced across the country.

But the waters of Hurricane Katrina also washed away our national denial of the shockingly high number of Americans living in poverty and our reluctance to admit the still-persistent connection between race and poverty in America. The pictures from New Orleans stunned the nation. They exposed the stark reality of who was suffering the most, who was left behind, who was waiting in vain for help to arrive, and who would now face the most difficult challenges of recovery. The faces of those stranded in New Orleans were overwhelmingly poor and black, the very old and the very young. They were the ones who could not evacuate; had no cars or cash for gas; no money for bus, train, or airfare; no budget for hotels or no friends or family with room to share or spare. They were already vulnerable before this calamity; now they were totally exposed and on their own. For days, nobody came for them. And the conditions of the places they were finally herded to ("like animals," many testified) sickened the nation.

The truth was revealed – those left behind in New Orleans had already been left out in America. From the reporters covering the unprecedented disaster to ordinary Americans glued to their televisions, a shocked and even outraged response was repeated: "I didn't realize how many Americans were poor."

"We have now seen what is under the rock in America," said a neighbour in Washington, D.C. The vulnerability of the poorest children in New Orleans was riveting to many Americans, and especially to other parents. Many said they had trouble holding back their tears when they saw mothers with their babies stranded on rooftops crying for help, or jammed into dangerous and dirty places waiting for someone to save them.

As a direct result of Katrina and its aftermath, and for the first time in many years, the media were reporting on poverty, telling Americans that New Orleans had an overall poverty rate of 28 per cent (84 per cent of them African American) and a child poverty rate of almost 50 per cent – half of all the city's children (rates only a little higher than other major cities and actually a little lower than some others). Ironically (and some might say providentially), the annual 2005 U.S. Census poverty report came out during Katrina's deadly assault, showing that poverty had risen for the fourth straight year and telling us that thirty-seven million Americans were below the poverty line. These were the people most stuck in New Orleans.

Katrina revealed what was already there in America: an invisible and often silent poverty that most of us in the richest nation on earth have chosen not to talk about, let alone take responsibility for. After the storm hit, we all saw it – and so did the rest of the world. It made Americans feel both compassion and shame. Many political leaders and commentators, across the ideological spectrum, acknowledged the national tragedy, not just of the horrendous storm but of the stark realities the floodwaters had exposed. And some suggested that if the aftermath of Katrina finally led the nation to demand solutions to the poverty of upward of a third of its citizens, then something good might come from this terrible disaster. We are still waiting for that redemption.

What the waters revealed was the moral scandal of America's poverty in the midst of enormous wealth. We live in the richest nation in the history of the world, with choices, comforts, and luxuries beyond the dreams of most of the world's people in all of human history. Yet, every morning in America, thirty-seven million people wake up in poverty. And that includes thirteen million children. Forty-seven million people are without health insurance. Thirteen and a half million are called "food insecure," meaning that at some point during the year they had difficulty providing enough food for all their family members; and four and a half million of those are "insecure" to the point where family members went hungry.

Again, all this must become personal. Over dinner recently, a good friend of mine was recalling his childhood of abject poverty in one of our major cities. Now a dynamic young black Christian leader with a rising national reputation, he told me he still fears falling back into that poverty. "When I see a young black kid getting on a bus, my mind goes back to my school years when I had to choose most days between using my lunch money to eat or for bus fare to go home. I either had to suffer the hunger and social embarrassment of not eating any lunch, or to beg people on the street for bus fare to get back home at night. Those memories and feelings are still very powerful in me."

Decades before Katrina, another flood visited destruction on the city of New Orleans. In his provocative book *Rising Tide: The Great Mississippi Flood of 1927 and How It Changed America*, historian John M. Barry describes how the disaster revealed both racial and economic inequalities. The response to the disaster by local authorities directly exposed the brutal inequities of race and class and provoked a deep populist anger. People demanded new responses from the federal government, and the 1927 flood helped pave the way for the New Deal. Earlier, a Johnstown, Pennsylvania flood in 1889 that killed hundreds opened people's eyes to great inequities and also helped prepare the way for the turn-of-the-century progressive movement.

Citing both Johnstown and 1927 New Orleans as examples, columnist David Brooks wrote insightfully in *The New York Times* immediately following Katrina, "Hurricanes come in two waves. First comes the rainstorm, and then comes what the historian John Barry calls the 'human storm' – the recriminations, the political conflict, and the battle over compensation. Floods wash away the surface of society, the settled way things have been done. They expose the underlying power structures, the injustices, the patterns of corruption, and the unacknowledged inequalities. When you look back over the meteorological turbulence in this nation's history, it's striking how often political turbulence followed." Such natural disasters, said Brooks, can become "civic examinations".[5]

Interviewing Barry on *Meet the Press,* Tim Russert asked, "Do you see the same thing happening now in terms of the re-emergence of class and race and poverty as political issues?" Barry replied, "I think it's certainly possible and maybe likely. But it's obviously too early to tell." The storm "ripped off the cover" from America, said Barry, revealing what happens to people without resources. The question, said the historian, is whether Katrina would cause a "shift in public thinking" about our collective responsibilities to people in need.[6]

That shift in thinking cannot be just the reassertion of old social and political agendas and ideologies that have been at war over the issue of poverty. The truth is that our failure of the poor is a collective one: both conservative and liberal agendas have proved inadequate and left us with a very large underclass of poor people – adults, children, families – in America. Both sides have important insights that must be factored into any real solutions, but both have fallen far short of providing real answers.

The very alarming facts are that most poor people work, and work hard, but still fall below the poverty line, and are often without health insurance or decent and affordable housing. One recent study showed that more than nine million families have at least one full-time worker in the household working one or more jobs – but still raise their children in poverty. That should be unacceptable in America. To change that, we will need a new commitment, a new approach, a new strategy, and a new alliance to overcome poverty in America.

A New Relationship and a New Strategy

Without re-establishing relationship with the rest of us, the poor will continue to be on their own, which usually means invisible and forgotten. It will take a moral and even religious imperative to change our priorities, but the time has come to do so.

Evangelical Christian leader John Perkins has always talked about the three R's: relocation (by which he means living in the community one is working to serve), reconciliation (reconciling people to God and to other people), and redistribution (a just distribution of resources by utilizing skills and resources to address the problems of the community). Those principles have led to more than five hundred urban revitalization projects across America through the Christian Community Development Association. In December 2005, the seventy-five-year-old Perkins came to Washington, D.C., and was arrested in a prayer vigil opposing the nation's budget priorities, which were ignoring the people he had come to love. "It's my last stand," he said, inspiring us all as he has for forty years of faithful ministry among the poor. When John preached the night before in the church service that prepared us to act the next day, he told the story of his mother's death – it was from a nutritional disorder when he was only seven months old and still breast-feeding. "For many years, I thought I had killed my mother," he recalled. "I later learned how a white society didn't care much for the nutritional needs of poor black women and their children. Now they want to cut food stamps again to mothers like mine."

The Washington, D.C., gathering was the culmination of a yearlong effort by people of faith to teach our nation's political leaders that "a budget is a moral document". In the final stages of the budget process, after praying and making our best arguments from afar, we decided to brave the cold of a bitter December morning and take our prayers and presence to the steps of the Cannon House Office Building. After some powerful preaching on the steps and a press conference that was more like a revival, one hundred and fifteen pastors and urban ministry workers continued our praying and singing in front of the entrance, symbolizing the denial of access to Congress for low-income people. We sounded like a choir (and a good one at that) as we sang Christmas carols while being arrested, handcuffed, put into buses, and taken to a large holding cell roughly a mile away.

"Come walk with us," said Mary Nelson, founder of the Bethel New Life ministry on the west side of Chicago. With congressional staff looking down from their Cannon Office Building windows and members of Congress stepping over the kneeling Christians on their way to vote, they heard Mary invite them into relationship: "Come walk with us and meet the children on the other end of your cuts to critical nutrition programs, the families who will lose their health care, the students who will lose their chance to go to college. Come walk with us!"

I believe it is only that kind of credibility and that kind of invitation that will change how Washington, D.C., prioritizes the poor.

But we also need a new strategy. We have been paralyzed by the debate between liberals and conservatives on which solutions to pursue, with the right favouring cultural changes and the left endorsing policy changes. But new relationships with the poor could change that impasse, too. Who can credibly say that family breakdown, out-of-wedlock births, substance abuse, bad individual choices, and the eroding of both personal responsibility and strong moral values are not factors that further entrench poverty? And who can honestly say that the lack of decent wages, quality health care, affordable housing, educational opportunity, and safe neighbourhoods are not factors that erode family values and imprison poor children in poverty? It will take a renewal of both social and personal responsibility to overcome poverty. Biblically, that responsibility begins with those "to whom much has been given".

It's time to insist that we be disciplined by and accountable to outcomes for poverty reduction. It's time to move from the politics of blame to a politics of solutions, from sound bites to sound strategy, and from rhetoric to results. Liberals must start talking about the problems of out-of-wedlock births and about strengthening both marriage and parenting, while conservatives must start talking about strategic public investments in education, health care, affordable housing, and living family incomes. That would be the new "grand alliance" we so desperately need to begin making progress on poverty in this country.

Together, we must end the debate that's limited to the choices of big or small government and, rather, forge a common commitment to good and effective government. We need a three-legged-stool strategy, one that utilizes the strengths of the private sector (businesses and unions), the nonprofit sector (including faith-based organizations), and the public sector (government on all levels – local, state, and national). Each sector must do its share and focus on what it does best. We need to strike a strategic balance between all three sectors. Because, when one leg of the stool breaks, the whole society falls over. Real progress will require a combination of public and private initiatives, the merger of personal and social responsibility, the rebuilding of both families and communities, and a more honest assessment of both the individual decisions and the social systems that trap people in poverty. We need nothing less than a call for a new moral and political will to overcome needless poverty.

Katrina provided a teachable moment, but at the level of political leadership we seem to lack good teachers. What have we all learned, how must we change, where will we transform our priorities, and when will we commit ourselves to forging a new strategy that might actually work to defeat the cruel and senseless cycle of poverty?

Most of all, a new commitment will require us to make different choices. The critical needs of poor and low-income families must become a first priority of our federal and state legislatures, not the last. Moreover, the blatant inequalities of race in America – especially in the critical areas of education, jobs, health care, housing, and criminal justice – must finally be addressed. Congressional pork-barrel spending that aligns with political power more than with human needs must be challenged as never before. And that will require a complete reversal of the political logic now operating in Washington and in state capitols around the country: a new moral logic must reshape our political habits. Former Senator John Edwards has now made overcoming poverty his mission and calls us to higher ground:

> All over this country, too many children are growing up in harm's way – and too many lives are being washed away – because the levees we've built are too weak and too low. When a 13-year-old girl thinks there's nothing wrong with having a baby that will drive them both toward lives of poverty, we haven't built the levees high enough. When 15-year-old boys become fathers, then walk away, get shot, or go to jail, we haven't built the levees high enough. When young people spend more time going to meth labs than chemistry labs, we haven't built the levees high enough. We know better, but we don't act because we don't want to look. If we believe in community, we must find the courage to do what communities do: Together, we must stand side by side and man the levees.[7]

Restoring the hope of America's poorest families, renewing our national infrastructures, protecting our environmental stability (which so directly affects our poorest citizens), and rethinking our most basic priorities will require nothing less than a national change of heart and direction. It calls for a transformation of political ethics and governance, a move from serving private interests to ensuring the public good. If Katrina ultimately changes our political conscience and reinvigorates among us a commitment to the common good, then even that terrible tragedy might be redeemed.

Three Steps to Inclusion and Justice

We will make no real progress on the issue of poverty until our basic perception of the problem and the solutions undergoes a radical change. Presently, the poor are assumed to be relatively helpless in their ability to help themselves. For decades the stereotypical response of political conservatives was to abandon the poor, and blame their condition principally on themselves, while the stereotypical liberal response was to subsidize the poor and virtually maintain poverty. Neither side was looking for solutions, but rather how to blame the problem of poverty on the other side – either cruel abandonment or subsidized dependence.

Neither the political conservatives nor the liberals engaged much with actual poor people. Most conservatives did not know any poor people or families to test their assumptions about poverty and, if they ever did come into real contact, those assumptions often changed. Many liberals had little more relationship to poor people than conservatives, and generally regarded "the poor" as objects more than as subjects in social problem solving. Doing things *for* rather than *with* poor people became the liberal strategy.

In recent years, though, religious conservatives have been rediscovering the biblical imperatives to serve the poor and are opening up new engagements with poverty both internationally and in their own neighbourhoods. And liberals have become more critical of their past paternalism and failed programmes, with at least some seeking more pragmatic solutions that actually involve the poor themselves. There is an opportunity here.

It is now time to move through three critical steps on the way to solving the vexing issues of poverty that so shape the world's painful realities today. And the strategies of both inclusion and justice may help get us there.

Compassion for the poor is usually the first step, but it is only the doorway to change. Finally seeing and feeling what life is truly like for half the world's people and an embarrassing number of our fellow citizens in America is always the beginning of change. Social services, religious ministries, and volunteer opportunities expose millions of middle-class people to a new world of hurt and injustice, and their conscience is pricked for the first time. Caring is certainly the beginning of change; but it is only the beginning.

Second is the call for social justice, which flows directly from compassion. Feeding hungry people isn't enough; asking why they are hungry is the justice question. Caring for HIV/AIDS sufferers is wonderful, but asking why affluent AIDS patients can buy their health and their futures with lifesaving antiretrovirals while the disease is literally a death sentence for the poor is the justice question. Working on a new Habitat for Humanity home for a poor family or volunteering in a homeless shelter is an inspiring experience, but asking why there isn't more affordable housing available or why home ownership is only for the middle class is the justice question. The same is true about the relationship between tutoring an inner-city kid and fixing failed school systems, starting a health clinic and reforming the health care system, rescuing women and children from sex trafficking and fighting the practice and the industry. But even in calling for social justice, there is still the possibility of keeping a safe distance from the poor themselves, still the temptation to see the problems to be fixed as concerning "them" and not "us".

The third step is the critical movement into solidarity, community, or interdependence with the poor. That only comes when we see our destinies ultimately tied up with one another. It is the insight that what happens to the poor, or any of my neighbours, will finally also affect me and the people I love. James Wolfensohn, former president of the World Bank, made much the same point when he said, "There is no wall." Walls don't protect us from environmental degradation and pollution, the social costs of poverty, the social instability of inequality, the political costs of anger and resentment, and the results of injustice and hatred in the forms of crime, insurrection, terrorism, and other forms of random violence. The costs of the urban poverty we accept for children of colour in America are finally revealed in a dysfunctional criminal justice, in crumbling social safety nets, unsafe neighbourhoods, and dangerous social alienation. And the consequences of global poverty are evident in the spread of pandemic disease, environmental degradation, endless military conflicts, and the regional anarchy that leads directly to chaos and terrorism.

Conversely, the benefits of solidarity with one another are a rewarding interdependence and the safe and satisfying experience of community.

We actually come to believe that we need one another, that everybody has things to give and to receive, and that in mutual aid we find our truest security. Our diversity becomes a rich bounty of blessings rather than a threat driving us behind tribal boundaries that are both costly and dangerous. What is fair, just, and "enough" become questions of social equity and community relationships. And "justice" reassumes its biblical meaning, which is "right relationships". Personal responsibility is also restored as nobody can be just a recipient of other's social responsibilities but must also become a contributor, in his or her own way, to the common good. We all give and we all receive, which is how real life is.

The movement is to compassion for others, to the requirements of justice, to the reality of community and interdependence. The biblical strategy of inclusion and the biblical imperative of justice lead directly to that experience of community – a just and healthy community. Only then will we break the hold of the separation, the paternalism, and the inequality that have kept us apart. We are not the same in gifts, talents, advantages and disadvantages, joys and sorrows, but we still need each other; and our common humanity, more than our differences, is the key to our future. We are a community one way or another, either with destructive and dysfunctional relationships or with creative and healthy ones. The issue is one of solidarity, and it is the decisive choice we must make. When we make that choice, we all win. And when we don't, the world is divided into winners and losers, but the losses of the losers will finally taint and undermine the victories of the winners.

Shelter

Safe and affordable housing is an increasingly scarce resource, even for many working families in the United States, and enormous numbers of people worldwide live in slums and shantytowns in utter insecurity. Homelessness is greater than most people think, even in America, and the demographics of the homeless have changed – from addicted men to families with children.

Faith-based organizations such as Habitat for Humanity are moving beyond building houses for low-income families to making serious advocacy commitments to end "poverty housing". Is shelter meant to be a mere commodity based on prices determined by market forces alone, or is decent and secure housing for all of us a part of what justice requires? It's time to extend the blessings of good housing down the economic ladder, including making home ownership possible for poor families.

It's also time to explore what it would mean to disperse poverty rather than keeping it concentrated. One of the reasons for lack of relationship with the poor is that low-income families have been geographically concentrated and consistently isolated. The perpetual segregation of the poor – in New Orleans's Ninth Ward, on the fragile Asian coastlines hit hardest by the tsunami, or in Africa's and Latin America's isolated but teeming shantytowns – serves to separate poor families and children from broader relationships, good schools, efficient transportation, essential services, and safe places to live. The ghettoizing of poor people also concentrates the pathologies of poverty – family breakdown, substance abuse, poor education, rampant crime, and lack of social services are all endemic in poor neighbourhoods. So why keep all the poor people in poor neighbourhoods? Why not let them live in all kinds of neighbourhoods, go to better schools, have classmates with intact families, live in safe places, and participate in the multitude of services and activities that are so much more available in more stable neighbourhoods? The children of single parents could be included in multiple community activities supported by a critical mass of two-parent families. But that's hard to do when most of the families in a neighbourhood are single-parent ones. Robert Lupton's FCS Urban Ministries has developed creative programmes of mixed housing and zoning and attracted middle-income people of faith to mixed-income neighbourhoods in Atlanta. Similar programmes are taking root in other cities.

Healing and Health Care

Healing is both a major subject of faith and now a global crisis with the breakdown of public health care systems and the breakout of pandemic diseases. Megachurch pastors hold conferences on HIV/AIDS and malaria, while faith-based organizations are often in the forefront of responding to the world's most lethal diseases. The grotesquely unequal access to lifesaving drugs and medical care has made death a social disease. Proclaiming that the market has utterly failed in regard to health care, Bill Gates has become an expert philanthropist on the world's most neglected diseases, and Bill Clinton has begun a new global initiative with global health at its centre.

To guide our search for more humane and effective health care, we will need to establish some principles: for example, that health should be a human right and not a commodity for sale, and that wealth should not determine one's share of health in our world. We need to build consensus on principles and priorities if we are to address successfully the enormous challenges of public health in a world of massive inequalities. And until something is done to make universal health care a reality in America, millions of families will remain poor. There are a variety of proposals that might work, but a new principle of health as a human right must guide us.

Jesus made healing a principal sign of his ministry and of the presence of the kingdom of God. From a biblical point of view, it is simply wrong when health becomes a commodity and accessibility depends upon wealth.

Time for a Change

The Hebrew prophets consistently say that the measure of a nation's righteousness and integrity is in how it treats the most vulnerable. Jesus says the nations will be judged by how they treat "the least of these" (Matthew 25).

A global conversation is now going on about this very subject, among grassroots organizers and activists, among young people, and, increasingly, in the churches. Even at the level of the world's elites, there is now recognition that our enormous problems of inequality must be solved and that we ignore them at our own peril.

Once each year, the quiet and spectacularly beautiful Swiss mountain village of Davos is taken over by top business and political leaders from around the globe for the World Economic Forum. The motto of the event is "Committed to Improving the State of the World". Some critics of Davos have challenged the high-powered gathering and wondered for whom it is improving the world. More than a thousand of the world's elite gather, carefully protected by eight thousand security personnel. The topics are wide-ranging, the panelists among the most famous people in the world, the discussions often quite provocative.

The kind of globalization that seeks unbridled economic growth and unlimited corporate profits while imposing financial conditions on poor countries – usually to their detriment – has been a persistent obstacle to real development in the global South and an offence to the requirements of justice. But even at Davos there is a growing critique of those very practices and structural problems, especially in regard to the global health care crisis and the tragedy of extreme poverty.

Since 9/11, a few religious leaders have been invited to join the Davos conversation with the hope of creating interfaith dialogue to breach dangerous divides and add broader moral and ethical perspectives to the deliberations over the "state of the world". A small group of religious leaders now comes from around the world to talk with one another and with the gathered leaders of governments, corporations, and civil society.

I have been encouraged by the frank conversations at Davos about global poverty and disease that so adversely affect the world's poorest people. In one session it was pointed out that of the ten million children who die every year, one quarter could be saved by the vaccinations that routinely prevent their diseases in developed countries but are still not widely available in developing nations. About a twenty-year gap exists between when new lifesaving and life-enhancing drugs are introduced in the rich and poor parts of the world, and the difference in life expectancy between the two parts is now as high as a shocking forty years.

In one session Bill Gates pointed to the "market failures" of a health care system that caters to the rich world and called for "grand risk-taking" to save many lives. It was impressive to see how the world's greatest architect of computer software has so thoroughly educated himself on the world's greatest health crises and begun to invest so much of himself and his fortune in finding answers. Underneath the discussions was the dramatic disparity and acknowledged moral indictment of how life is much less valued in the world's poor places than its rich ones – about one hundred times less, one presenter estimated.

I was asked to address a session called "Should We Despair of Our Disparities?" I cited the Hebrew prophets and how they always seemed to speak up when the gaps in society grew too large (as they are today). When the gulf widened and injustice deepened, the prophets rose up to thunder the judgment and justice of God. Their words reveal that God hates inequality and we should, too. When our disparities become too great, they also become a very destabilizing force in the world, an incubator of resentment, despair, and violence. Former President Bill Clinton packed the house at Davos in 2006 when he spoke of the three greatest threats in the world today – global climate change, social and economic inequality, and religious and cultural conflict – but called the assembly of talented and powerful people to believe that these problems have solutions if we work hard and persevere.

The time has come to call poverty what it is. Just as our religious forebears in the Second Great Awakening declared that slavery was morally intolerable, we must now insist that widespread poverty in the midst of plenty is a moral wrong and a religious offence that we refuse to accept any longer. Poverty is the new slavery – imprisoning bodies, minds, and hearts. It is time to lift up practical policies and practices that help the poor escape their poverty and clearly challenge the increasing wealth gap between rich and poor.

In a time when political and social issues threaten to divide the church, many people of faith are coming together to affirm that justice for those who live in poverty is a deeply held religious commitment on which we are all firmly united. Increasingly, religious leaders from across the theological and political spectrum are building new common ground around a fundamental commitment to the most vulnerable, who were such a special concern of Jesus.

The Washington National Cathedral was buzzing on a June night in 2005. More than one thousand people of faith had gathered for a convocation focused on the world's hungry people. An amazing procession of religious leaders from almost every major faith tradition in America led the service. Evangelical leaders stood beside heads of mainline Protestant denominations, a Catholic cardinal, bishops from the historic black churches, Jewish rabbis, and Muslim imams. The main homilist, Anglican Archbishop Njongonkulu Ndungane of Cape Town, South Africa, noted the moral convergence of such a wide spectrum of American religious life and pronounced this a *kairos* moment – when regular time (*kronos*) gives way to a spirit-filled moment in history and a new sense of time takes over.

The massive reality of global hunger and poverty has revealed our own spiritual poverty and is bringing us together. Most of those gathered were committed to the Millennium Development Goals and were hoping to bring the religious community's moral energy and agency to bear on the world's pre-eminent moral issue. Despite our many deep and sometimes painful divisions, the growing crisis of the world's most vulnerable people is serving to bring many of us back together. It is a sign of hope in a world that desperately needs some right now.

But *kairos* is not a time for quick fixes or easy victories. Generating the necessary political and moral will to end extreme global poverty will require building a movement that is capable of changing the wind around the interlinked issues of increased and better aid, 100 per cent debt cancellation, and trade justice. Movements often fail when their vision becomes too shortsighted or compromised by the desire to claim immediate victory. We must acknowledge and celebrate every step that is made in moving us toward this vision, but continue to be prophetic about what is needed to truly make poverty history. We need a commitment to move from a lens of charity to justice and from paternalism to empowerment.

We must deal with the corruption in both the developing countries and the developed world. How do we find the right relationship between the empowerment of poor countries and the responsibility of wealthy nations?

Many have written about the inevitability and unstoppable momentum of globalization. If globalization is unstoppable, what are the moral ethics of globalization? Do unfettered economic growth and unlimited corporate profits really serve everybody best? Should there be any rules and, if so, whom should they protect? What are the ethics for rich nations in their relationship with the poor nations, and what are the responsibilities of poor countries for their own development and for the problems of the rest of the world? Is free trade the goal, or should it be fair and just trade? And how do individuals and communities make trade justice possible? In an interconnected world, how do we develop a new moral ethic for globalization?

In our own country, how do we end the needless poverty that persists in the world's richest country? How do we merge personal and social responsibility and transcend the liberal/conservative battle between cultural values and public policy that continues to keep the poor trapped in the political debate about poverty? Since most of America's poor already work, how do we make work really work in America so that families can sustain themselves? Poverty is not a family value, and most people in America believe that parents who work responsibly shouldn't have to raise their children in poverty. How do we all work together (not just government or charitable organizations, but all of us) to change that? Will we listen to the biblical prophets' insistence that the poor be protected from the abuse and exploitation of the rich, and their clear teaching that massive inequality greatly threatens a society's health, balance, and well-being? What does the Bible say about good work, just wages, the responsibilities of employees and employers, and the ethics of business?

The Commitment

We need some new commitments. The good news is that things may be starting to change. Increased media attention to the disasters and sufferings poor people face, new and highly visible antipoverty campaigns, the globalization of information via the Internet and the increasing mobility of a new generation, and a new focus of faith on poverty are all heightening the priority of the poor. An exit poll following the 2006 election indicated that 57.5 per cent of the voters considered poverty/economic justice and greed/materialism the most urgent moral crises in America.[8] Some polls even suggest that middle-class people would be willing to pay more taxes if that ensured that everyone would get health care. A June 2007 Zogby poll showed "58 per cent of likely voters saying they would be more likely to vote for a candidate who set a national goal of cutting poverty in half within a decade."[9] The labour movement and local grassroots community organizing are beginning to experience some new life and vitality. And at least a few courageous political leaders are identifying poverty as a central concern.

At a personal and family level, we need to relocate and redirect our lives so that relationship to the poor becomes a priority. Where we live, how we live, where we take our kids, whom they get to meet, and how their world can be expanded to include awareness of all God's children must become key conversations and decisions for parents. The best part of our family Christmas last year was after our two young boys opened their gifts and then went to the World Vision Web site to buy gifts for poor families in Africa. After thinking about the impact of the various choices, Luke bought one family a goat and Jack chose a sheep for another; we were amazed at how much more excited they were about the gifts they gave than the ones they received. Small practices like that don't change the world, but they do change young hearts and minds and help form a long-term social conscience.

An increasing number of college graduates are spending a year or more in voluntary social service internships rather than going on right away to jobs or graduate school. One of the best volunteer programmes, the Jesuit Volunteer Corps, has a wonderfully creative and subversive motto: "Ruined for life." Ruined for typical middle-class existence, most of those who move through one of the many volunteer programmes become very different kinds of teachers, doctors, lawyers, business and social entrepreneurs, community organizers, nonprofit professionals, journalists, citizens, parents, clergy, and lay church leaders than they normally might have become. The decision for voluntary years of social service and justice advocacy can make a life-changing difference. And it's never too late to get active for people of all ages and circumstances. A ninety-year-old recently came up to me after an event to say, "I see you're getting a lot of response from young people, but do you have anything for somebody like me to do?" Absolutely, I told him. We've had interns in their seventies, and the older generation is critical precisely for the mentoring of the young.

At the communal or congregational level, we need bold new leadership. Faith is not just between "me and the Lord", nor even just to share with our brothers and sisters in the community of faith. As we saw in chapter 3, the kingdom of God is not "from" this world but is decisively "for" this world, and in particular, the gospel that Jesus proclaimed is intended to "bring good news to the poor". It's time for congregations to ask, What would be "good news" to the poor in this community, in this city, in this nation, and in our world? What do people really need, and what gifts and resources are present in our congregation or community group to meet those needs? "Love is the answer," we often hear Christians say, but the love of God is meant to be taken to the streets and tested in the streets. The meaning of the incarnation, in Christian theology, is nothing less than this – in Christ, God hits the streets.

Local churches, especially some of those experiencing great spiritual growth, are moving into their communities with ministries of social service and neighbourhood economic development, and more are making the necessary connection to political advocacy, insisting that "budgets are moral documents". Church mission trips to rebuild houses in the devastated Gulf Coast or to serve the children who live on garbage dumps in Mexico are changing perspectives. Church youth groups are getting more excited about spring-break poverty plunges than about spring-break drunken orgies.

But we also need some public policy commitments – those that can change politics in the United States and around the world. More voices are calling for a results-based approach to poverty reduction rather than an endless ideological debate, and are insisting that overcoming poverty must be placed on a nonpartisan agenda and become a bipartisan cause. In Washington, D.C., we have relationships with senators and members of Congress on both sides of the political aisle who genuinely care about the myriad issues surrounding poverty. Things seem to be ripe for change. But we need to agree on some basic principles to shape new public policies.

Work is central to overcoming poverty. Just wages for good work is a consistent biblical value. We must focus on making work really work for low-income families. And it's time to make work pay. The combined effect of a higher minimum wage, an expanded Earned Income Tax Credit, tax policies that reward family stability, and creative thinking about work-support programmes would help ensure that those who work hard and full-time in America will not have to raise their children in poverty. We need fair employers who consider their employees part of their bottom line; we need strong unions who can again help make workers secure. Good and fair tax policies will help with more breaks and credits for those at the bottom than those at the top. Let's remember that work supplements and supports are not entitlements; they are the means to empowerment and should be supported by both liberals and conservatives. Let's begin the process of asset and wealth creation for all of America's families – including the poorest.

We are making progress in ending extreme global poverty. The U.N.'s

2007 Report on the Millennium Development Goals said: "We are now at the midpoint between the adoption of the MDGs and the 2015 target date. So far, our collective record is mixed. The results presented in this report suggest that there have been some gains, and that success is still possible in most parts of the world. But they also point to how much remains to be done. There is a clear need for political leaders to take urgent and concerted action, or many millions of people will not realize the basic promises of the MDGs in their lives. The MDGs are still achievable if we act now."[10]

The Micah Challenge is a new and promising network of churches and organizations from the global South who are focusing on the Millennium Development Goals. Led by churches in Africa, Asia, and Latin America who join with partners in the U.K., Europe, Australia, and North America, Micah Challenge is uniting the international body of Christ for justice. These are goals that must be met, and it will take a real mobilization in the faith community to accomplish that. A commitment to take that action is essential to improving the lives of billions of people around the world.

Overcoming poverty has been a priority for Sojourners since the very beginning. In 1971, when we were a group of young seminarians, we centred our work on a low-income community in Chicago and then in an inner-city Washington, D.C., neighbourhood that the media had called a war zone. Through organizing an after-school programme for young people and opening our homes to our neighbours, we committed ourselves to living with and intentionally forming relationships with the urban poor. After some time, we began to see that if we wanted people to have the opportunities they deserved, we had to change the way our political and social system works. Therefore, to serve our immediate community, Sojourners got involved with housing advocacy, food security issues, and welfare reform. Our services grew to encompass both direct relationships with the poor and advocacy for change in our political system to change the landscape in which our people were living.

Today, our work in Washington and around the country stands on this foundation. We work to eradicate poverty with a passion for personal relationships and community. At our 2006 Pentecost conference, we launched the Covenant for a New America, our solutions-based antipoverty policy vision. The Covenant outlines a series of broad commitments to make work "work", eradicate child poverty, and end extreme poverty around the world. With more than thirty endorsing organizations, the Covenant framed much of our work over the ensuing year. The Vote Out Poverty Campaign, launched at the June 2007 Pentecost, puts the Covenant into action. The campaign demands that political candidates commit to cutting in half the number of Americans living in poverty over the next ten years and to achieving the Millennium Development Goals. We presented the Vote Out Poverty challenge during a vibrant worship service early in the conference. After a time of prayer and worship, we gave the congregation a call to action: commit to reducing poverty by making these goals a priority in your own life. Every person in the sanctuary stood up and answered the call, signing their names to this pledge. It was a moving expression of what is becoming a unified Christian voice in our country.

Our efforts to put poverty on the national agenda for 2008 are already paying off. Thousands of individuals have already signed the Vote Out Poverty Pledge, and several leading presidential candidates are now making poverty a key issue in their campaigns. Issues around poverty are already part of our national political conversation, and we will push for them to be central in the 2008 presidential elections and beyond. Thirty-five years after Sojourners began in Chicago, we continue to work to overcome poverty every single day.

You can join us in that work by coming to Sojourners' Web site, Sojo.net, or by joining Bread for the World, the ONE campaign, the Micah Challenge, or many other local, national and international faith-inspired efforts to overcome poverty.

A Renewed Commitment to Overcome Poverty

In February 2007 a new network of Christian Churches Together (CCT) was formally launched in Pasadena, California, after almost six years of conversation, fellowship, worship, and prayer together. Thirty-six churches and national organizations from all the key U.S. church groups formally joined with one another, culminating in a powerful worship service with the church "families" visibly coming together: evangelical and Pentecostal, historic Protestant, Catholic, Orthodox, and racial/ethnic churches – Black, Latino, and Asian Christians – all gathered together.

A consensus was reached on the key importance of evangelism and the biblical imperative to overcome poverty – and those two most basic commitments will shape the new fellowship. A statement adopted by the church leaders says:

> As Christian leaders in the wealthiest society on earth, we are called by God to urge our churches and nation to strengthen and expand efforts to address the scandal of widespread poverty in the United States and around the world. The Gospel and our ethical principles place our service of the

poor and vulnerable and our work for justice at the centre of Christian life and witness…

Our faith in Christ who is the truth compels us to confront the ignorance of and indifference [to the scandal of widespread, persistent poverty in this rich nation]… We must call this situation by its real names: moral failure, unacceptable injustice… As leaders in Christian Churches Together, we believe that a renewed commitment to overcome poverty is central to the mission of the church and essential to our unity in Christ. Therefore in order to obey our God, respect the dignity of every person, and promote the common good of society, we must act.[11]

It has been a very long time since the churches had this kind of unity, and the issue on which they first chose to speak with a common voice was poverty. They are not alone; people from other faith traditions and those with no faith at all are ready to make new commitments to end the long isolation of poverty and invite God's poorest and most vulnerable children to the banquet table. And God will be smiling.

If we are to take seriously the opening sermon of Jesus at Nazareth recorded in Luke 4, his "mission statement" in which he proclaims that "The Spirit of the Lord is upon me, because he has anointed me to bring good news to the poor," there can be only one conclusion: no matter what else the gospel does in our lives, if our gospel message is not "good news to the poor", it is simply not the gospel of Jesus Christ.

6

STEWARDSHIP AND RENEWAL
The Earth is the Lord's

My son Luke asked me one day to explain what global warming is. I told him that the warming of the earth, climate change, is primarily caused by human activities, especially those that release carbon dioxide into the atmosphere, and that for more than a decade the scientific evidence has been conclusive: global temperatures are rising at a steady and alarming pace, because of these human activities. I told him of the likely consequences for the world and its people from significant rises in the earth's temperature, and that we don't really know how fast those things will occur. He listened carefully, and finally replied, "So I'm guessing that Hummers are a problem." He gets it, and so does most of the younger generation.

The Original Story

In the beginning… God created the heavens and the earth. (Genesis 1:1)

Then God said, "Let us make humankind in our image, according to our likeness; and let them have dominion over the fish of the sea, and over the birds of the air, and over the cattle, and over all the wild animals of the earth, and over every creeping thing that creeps upon the earth." So God created humankind in his image, in the image of God he created them; male and female he created them… God saw everything that he had made, and indeed, it was very good. (Genesis 1:26–27, 31)

The LORD God took the man and put him in the Garden of Eden to work it and take care of it. (Genesis 2:15, NIV)

The earth is the LORD's and all that is in it, the world, and those who live in it; for he has founded it on the seas, and established it on the rivers. (Psalm 24:1–2)

Sometimes it's necessary to return to our original story to see where we have gone wrong, to go back to the beginning to see how we might get on the right track again. These biblical narratives tell our original story, the story of God's good creation, given as a gift to those created in God's own image – but as a gift and not a possession. God told human beings to "have dominion" over creation (Genesis 1:28), a commission that has far too often been interpreted as the right to destroy. The original story says that God retains ownership and control of creation (Psalm 24:1–2) and has given it to humankind "to work it and take care of it" (Genesis 2:15, NIV). As *The Message* translation puts it, we are to "Be responsible for fish in the sea and birds in the air, for every living thing that moves on the face of Earth" (Genesis 1:28).

Good theology clarifies who God is and who we are. The original story speaks of God's vocation as Creator and our vocation as the stewards of God's creation. The "earth is the LORD's", the psalmist writes. But human beings have often sought to take the place of God as the owners of creation and no longer a part of it. "Dominion" has become domination and not stewardship. And a "dominion theology" has arisen that ends up appearing to justify the neglect and even exploitation of the environment. The dictionary definition of *stewardship* is "the careful and responsible management of something entrusted to one's care". The issue here is right worship; indeed, the environmental irresponsibility of human beings can rightly be called idolatry: replacing the Creator's role with our own, by human arrogance and shortsightedness.

The neglect of our natural environment and its degradation is not just bad policy; it is bad theology. And getting our theology wrong has put our natural environment and our children's future in great jeopardy. Our private religion has fostered an individualism that has not only diminished our social conscience for the poor but also separated us from the earth itself. Our cultural conformity and personal subservience to "market values" and our spiritual addiction to consumerism have wreaked havoc on the created order and devastated the environment we depend upon for our life and sustenance. Our lack of respect for God's creation has disrupted the very cycles of nature. And a distorted eschatology of the "end times" and so-called biblical prophecy has denigrated the importance of the natural world, giving wayward believers a false religious licence for environmental destruction. The wildly successful *Left Behind* book series promotes the view of a future defined by "apocalyptic events", which diminishes the importance of caring for the earth.

Christians, in particular, have too often seen the earth as merely a way station to heaven, an unimportant stage prop for the human drama of salvation. A singular emphasis on eternal life has been used to justify a utilitarian environmental ethic that treats the natural order as a merely temporal, throwaway resource. If Psalm 148 suggests that every part of the creation offers praise to the Creator, our mindless destruction of so many species of plant and animal life has served to actually diminish the worship and praise that God now receives, as evangelist Tony Campolo has pointed out – there are now fewer species to praise God. That startling revelation serves as a metaphor for our environmental failure to worship God.

The original story makes it clear that the earth matters. God cares about the creation and expects much of those commissioned as its stewards. The biblical prophets insist that God's demands are not just for a future time, future life, or future earth. They are precisely for life on this earth, for here and for now. Throughout the Hebrew scriptures, God provides instructions to humanity on how to take care of creation and offers lessons on stewardship: regulations for protecting animals (Deuteronomy 21:6, 25:4); instructions not to hurt fruit trees even during war (Deuteronomy 20:19); and provisions for periodic Sabbath rest for the land (Leviticus 19:1–7), among others.

Jesus' message of the kingdom of God is full of references to the earth, the natural cycles, and God's many creatures (Matthew 13:24–32; Mark 4:26–27; Luke 6:43–45). In his parables it is clear that the birds of the air and the lilies of the field have much to teach us (Matthew 6:26–30). Most profound, the prayer that Jesus taught his disciples to pray asks that God's will be done "*on earth* as it is in heaven" (Matthew 6:10, emphasis added).

Recovering the Genesis Story

Theologian Ched Myers reminds us that the rediscovery and reappropriation of the Genesis story may be the key to our future.[1]

"Origin stories matter," explains Myers. "Our relationships with one another, God, and the Earth are deeply shaped by them." He points out how the original stories of creation and the clear vocational purposes for human beings in the created order have been replaced by the new stories of modernity, the "powerful Enlightenment ideologies of positivism, capitalism, and rationalism that first challenged, then deconstructed, and eventually eclipsed the biblical tradition, replacing it with the heroic myth of Progress. This is our official civilization story today, mediated in myriad ways through discourses of science and popular culture alike."

Our interdependence with nature was forgotten and changed to our domination over it, with results that now threaten human civilization itself. Myers says that modern society moved away from a relationship of mutuality between human beings and the natural world, reducing nature to a mere "instrument," without spiritual significance, to be used for human benefit. "By marginalizing (or banishing) God and exalting an autonomous and ingenious humanity," Myers writes, "the Enlightenment produced a compelling historical fable about the nobility of civilization and its 'redemption' of a deeply flawed natural world." The modernists held on to one part of the Genesis tradition: God's granting to human beings of "dominion" over creation and instructing them to "fill the Earth and subdue it" (see Genesis 1:28). Myers explains that this text was used to help "rationalize and even mandate ecological destruction in the name of civilization's sovereignty".

This "dominion theology, substituting domination and degradation of the environment for stewardship" has indeed resulted in disastrous consequences for the earth and for human society. For many decades, however, it was hardly questioned by the religious mainstream. Indeed, some secular environmentalists have put the blame for much of our environmental degradation precisely on the Christian dominion theology that was all too common across the spectrum of the churches.

Some Christians, of course, have taken a very different theological approach. Brian McLaren is one of them. As a volunteer doing wildlife surveys in his native Maryland, he searches for species of endangered turtles. McLaren, who is also a theologian, reports that on one such survey he was thinking about why a profound environmental shift is taking place "as I was thigh-deep in muck. Clad in hip waders, I'm slogging through a spring-fed bog in northern Maryland. I'm surrounded by tussock sedge, alder, jewelweed, skunk cabbage, and swamp rose. And I'm having a great time."[2] Like many evangelicals, McLaren now finds himself in an emerging new theological habitat where care of creation is central to mission. He also reports that when he meets professional wildlife biologists, they are surprised that an evangelical pastor would be out there in hip boots looking for the rare little "turtles of the fields".

He happily recounts, "They're not used to seeing mud-smeared pastors who aren't afraid to grope around in bog muck for turtles or who keep track of chorus frogs and Baltimore checkerspots and Indian paintbrush. I know what they're thinking: Christians, especially ones associated with the term 'evangelical', are part of the problem, not part of the solution. They listen to James Dobson and Pat Robertson and James Kennedy, not Wendell

Berry and Herman Daly; they focus on the family and the military, not the environment."

The good news is that a fundamental challenge to dominion theology has begun to arise that seems to be fired by a revival of the original Genesis stories. That development holds great promise for the earth and our relationship to it; it signals the possibility of a turnaround in our thinking and actions, one that the whole creation seems to be literally "groaning for".

I once spoke at a meeting of the CEOs of the country's top environmental organizations, along with Rabbi David Saperstein of the Religious Action Center of Reform Judaism. A Christian and a Jew were going to address the nation's key environmental leaders, who had good reasons for scepticism when it comes to the religious community on this issue. We knew that few of the environmental leaders present were religious believers. We started by acknowledging that fact but said that nonetheless "we want to thank you for doing the Lord's work!" They seemed taken aback but pleased to hear such an affirmation. We also told them of a new generation of the faithful who were experiencing a profound conversion on the matter of the environment and might indeed become a critical constituency for fundamental lifestyle and policy change. The thought of a new alliance between environmental activists and the community of faith was an exciting prospect for everyone in the room. Many important efforts now reflect that promise, including groups such as the interfaith Religious Partnership on the Environment and the newer Evangelical Environmental Network.

Bad theology is best challenged by good theology. The renewal of the Genesis story among a new generation of believers is one of the most hopeful current developments. The misappropriation of the Genesis texts is being replaced by deeper reflections and new applications.

Ched Myers puts it well. "The misappropriation of Genesis 1:28 thus continues to be deeply consequential," he writes. "Rather than conceding its interpretation to environmental imperialists, however, or throwing it out as hopelessly problematic, we would do well to re-place this text within its cultural and narrative context. Genesis 1–2 tells a very different story about the relationship between human society and the rest of creation than the one we moderns tell ourselves. It offers old wisdom that, if heeded, may yet help us step back from the brink of ecological catastrophe."

Those original Genesis texts tell the story of a beautiful and bountiful creation with abundance for all, but one that depends on the faithful vocation of its human caretakers. The Hebrew word *tov,* which God uses to describe the creative work he has done, is often translated as "good" but is better rendered as "fantastic", according to Myers, in what Old Testament theologian Richard Lowery in *Sabbath and Jubilee* calls "God's cosmic WOW".[3] Moreover, the richness and abundance of God's creation contrasts with modern notions of scarcity and competition. From Genesis we derive the two central principles of biblical economy: first, there is enough, and second, it is for all creation to share.

Myers summarizes: "The human vocation is summarized in Genesis 2:15: The human being is to 'till and keep' (*'abad* and *shamar*). Outside the Eden story *'abad* connotes servitude, not management, while *shamar* is used for conservancy of life or observance of covenant. So the phrase is better translated 'serve and preserve' – this is what it means to 'rule' faithfully." The idyllic picture of creation and relationship in the Garden of Eden was shattered when the human beings ate from the tree of the knowledge of good and evil and decided they knew better and could do better than God. Myers describes the balance of the narrative in Genesis 3–11 as "a warning tale that identifies the Fall with our alienation from the Earth, its creatures, and the Creator, and goes on to offer a withering critique of civilization and its discontents". Clearly, dominion theology simply doesn't grasp the vision and purpose of the Genesis story and, in fact, contradicts it. Rather, it is revealed as a false theology used for the malicious interests of environmental destruction in the name of so-called progress. A truer picture of the Genesis accounts reveals an ethic not unlike the origin stories of some indigenous peoples, where all living things are vitally connected and stewardship means applying the test of thinking ahead seven generations. Concludes Myers, we are "tightly woven together with the rest of creation" with whom we live in "a symbiotic relationship. The modern myth of our 'lordship' over nature clearly will not serve a sustainable future. Perhaps the older, wiser creation story of Genesis, when more carefully handled, will restore to us the instructive memory of where we came from, so we can turn around from where we are headed."

The New Theological Habitat

A remarkable conversion on the matters of creation and the environment is now occurring in the religious community, and most strikingly among the evangelical Christian community. This holds hopeful possibilities for significant changes in environmental directions and policies.

Brian McLaren explains why things are changing: "People who are sensitive to creation know that creation is in constant flux. Continents drift, climates change, magnetic poles flip-flop, and bogs like this one [where he searches for endangered species] gradually give way to wet meadows and then various kinds of forests. There's a natural succession out here under the sun, and I think there's a kind of natural succession going on theologically for many Christians as well."

McLaren lays out three principal reasons for that "natural succession", the significant shift now occurring among Christians in particular. First, McLaren says, "increased concern for the poor and oppressed leads to increased concern for all of creation", and many Christians now decry a "spirituality that cares for souls but neglects bodies, that prepares for eternity in heaven but abandons history on earth".

Second, McLaren writes, the "eschatology of abandonment" is being replaced by an engaging gospel of the kingdom. In the past, he explains, the "phenomenon of evangelical-dispensational eschatology (doctrine of last things or end times)" offered a model in which "virtually no continuity exists between this creation and the new heavenly creation; this creation is discarded like a non-recyclable milk carton. Why get sentimental about a cheap container destined for the cosmic dumpster of nothingness?" But in recent years, McLaren says, "as more and more of us rediscover Jesus as master-teacher, we are struck by the centrality of 'the kingdom of God' in Jesus' message (and Paul's too). And it is clear to us that this kingdom is not just about heaven after we die: It's about God's will (or wish) being 'done on earth' now, in history. In this kingdom... everything God made matters. God sent Jesus into the world with a saving love, and Jesus sends us with a similar saving love – love for the orphans and widows, the prostitutes and lepers, the poor and forgotten to be sure, but also for the little creatures who suffer from the same selfish greed and arrogance that oppress vulnerable humans."

The third reason McLaren offers is that the "hallowed concept of private ownership" is being challenged by the biblical notion of stewardship. He explains:

> For increasing numbers of us who consider ourselves post-liberal and post-conservative, words like private (meaning personal and individual), ownership (meaning autonomous personal and individual control), and enterprise (meaning autonomous, personal, individual control over projects that use God's world for our purposes) seem to fly in the face of kingdom values. Values such as community (meaning seeing beyond the individual to the communal), fellowship (which means sharing, holding in common with the community, not grasping as "mine!"), and mission (meaning our participation in God's projects in God's world for God's purposes).

A stewardship economy, McLaren says, "doesn't see every majestic mountain as a potential site for strip-mining operations, nor does it see forests as board-feet of marketable lumber, nor does it see this spring-fed emergent wetland (drained and bulldozed) as a lucrative site for a housing development… Rather, whatever we 'own'… is really lent and entrusted to us by God, received by us and reverently used for a time."

McLaren's words are revolutionary in their break with the old dominion theology. They actually debunk and reverse it and have the potential to set us on an entirely different course. Given the enormity of the environmental crisis humanity now faces, there could be no more welcome or hopeful words.

Sitting in his bog with muddy boots, McLaren reflects on what this big theological shift in the Christian community's view of the environment might mean:

> So, what do we do differently in this emerging theological habitat, this new stage in the spiritual forest succession? That remains to be seen. But for starters, we see differently, and we care differently, and we value differently – and if those differences catch on, with Christianity being the largest religion in the world, there are bound to be good effects in our world. Ultimately, those effects will have to go beyond the important but limited conservation actions of individuals (recycling, reusing, abstaining, etc.). The effects of caring will have to change our systems – transportation systems that depend on fossil fuels and that divide and devastate our nonhuman neighbors' habitats, housing systems that maximize human impact through suburban sprawl, farming systems that violate rather than steward land, advertising systems that make us want more stuff that we don't need and that will soon fill even more square miles with trash.

Creation Care

McLaren is not alone in his work toward a new theology of the environment. For more than a decade, a series of environmental initiatives have been coming from an unexpected source: young evangelical activists. Mostly under the public radar screen, they have included new and creative projects such as the Evangelical Environmental Network and *Creation Care* magazine. In November 2002, one of these initiatives – a campaign called "What Would Jesus Drive?" – received some national attention. The campaign was launched with a Detroit press conference and meetings in which automotive executives talked with ecumenical and interfaith leaders.

Since then, more establishment evangelical groups, especially the National Association of Evangelicals, have also spoken up on the issue of creation care. Leading the way was Richard Cizik, NAE vice president for governmental affairs, who, on issues like environmental concern and global poverty reduction, began to sound like the biblical prophet Amos. Evangelical leaders began attending critical seminars on the environment, and climate change in particular, and were describing their experiences of "epiphany" and "conversion" on the issue.

In 2004, the NAE adopted a new policy statement, "For the Health of the Nation: An Evangelical Call to Civic Responsibility", which included a principle titled, "We labor to protect God's creation." It said: "We are not the owners of creation, but its stewards, summoned by God to 'watch over and care for it' (Genesis 2:15). This implies the principle of sustainability: Our uses of the Earth must be designed to conserve and renew the Earth rather than to deplete or destroy it... We urge Christians to shape their personal lives in creation-friendly ways: practicing effective recycling, conserving resources, and experiencing the joy of contact with nature. We urge government to encourage fuel efficiency, reduce pollution, encourage sustainable use of natural resources, and provide for the proper care of wildlife and their natural habitats."[4]

Cizik was notably quoted by *The New York Times* as saying, "I don't think God is going to ask us how he created the earth, but he will ask us what we did with what he created."[5] The March 2005 article noted that "A core group of influential evangelical leaders has put its considerable political power behind a cause that has barely registered on the evangelical agenda, fighting global warming." The politics of global warming changed overnight in Washington, D.C. Previously, advocates around climate change and other environmental issues were simply not a part of the Bush administration's political base and their concerns were not on Washington's political agenda. But the NAE constituency had mostly been part of the Republican base, and its new environmental concern did not go unnoticed by the White House – the day the article came out, the Bush White House called the NAE to ask what policies they were most concerned about. We began to see evangelicals participating at many major environmental meetings, both domestically and internationally, and a series of press stories about the new evangelical environmentalists appeared.

But the Religious Right finally reared its head. A 2006 letter addressed to the NAE and signed by twenty-two of the Religious Right's prominent leaders, said, "We respectfully request... that the NAE not adopt any official position on the issue of global climate change. Global warming is not a consensus issue." It was a clear attempt to prevent the NAE from taking a stand on environmental issues and even to veto the whole effort. Five years earlier, so powerful a group of conservative Christian leaders probably could have tamped down a new evangelical effort such as this. But this time, it didn't work.

A month after the letter was sent, a full-page ad appeared in *The New York Times* with the headline "Our commitment to Jesus Christ compels us to solve the global warming crisis." The statement said in part, "Love of God, love of neighbor, and the demands of stewardship are more than enough reason for evangelical Christians to respond to the climate change problem with moral passion and concrete action... we are convinced that evangelicals must engage this issue without any further lingering over the basic reality of the problem or humanity's responsibility to address it."

The striking ad announced the Evangelical Climate Change Initiative. It was signed by eighty-six prominent evangelical leaders, including the presidents of thirty-nine Christian colleges.[6] I was speaking at one of those schools shortly after the ad appeared and talked to their president, who was one of the signers. "I'm tired of those old white guys telling us what to think and do," he said. He had decided to take a stand for the first time, even if it was against the old guard of the Religious Right.

These events signal a sea change in evangelical Christian politics: the Religious Right has lost control on the environmental issue. The "greening" of the evangelicals in particular is a major new development. Right-wing Christian groups tried to prevent this from happening, but they failed, and in so doing lost their hold on the evangelical political agenda. They labelled the issue a distraction from the issues that they have focused on, but caring for God's creation is now a mainstream evangelical issue, especially for a new generation of evangelicals. Key groups like the National Association of Evangelicals are firmly committed to "creation care" and to the issue of global warming in particular.

The concern over global warming is even stronger among young evangelicals who have made environmental stewardship central to their faith. Many evangelicals now say that global warming is a "life issue" for them and a fundamental part of Christian ethics. I've spoken to many leaders of environmental organizations who are beginning to realize how the new evangelical environmental movement could provide a key constituency in turning the nation around in the urgent crisis of global warming. If scientists and evangelicals made this a common cause, there's no telling how much could happen.

Many Christians, including evangelicals, now ask if political candidates support protections to clean air and water, if they will work to reduce the dangerous emissions that cause global warming, if they favour a shift from our addiction to oil and fossil fuels to cleaner, safer, and more renewable energy sources. Do political leaders support the transformation to conservation and new energy sources that could provide jobs, reduce our dependence on foreign oil, help solve the Middle East crisis, and even reduce the threats of terrorism?

The new evangelical concern for environmental sustainability is a direct counterpoint to the more fundamentalist stance of those behind the *Left Behind* books who predict the imminent second coming of Jesus Christ and use their apocalyptic theology as an excuse to ignore environmental issues and other concerns about this world. Being good stewards of God's creation and caring about what happens in all God's world is simply much better theology than the bad eschatology (of the "end times") that leads to a cop-out of Christian responsibility in the name of alleged biblical prophecy.

God and Climate Change

In 2007 the Religious Right again went on the attack, orchestrating a new campaign that sought to undercut the growing evangelical commitment to reversing climate change. In a letter to the chairman of the National Association of Evangelicals, James Dobson, Tony Perkins, Gary Bauer, Charles Colson, and others claimed that "The existence of global warming and its implications for mankind is a subject of heated controversy throughout the world."[7] Again they called the issue a distraction from "real" moral issues. In his sermon that week, Rev. Jerry Falwell claimed that the debate over global warming is "a tool of Satan being used to distract churches from their primary focus of preaching the gospel". But their attack showed just how far outside the evangelical mainstream the Religious Right's views on the environment have become.

There is little reasonable doubt left about the threat posed to the earth by global warming. A broad international consensus now exists among scientists, religious leaders, business leaders, and economists that we must act and act soon to preserve a world for our children. In early 2007, the leading international network of climate-change scientists, the Intergovernmental Panel on Climate Change, concluded for the first time that the evidence of global warming is "unequivocal" and that it is with 90 per cent certainty caused by human activity. *The New York Times* called the report "a bleak and powerful assessment of the future of the planet". Many have also reported that the results of climate change will take their greatest toll on the world's poorest people, who are least prepared to protect themselves from the consequences of global warming, for which they are also least responsible. It is a sad case of moral double jeopardy. And what do we make of this moral issue? The United States, with only 4 per cent of the world's population, contributes more than 25 per cent of the world's carbon dioxide emissions.

Global warming has become a bipartisan issue. Senators John McCain and Joe Lieberman declared in a *Boston Globe* op-ed piece, "The debate has ended over whether global warming is a problem caused by human activity... There is now a broad consensus in this country, and indeed in the world, that global warming is happening, that it is a serious problem, and that humans are causing it."[8] In a powerful commentary in *The Washington Post,* David Ignatius wrote, "The scientific debate about whether there is a global warming problem is pretty much over... Skeptical researchers will continue to question the data, but this isn't a 'call both sides for comment' issue anymore. For mainstream science, it's settled."[9]

Former Vice President Al Gore has, of course, become even more famous than he was before because of a PowerPoint presentation made into an Oscar-winning documentary film about climate change called *An Inconvenient Truth.* The compelling presentation describes the potential consequences of climate change in the melting of glaciers, the rising of global sea levels and devastating flooding of coastal areas, the increase of major droughts, catastrophic storms, and intense heat waves, the spreading of disease to higher altitudes, and the impact on thousands of plant and animal species. In the fall of 2007, Gore was awarded the Nobel Peace Prize for his efforts as an environmental evangelist.

One might say this could be an environmental crisis of "biblical proportions". For too many years, we have destroyed other species without thought, but now we risk destroying our own species. We could also say that the crisis of climate change calls for a biblical response. With a consensus now emerging regarding the reality and seriousness of the problem, we still have a chance to make a difference – not in the incremental ways that will be too little and too late, but through fundamental changes in both personal behaviour and public policy. The response of the religious community, in particular, could help provide the driving spiritual energy for change.

The letter from the Religious Right opposing climate-change initiatives sparked several postings on the God's Politics blog. One came from Lyndsay Moseley, associate representative for faith partnerships with the Sierra Club, who wrote that we should "emphasize that the story is not finished! The scientists tell us that we have time to avoid the most devastating impacts of global warming if we begin to act now." Moseley pointed to the biblical story of Jonah, who warned about the coming destruction of Nineveh. "The people heeded his warning and turned from their ways, repenting and seeking God's mercy and forgiveness," she wrote. "We, like the people of Nineveh, can heed the warnings and take steps to be better stewards of the earth – not only for ourselves, but for our neighbors, our children, and God."

Moseley also pointed to Deuteronomy 30:19: "I have set before you life and death, blessings and curses; therefore choose life, that you and your descendants may live." She said that around the country she sees "evangelical Christians and people of all faiths choosing life, embracing their call to environmental stewardship in unique and inspiring ways... With this growing momentum, people of faith can turn the tide on global warming and other threats to God's creation."[10]

Brian McLaren added a post pointing to the biblical story of Joseph's warning of a coming drought. "The leadership of Egypt heeded his warning and began stockpiling food so that their people wouldn't starve if and when the drought materialized." Is there a message for us today in that story? McLaren wrote, "As scientists go beyond identifying the threat of climate change to predicting its impact on global civilization, I wonder what it might look like for our nation and the nations of the world to take joint ameliorative action regarding greenhouse gases, and to take precautionary action regarding water and food. I wonder what it might be like for people of faith, like Joseph, to take a catalytic role in these efforts."

McLaren also raised the biblical story of Noah, "because so many species have already been pushed to the brink of extinction and beyond, and with rapid climate change, this tragic trend is likely to skyrocket". He asked what it would be like for people of faith to follow Noah's example in preserving species wherever possible – by preserving natural habitat, and in other cases, by "creating 'arks' to preserve species whose natural habitats are destroyed by flood or drought or melting ice or rising sea levels. People of God, both the Joseph and Noah stories suggest, are keenly interested in the common good – the good of all human beings and the good of all living creatures."[11]

Time to Step It Up

One of the clearest voices on the environment, and global warming in particular, is professor and writer Bill McKibben. In spring 2007, he and his students at Middlebury College in New Hampshire launched the first nationally coordinated actions on climate change. It was called Step It Up and included approximately fourteen hundred diverse and very creative actions in all fifty states, all responding to the crisis of global warming. *The New York Times* reported:

> The day's events were as varied as national weather patterns. There were film screenings and poetry readings, bicycle rides and hiking expeditions, drum circles and tree plantings. People dived underwater to wave a sign reading "It's Getting Hot Down Here!!" at a coral reef off Key West, Fla. In Jacksonville, Fla., demonstrators used an unusual visual aid to illustrate rising sea levels: Alltel Stadium, home of professional football's Jacksonville Jaguars, where they hoisted a boat 20 feet in the air outside an entrance.
>
> At a rally that drew about 400 people to Boston Common, dozens of schoolchildren and their parents carried "recycling rope", blue twine decorated with milk cartons, egg cartons and aluminum cans. In the San Francisco Bay Area, thousands turned out in the rain at a series of demonstrations and town hall meetings.[12]

The point was that slow incremental action to counter climate change is no longer enough, that only dramatic and transformational action will now suffice.

Saying that we need a movement, McKibben reports:

> Parts of the faith community are stepping up to the challenge with real vigor. Not only evangelicals but also Unitarians, Presbyterians, Orthodox Jews, and everyone else who can feel the horror of the de-creation we're now engaged in... But we need more religious involvement, because it's one of the ways we can show wavering members of Congress that this isn't an "alternative" movement – that instead it comes straight from the heart of America. And straight from the heart of the gospel tradition, with its paramount call for love of neighbor. At the moment, the 4 per cent of us in this country produce a quarter of the world's carbon dioxide – once you look at maps of rising sea levels and spreading mosquitoes, you realize that we've probably never figured out a way to hate our neighbors around the world much more effectively. That's got to stop.[13]

McKibben also reports on the scientific clarity concerning global warming. He writes that the Intergovernmental Panel on Climate Change, the world's leading climatologists, "assessed all the peer-reviewed research of the last decade and calibrated all the planet's computerized climate models, concluding from their work that unless we take dramatic action to reduce our use of coal, gas, and oil, the temperature of this particular planet will increase something like five degrees Fahrenheit before the century is out. That would make it hotter than it has been on this particular planet for tens of millions of years."

McKibben puts that in perspective. "Even with our current increase of one degree Fahrenheit," he writes, "every major glacial system on earth is melting, the seasons are shifting radically, and both drought and deluge are on the increase." As is often the case, McKibben says, such changes will disproportionately harm "those living on the margins… many credible estimates suggest that the number of environmental refugees in this century will outnumber the political refugees of the bloody century we've just endured. And the rest of creation? An extinction crisis at least as bad as the last time a major asteroid hit, some ninety million years ago. Except that this time the asteroid is us."

The question is whether Americans will do what it would take to reduce global warming – higher costs for fuel, investing in renewable energy and sharing it with the developing world. McKibben explains that one hundred years from now, the economy will not be powered by fossil fuels as it is now, but wonders how quickly the change can be made. "The temptation," he says, "is always going to be to postpone the pain for the next one in line. Let the next Congress deal with it; let our kids deal with it."

Moving away from fossil fuels could have positive consequences, McKibben says. "If we got serious about this transition now, we could not only head off some of the climate trouble, we could also do great things for our communities. Imagine a world where people drew their juice from an array of wind turbines a few miles away. Imagine a vastly decentralized power grid that didn't depend on the brute power of Exxon Mobil and the 82nd Airborne – that didn't require slave labor to build pipelines through dense jungle, that didn't need young men and women to travel halfway around the world to shoot at and be shot by people who had the great misfortune to live atop reservoirs of crude. Imagine a defensible energy supply – physically defensible, and morally too."[14]

The Commitment

So, how can we get down to work?

For starters, families can listen to our children, who have a deeper intuitive sense of the environmental issues that most of their parents do. Teach them to respect and enjoy the world of nature. Spend time helping them get to know the magnificently abundant and spectacularly diverse species of God's good creation. Watch sunrises and sunsets together. On a recent family vacation, when my son Luke woke me up very early to show me the sunrise, I knew I needed to replace tired annoyance with childlike wonder. Learn personal and family habits of conservation, recycling, energy efficiency, and good stewardship of resources. Actively and openly resist advertising and consumerism.

Churches and other religious communities could play a major role here. Biblically rooted environmental education and creation-care instruction could be made a part of Sunday school curricula for all ages. Sermons could help the people of God remember, revive, and reinterpret the Genesis narratives and apply them to the most urgent environmental crisis of our time. What if the environmental "sins" of omission and commission were denounced from the pulpit and repentance called for? And what if local congregations made the commitment to energy conservation, beginning with their own buildings and facilities? What if our houses of prayer and worship demonstrated the worship of their Creator with creation-friendly energy practices? Given the large number of religious facilities throughout the nation, that would itself contribute to the solutions for global warming and, at the same time, provide the most powerful of examples to the rest of society and our elected leaders. This is a place where the religious community can really lead.

At Northland Church in Orlando, Florida, "volunteers... sift through the church building trash... to learn ways to make a bigger impact in their community by making a smaller impact on the environment. The church plans to purchase more recyclable products when it moves into its new 3,200-seat sanctuary in mid-August... Other green-friendly design ideas include: automatic utility shutdown systems, heavy insulation, a surfeit of tinted glass and landscaping with native plants to reduce water usage. Paving will yield to grass for much of the parking needs... 'It was the first order we got when we got down here,' Pastor Joel Hunter says. 'God said to Adam, "I'm giving you this garden to develop and to protect." There's a direct mandate (to) protect the garden that we've been given.'"[15]

Being environmentally responsible can also save money. *The Christian Science Monitor* reported some examples: "By installing solar panels on the roof and changing lighting, Christ Church in Ontario, Calif., saw its summer utility bills drop from $600 to $20 a month. All Saints Episcopal Church in Brookline, Mass., which installed a new boiler with zoned heating, programmable thermostats, and more efficient lighting, was rewarded with annual savings of $17,000. They've used 14 per cent of the savings to buy 100 per cent renewable energy, further reducing pollutants.

Hebron Baptist Church in Dacula, Ga., revamped its lighting system, converting fixtures and exit signs. They're saving $32,000 a year in church expenses and 450,000 kilowatt hours of energy."[16]

In many areas, the business community is taking a leading role. Companies are building new "green" facilities, producing energy-efficient products, practicing better waste management, and reducing emissions. The Pew Center on Global Climate Change was established in 1998 "to provide credible information, straight answers, and innovative solutions in the effort to address global climate change". Established at the same time was a Business Environmental Leadership Council[17] with "the belief that business engagement is critical for developing efficient, effective solutions to the climate problem." The council now has forty-three corporate members representing $2.8 trillion in market capitalization and more than 3.8 million employees. Many different sectors are represented, from high technology to diversified manufacturing, from oil and gas to transportation, from utilities to chemicals. Churches, which have many of those business leaders and legions of their employees in their congregations, could give such new environmental initiatives a moral boost. And church-business partnerships could provide the critical links between moral and technological innovation in local communities and around the world.

Eventually, some political leaders will take up the big idea of energy transformation, but it will likely take a movement to bring about that kind of dramatic political leadership. The benefits of a fundamental transformation in the ways our society creates, harnesses, and uses energy would be enormous. Massive numbers of jobs could be created – and good jobs beyond the low-paying service-industry work that now dominates expanded employment. Energy transformation could give a new focus to educational priorities and prospects, especially for lower-income people who are often faced with limited opportunities. Wouldn't that be better than more destruction of Amazon rain forests to create more pastures to graze more cattle to give more jobs to poor kids to make more hamburgers to make us fatter and unhealthier?

The conversion (and that's the right word) from our addiction to oil and other fossil fuels to cleaner, safer, and eventually more affordable sources of energy could also redeem our nation's foreign policies. There is perhaps no single greater cause for America's international hypocrisy and habitual drive to war than our dependence on oil. Does anyone really think that our nation's disastrous policies toward the Middle East and our wars in the Persian Gulf are not rooted in the oil addiction? If we are to change those policies and open up the possibility for genuine peace and democracy in the Middle East, the energy needs and policies of the world's most powerful nations will have to change. But what a welcome change that would be!

I recently heard a panel discussion in which former Senator Gary Hart spoke on the topic of "our addiction to oil". He said that America does indeed have an energy policy – to depend upon foreign supplies of oil for two-thirds or our energy needs and to fuel energy-inefficient vehicles. And if a cutoff of the foreign supply is threatened, we just sacrifice our young sons and daughters to get it turned back on. We've had two Persian Gulf wars so far, said the senator, and without a change in policy there will be more. He said that outside the United States there is nobody who doesn't believe that our Middle East policies and wars have something to do with oil. Of our $500 billion military budget, Hart said, half goes to protect oil supplies. And, he concluded, until people equate "blood with oil" and see this as a moral issue, a life-and-death issue, we will never see a change in policy. The other panelists, including former CIA director James Woolsey, were very positive about the huge market opportunities for clean energy alternatives, given the bleak oil option. They suggested that smart investment and the removal of barriers to alternative fuel sources could "destroy oil as a strategic commodity".

Psalm 145:9 says: "The Lord is good to all, and his compassion is over all that he has made." The implications of that psalm are boundless. When climate change and ecological pressures threaten the survival of civilization as we know it, how do we reassert an ethic of environmental stewardship that is rooted in our most basic moral and religious values? What does it mean to be good stewards of our endangered environment? And how do we integrate the need for economic growth, especially in the poorest nations, with the crucial need for ecological responsibility?

Energy transformation is the key – for personal renewal, social change, and political redemption. How can we take on the transformative challenge of a new energy ethics? How can individuals and families really change their lives? How could religious congregations lead by example in practising model ecological behavior, perhaps beginning by environmentally transforming their own facilities with new conservation practices and the use of more renewable energy sources, and becoming a serious moral and political force for political change? How could the ecological and energy refitting of the world also become a powerful engine of new jobs and economic sustainability? In particular, how could the religious community become the "tipping point" on a critical issue like global warming? All of that is now within our grasp if we make the deeply biblical commitment to be good stewards of God's creation.

7

EQUALITY AND DIVERSITY
The Race to Unity

Kenny's Barbecue was a neighbourhood institution. It was just a hole in the wall, with a couple of small Formica tables. Mostly carryout (takeaway), it was gooooood, and I must admit to being a regular customer. I had heard a rumour that Kenny's had changed hands, so the next time I went in I was curious to see who was there. As I walked into the cramped space, the familiar smells filled the air, but standing behind the counter was a little Vietnamese woman. I smiled at her and said, "I hear there's a new owner here." She grinned back at me and replied, "Me, I'm new owner." Wanting her to feel at home, I greeted her warmly, "Well, welcome to the neighbourhood! What's your name?" The new Asian immigrant to America, trying to master the arts of barbecue, beamed at me and proudly exclaimed, "Now my name is Kenny!" It was a metaphor for the whole new world of diversity that now shapes most American cities.

After this I looked, and there was a great multitude that no one could count, from every nation, from all tribes and peoples and languages, standing before the throne and before the Lamb, robed in white, with palm branches in their hands. (Revelation 7:9)

… for in Christ Jesus you are all children of God through faith. As many of you as were baptized into Christ have clothed yourselves with Christ. There is no longer Jew or Greek, there is no longer slave or free, there is no longer male and female; for all of you are one in Christ Jesus. (Galatians 3:26–28)

From now on, therefore, we regard no one from a human point of view; even though we once knew Christ from a human point of view, we know him no longer in that way. So if anyone is in Christ, there is a new creation: everything old has passed away; see, everything has become new! All this is from God, who reconciled us to himself through Christ, and has given us the ministry of reconciliation… (2 Corinthians 5:16–18)

Do you ever wonder what God might think of all our cultural conflicts? These texts suggest the opinions of God on the subjects we today call diversity, equality, and all the divisive matters surrounding the historic divisions of race, gender, and class.

The Revelation narrative is powerful and clear. This great multitude of people "from every nation, from all tribes and peoples and languages" are affirmed in their very diversity. They are different from one another and that is assumed to be just fine, even good. They are not amalgamated into one homogenized race or people but retain their cultural distinctiveness. They are present before the throne in all their diversities, we assume, of language, culture, race, gender, and class. But before the Lamb and the throne they are all absolutely equal. What unites them all here in the narrative is the worship of God, who recognizes no difference in value among them! The "great multitude that no one could count" from every nation and tribe stand before the throne "with palm branches in their hands", all testifying to the truth that "salvation belongs to our God who is seated on the throne, and to the Lamb!" (Revelation 7:9–10). What unites them in the Revelation story is their common affirmation in worship, and their humility before God – "they fell on their faces before the throne and worshipped God, singing, 'Amen! Blessing and glory and wisdom and thanksgiving and honour and power and might be to our God forever and ever! Amen'" (Revelation 7:11–12). Yet, if humility before God is a path to unity, it is hardly a characteristic behavior in today's painful and dangerous clashes between our "peoples and tribes".

The Galatians passage is absolutely seminal to the whole issue of diversity. It asserts unequivocally that because of the work of Christ, "There is no longer Jew or Greek, there is no longer slave or free, there is no longer male and female; for all of you are one in Christ Jesus." These three are the historic divisions and conflicts of humanity throughout history, the walls that divide and oppress – race, gender, and class. They are, indeed, the facts of oppression. However they are configured in different circumstances, race, gender, and class are usually involved in the oppression that human beings inflict on one another. Sometimes one factor is more prominent, sometimes another, but some or all are usually there, and the different oppressions generally exist in relationship to one another – they are usually interlocking and mutually reinforcing. Good social analysis can help us understand how these three great factors of oppression are involved in a situation and how they interconnect. But overcoming them is a much more difficult task than analyzing them.

The Galatians text is quite revolutionary in saying that despite all the human and societal things that would divide us, we "are all children of God through faith". It purports actually to overcome the historic facts of oppression. This text was so important to the early church that it was often used as a baptismal formula, during the induction of new converts into the life of the community. The new community of the church, the body of Christ in the world, would be based on a public repudiation of these three major factors of human division and oppression – racism, sexism, and class structures. The old divisions would not hold sway in the new community of Christ. Their authority and power were broken because a new humanity was coming into being – still diverse, but equal and reconciled.

Indeed, 2 Corinthians says that reconciliation of the world's divisions is one of the very purposes of the gospel and is at the heart of the church's mission. Paul says that the "human point of view" – meaning the normal and accepted human divisions and distinctions – is now pushed aside. And God's point of view will now replace the human point of view. Here is the big change: "From now on, therefore, we regard no one from a human point of view... if anyone is in Christ, there is a new creation: everything old has passed away; see, everything has become new!" Paul says that God has now given us the "ministry of reconciliation". "In Christ God was reconciling the world to himself," and is now "entrusting the message of reconciliation to us." We are therefore "ambassadors for Christ, since God is making his appeal through us," and we are literally commanded to "be reconciled to God," which also entails being reconciled to one another (2 Corinthians 5:19–20). This is not a suggestion but a command from God: "Be reconciled!"

Certainly, all this is extremely challenging and, "from a human point of view," many would say completely unrealistic. Yet without a doubt this is the vision that God expects us to carry out. So when Martin Luther King Jr. pointed out that the most segregated hour in America was 11:00 a.m. on Sunday morning (when most Americans go to church), he was really voicing the critique, opinion, and lament of God.

For despite God's wishes, racism continues dramatically to shape American life and politics. Our unrepentant sins of racism still poison the body politic. How do we overcome both the persistent prejudice of the majority and the resulting victimization culture of minorities? How do we both create and trust real opportunity? How do we move beyond easy multiculturalism by doing the hard work of racial justice and reconciliation?

And how do we navigate the new waters of multiethnic communities and conflicts in neighbourhoods across the country? America's newsreel isn't just in black and white anymore; bloody Technicolour conflicts between racial minorities are the tragic new addition to the landscape of racial strife in the United States. With race, we have original history and new history. How do we both recognize and affirm America's new multiracial family photo, but also never forget the particular sin of slavery and its aftermath of crushing discrimination, by taking responsibility for the unique experience of African Americans in the United States?

The conversion story of Zacchaeus may be instructive here:

> He entered Jericho and was passing through it. A man was there named Zacchaeus; he was a chief tax collector and was rich. He was trying to see who Jesus was, but on account of the crowd he could not, because he was short in stature. So he ran ahead and climbed a sycamore tree to see him, because he was going to pass that way. When Jesus came to the place, he looked up and said to him, "Zacchaeus, hurry and come down; for I must stay at your house today." So he hurried down and was happy to welcome him. All who saw it began to grumble and said, "He has gone to be the guest of one who is a sinner." Zacchaeus stood there and said to the Lord, "Look, half of my possessions, Lord, I will give to the poor; and if I have defrauded anyone of anything, I will pay back four times as much." Then Jesus said to him, "Today salvation has come to this house, because he too is a son of Abraham. For the Son of Man came to seek out and to save the lost." (Luke 19:1–10)

In the popular children's Bible story about the little man who had to climb a tree to see Jesus, a central point is often missed. Zacchaeus was a tax collector who had made a fortune based on corruption and injustice. When he was converted, he didn't just stop doing the unjust things, merely changing his behaviour. He also made restitution or reparations to those he had wronged, returning four times as much to anyone he had defrauded. Then Jesus said to him, "Today salvation has come to this house." Racial salvation has not yet come to the house of America, perhaps in part because the white majority has yet to take responsibility and make restitutions for the sins of slavery and racial discrimination.

Imagine if, after the end of slavery, the U.S. government had offered every newly freed slave a fresh start. In fact, General William T. Sherman issued an order in early 1865 that freed slaves were to be given "forty acres and a mule" for just that reason. Unfortunately, after President Lincoln's assassination, that order was overturned, and some former slaves who had already received the land had their titles revoked. How different might race relations be today if restitution for slavery had occurred at the beginning of emancipation, an offer of land, livestock, or capital that would have allowed the former captives to begin a new life as American citizens? Would there be so much anger today among African American young people who still struggle with a lack of opportunity, or such resentment from many white Americans about black complaints?

In other instances of oppression toward racial groups around the world, restitutions have indeed been made. Japan has admitted its offences against Korean women, who were systematically raped and forced to sexually service Japanese soldiers during World War II. Even the U.S. government made restitution to Japanese Americans who were forcibly detained in prison camps during the war. But are racial reparations even possible now in America, and what would they look like?

I have often described the near-genocide that white Europeans inflicted on America's indigenous Native American peoples and the human bondage forced on kidnapped Africans as "America's Original Sin". Today, our sin remains unrepented.

Apologizing for Slavery

About eleven million Africans and their descendants were enslaved from 1619 to 1865,[1] and about half of those kidnapped from Africa died in the notorious "middle passage" on the cruel slave ships. They were denied every respect and right of humanity: their families were ripped apart, their women raped, their men denied all dignity, and they, though human beings, were made into property. They were not allowed any benefit from their harsh labours. When finally freed, they were given nothing, no compensation for two and a half centuries of oppression. A few proposals to redress the grievance and offer a new start died quickly. Having been property themselves, the slaves were now propertyless. They were quickly relegated to the poorest underclass of America and became the focus of the most severe and often violent racial segregation and discrimination. Even after civil and voting rights legislation was finally passed in the 1960s, black Americans continued to be subject to personal prejudice, along with social, economic, and political discrimination.

The legacy of slavery, segregation, and discrimination is still woven into the fabric of American life, but, to this day, there has never even been an official federal government apology for slavery, the root of all these evils. And it was government policies that were both complicit in and directly responsible for this great inhumanity and injustice. Nobody alive in America today participated in slavery, many have no ancestors who did, and large numbers of families came to this land only after slavery was officially abolished – but all white Americans have benefited from the poisonous legacy of slavery and discrimination. And we have yet even to say we are sorry. The only exception that comes to mind is President Clinton's attempt in Ghana to apologize for slavery.

One positive sign in U.S. race relations is the spate of new resolutions in several states that explicitly apologize for slavery. In Alabama, a resolution passed the legislature in spring 2007 expressing "profound regret" for slavery. "We were not involved in that awful practice, but the government officials of that day were involved in slavery. For us to express our disapproval of what they did as representatives of the state is very appropriate," said Lowell Barron, chairman of the Alabama Senate Rules Committee.

"When I heard about Virginia [which had passed a similar resolution], I said we really need to do that because there is a great power in acknowledgment when you have hurt and injured someone," said State Senator Hank Sanders, who introduced the Alabama resolution, which recounts the reality of slavery, with its history of slaves being cruelly abused and brutalized and African families being torn apart. The extraordinary resolution says "an apology for centuries of brutal dehumanization and injustices cannot erase the past, but confession of wrongs can speed racial healing and reconciliation and help African-American and white citizens confront the ghosts of their collective pasts together". The resolution also reminded people that the legacy of slavery remains today: "for many African-Americans the scars left behind are unbearable, haunting their psyches and clouding their vision of the future and of America's many attributes".[2]

The North Carolina State House also officially apologized "for the injustice, cruelty, and brutality of slavery". Speaking to his white colleagues, an African-American lawmaker said, "Don't take it personal, but the lawmakers and policy makers of that time passed laws that made human bondage legal."[3]

The first of the slavery apologies was passed in Virginia, on the grounds of the former Confederate capitol, where the General Assembly voted unanimously to express "profound regret" for the state's role in the evil of slavery. The measure also expressed regret for "the exploitation of Native Americans". These apologies came as Virginia began its celebration of the four hundredth anniversary of Jamestown, the place in the new world where the first Africans arrived in 1619. The Virginia resolution powerfully admits that government-sanctioned slavery "ranks as the most horrendous of all depredations of human rights and violations of our founding ideals in our nation's history, and the abolition of slavery was followed by systematic discrimination, enforced segregation, and other insidious institutions and practices toward Americans of African descent that were rooted in racism, racial bias, and racial misunderstanding".[4]

Taking Responsibility

The slavery apology resolutions, especially coming from the South, are far more significant than is suggested by the meagre press attention given them. Their language is almost theological in places, clearly describing the moral issues that slavery and racial discrimination still pose to the nation and explicitly calling for healing on the basis of truth-telling. They could become a model for a nation that has yet to come to terms with its racial past and present.

The Zacchaeus story provides an example of "repaying" a debt of corruption and injustice and of making restitution for past sins. Exodus 22:1 says that whoever steals an ox or a sheep and slaughters it must pay back four or five to one. Numbers 5:5–7 says, "When a man or a woman wrongs another... the person shall make full restitution for the wrong, adding one-fifth to it, and giving it to the one who was wronged." The repentant tax collector, Zacchaeus, gave half of his possessions to the poor and paid his victims four times the amount he had stolen.

Most of the slavery apology resolutions in the southern states are just that – apologies without reference to restitution. Biblically, though, repentance is generally followed by a behavioural change bearing the "fruits" of repentance. Many today feel that such apologies should be followed by some form of "reparations" to the victims of American slavery. Without some form of restitution, apologies can ring hollow.

Antipoverty programmes can be judged both for their successes and for their failures, but they were never set up as "restitution" for the sin of slavery. Even "affirmative action" was never truly an effort to take national responsibility for racism, making demands on the whole nation and spreading the burden to all Americans, and has in fact been criticized for giving advantages to some Americans at the expense of others. Neither is true restitution.

In Virginia, the legislature took a step in 2004 toward "atoning" for the state's massive resistance campaigns in the 1950s and 1960s to the enforcement of federally mandated educational equality between the races. They did so by creating a scholarship fund for blacks whose schools were shut down between 1954 and 1964.

What form racial restitution or reparations should take is a matter of intense debate. I don't have the ideal formula or answer. But for the healing of the nation, and the genuine task of counteracting an injustice, some form of restitution could still be very significant. Few believe that solutions such as cash payments to individuals or families are the best option now, but there is a growing interest in exploring what might be the equivalent of "forty acres and a mule".

Today, that equivalent could be found in expanding educational opportunities for young black Americans who are still trapped in failing urban and rural educational systems – a modern subjugation to dangerous and substandard schools that is tantamount to a prison sentence, and too often leads to one. Education is the modern asset most important to success now, and perhaps most equivalent to the old "forty acres" start-up investment. It is a discussion that we must have.

We must come to understand that racism and sexism are part of the sea we swim in; they are in the air we breathe. They are so rooted in the systems and culture around us that just to accept things as they are is to be complicit in both racism and sexism. A better question to ask is, Who is responsible to repair the damage that racism and sexism have done? Unless we deliberately reveal the racism and sexism that surround us and permeate the environments in which we live, we will never break their power over us. That's what it seems the early church did – its members named and confronted racial, gender, and class distinctions and sought to overcome them. We don't need just more political correctness; we need a deliberate strategy to confront these cruel and divisive facts of the world and change them.

I had thought the most controversial week in my course at Harvard would be the one in which we discussed abortion and gay marriage. But that turned out not to be the case – it was the week focused on race. Most Harvard students think of themselves as liberal but were quite resistant to the idea of having any responsibility for racism themselves. When I suggested the principle that "benefiting from oppression means to be responsible for it", I could feel the push back. I didn't say guilty, I said responsible. We may not have personally had ancestors who owned slaves, as many of my students were eager to point out, but can anyone possibly deny that slavery and discrimination were oppressions intended to benefit the white majority at the expense of black people? Has anyone at Harvard, or in white affluent America, not benefited in this society? Recognition of responsibility doesn't come quickly or easily.

The discussion always reminds me of what happened when Sojourners put out its first study guide on racism called *America's Original Sin: A Study*

Guide on White Racism. My introductory piece opened by saying, "The United States of America was established as a white society, founded upon the genocide of another race and then the enslavement of yet another." I have never received more letters in response to a single sentence. The letters either called my sentence "courageous" or "outrageous" when, of course, it was neither, but rather simply a statement of the historical facts surrounding the nation's founding and economic development.

I used that infamous sentence at a 2006 conference in Cincinnati, Ohio, called "Race to Unity". It was hosted by Rev. Ray McMillan, senior pastor of Faith Christian Center, and a number of other local pastors, both black and white. They were concerned with truth-telling about race in America. McMillan was a gang leader in Chicago when he had a Christian conversion. As a young believer he was an eager learner and before long became a pastor himself. But eventually he became uncomfortable with some of the things his conservative white Christian brethren were saying, and not saying, about race. He noticed how some leaders of the Religious Right had labelled many of our founding fathers Christian "heroes". McMillan's studies revealed that many of the country's founders were actually not orthodox Christians at all, and many were slaveholders. How did they get to be "Christian heroes", he asked, and what does that imply for your black brothers in Christ? I had to smile when Ray accused these Christian leaders of "ancestor worship". He said, "our heroes are dividing us". McMillan's critique of the unwillingness of his white brothers to tell the truth about racism and directly confront it as the early church did was prophetic and compelling. He charged that many of them were, in the end, more American than Christian.

At the conference, I again received a shocked response to my controversial sentence and to the idea that those who benefit from oppression are responsible for it. But this time the shock was from black pastors and lay-people who had never heard a white person speak this way before. That struck me as a sad testimony. Why are black people always the ones to have to speak up on the subject of racism, or women on sexism? Why is it always their job? Why do the subjects often not even get mentioned in this obviously racist and sexist society unless a person of colour or a woman raises them? Is that fair or right? Ask people of colour and you will find how tiring it is always to have to be the ones who raise the issues of race. It was Paul, a Jew, who most confronted his Christian community and fellow Jews on their reluctance to embrace and include the Gentiles in the new community of the church. It's time for white people to talk about race, and for men to talk about gender justice.

White privilege is the nice, contemporary way of describing white supremacy. The assumption of white privilege is still very deep in the psyche and expectations of most white Americans. On a theological level, white privilege, domination, and supremacy are an idol – the idol of whiteness. Idol worship is always an affront to God, indeed a competition with God for allegiance. Many years ago William Stringfellow, a white lay theologian and lawyer working in Harlem, identified white racism as idolatry and said the real issue at stake in racism is the meaning of our baptism. Who God is and who we are, are the ultimate questions. For real racial reconciliation to occur in the American church and nation, we will have to give up all of our idol worship.

As I said earlier, Hurricane Katrina provided a searingly powerful illustration of the enduring and insidious effects of racism. Racism has become institutionalized in America and shows up in all our discussions of the life opportunities for all of our citizens. While more covert than the personal expressions of racism that in many places are on the wane, institutionalized racism is equally pernicious.

Welcoming the Stranger

I believe the issue of immigration is a religious issue, a biblical issue. We people of faith call it "welcoming the stranger", and we are under an obligation from God to do so. Immigration has become a very controversial subject in America and throughout the world. The recently divisive national debate over immigration reform was shaped by real concerns about economic insecurity and respect for the law, but also, sadly, by prejudice and fear about the America we are becoming. The unprecedented rallies and demonstrations of 2006–2007 could signal the birth of an immigrants' rights movement, but that movement must translate marches into real political change.

What would comprehensive immigration reform in America look like? How do we both "welcome the stranger" and preserve a nation of laws? What is both humane and just? How do we prepare for an America that will look like a completely different nation in a very short time? (Certain parts of the country already look like the new America.) By 2050, most Americans will trace their ancestry to Africa, Latin America, or Asia, and white Americans with European roots will, for the first time, be the minority population. Quite honestly, most white Americans are not ready for that. Who will help get them ready? Who will engage in the now-critical mission of reconciliation?

How we treat the stranger is, indeed, a critical religious issue. The biblical story continually shows God's concern for the migrant and the outcast. "The alien who resides with you shall be to you as the citizen among you; you shall love the alien as yourself, for you were aliens in the land of Egypt: I am the Lord your God" (Leviticus 19:34). Similarly, throughout the New Testament, Christians are called to care for the outcast and the stranger. Jesus identified with these neighbours when he said, "I was a stranger and you welcomed me" (Matthew 25:35).

As Christians from majority cultures, we must show compassion and pursue justice for immigrants and their families. Immigration is a deeply relevant issue for all Americans. We are a nation of immigrants, one that has been continually reshaped by new groups of people bringing diverse cultures, perspectives, and resources. Immigration issues are also poverty issues. Immigrants – both legal and undocumented – are more likely to live in families with incomes below the poverty level, and children of undocumented immigrants are especially at risk.

Twelve million people are now in the United States without documentation, whether or not we like how they got here. There is no way to round up all of them or send them back. If some kind of guest-worker status with an eventual earned path to citizenship is not provided for undocumented immigrants, our country will have a permanent underclass of illegal and vulnerable undocumented workers – people who work, live, pay taxes, and go to school in the United States but cannot attain better and more secure lives for themselves and their families.

We must be a nation of laws, and the current anarchy at our borders is not good for anyone. But legal enforcement must be humane as well as firm, and comprehensive immigration reform of the whole broken system is long overdue. Those reforms should be pro-work and pro-family, they should respect the law, and they should create new opportunities to strengthen the common good of families and employers alike, thus enriching the vitality of America.

The church has a unique role to lift up the moral and human aspects of immigration reform. We believe immigrants are children of God, entitled to dignity and respect. An increasing percentage of our congregants are immigrants, and our church social service agencies, schools, and health clinics work with them and their families on a daily basis. That moral grounding and day-to-day experience give us the authority to speak to political leaders, as Catholic Cardinal Roger Mahony of Los Angeles did when he prophetically warned public officials not to make into illegal acts the ministries of the churches who serve undocumented immigrants. If you make our church's ministries illegal, we will break your laws, he said. It is unusual for a cardinal to threaten civil disobedience. But this is a question both of theological principle and of pastoral relationship.

A very broad coalition of Christians has come together to support the principles of comprehensive immigration reform. Across many divisions and despite other disagreements, a wide group of evangelical, Pentecostal, Catholic, and mainline Protestant church leaders have joined in unity. We oppose the raids by agents of the U.S. Immigration and Customs Enforcement (formerly the INS), which are breaking up families and separating immigrant children from their mothers and fathers. We all agree that the system is broken and needs to be fixed. So let's fix it, but with compassionate and humane enforcement and with policies that also offer immigrants the chance to work legally and even pursue a path to earned citizenship.

Walls, fences, and law enforcement are not enough. The concerns about immigration often come from people's own economic insecurity, their fears of new influxes of people, their worries about terrorism, and sometimes their prejudice, narrow nationalism, misinformation, and xenophobia. But those are finally not religious motivations. We have yet to hear of a hotel housekeeper from Mexico turning into a suicide bomber. And the genuine economic insecurity of people on the bottom cannot, accurately, be blamed on others also at the bottom – the poor blaming the destitute – but rather on the national economic policies, the morally flawed budgets, and the lack of living wages and benefits from huge corporations whose enormous profits go disproportionately to their top executives rather than to their poorest workers. People of faith can be a voice on this issue for compassion, humane reform, and good immigration laws. As Rev. Samuel Rodriguez, president of the National Hispanic Christian Leadership Conference, said at the national launch of a new immigration reform group, "We propose that Congress pass comprehensive immigration reform that reflects the American commitment to the three formative pillars of our nation: the rule of law, our faith value system, and the pursuit of the American Dream."[5]

In the summer of 2007, the failure of legislation to fix this broken system showed just how divisive the issue of immigration still is in America. In the absence of federal legislation, people of faith must resist more punitive and draconian legislation at the state and local levels while working to change hearts and minds.

Noel Castellanos of the Christian Community Development Association eloquently sums up the issue for people of faith.

Regardless of our political persuasion, at the very least we as believers ought to be loving and merciful and compassionate towards those who are taking care of our kids, mowing our lawns, dry-walling our new homes, picking our crops, serving our meals, fighting in Iraq, and worshipping in our churches. At the very least, we should understand the agony that many of these parents feel; their willingness to do whatever they can to find a better life for their families and children – even if it means risking their lives. At the very least, our hearts should break when we hear about children being torn from their fathers and mothers by immigration raids that are, at best, a cold-hearted attempt to "fix" broken immigration laws. At the very least, those of us who really don't understand the issues related to immigration reform should take the time to get informed.[6]

And while Europeans have often been quick to judge America's racial problems, the new immigrations into Europe have now revealed their own ethnocentricities and are transforming European culture and politics. The truth is that racial, gender, and class divisions are a feature of almost every nation on the planet. We all have a stake in the race to unity. It's no wonder that the earliest Christians decided this was so important.

The Triple Burden That Women Bear

The inequality of men and women remains deeply embedded in American society and in global realities, including unequal pay, legal and political structures, corporate practices, definitions of marriage and child-raising responsibilities, cultural rules, popular culture roles from sports to entertainment, and the leadership of religious communities. In the United States, of the thirty-seven million people below the poverty line, twenty-one million (57 per cent) are women. Heather Boushey, senior economist at the Center for Economic and Policy Research, writes, "Most women are in the labor force, including over 70 per cent of all mothers. Yet, women continue to earn less than men even if they have similar educational levels and work in similar kinds of jobs. The typical full-time, full-year working woman earns only 77 per cent of what her male counterparts make. About 40 per cent of this gap in pay cannot be explained by women's choices."

According to Boushey, "Closing the gender pay gap requires that policy-makers do more to help families balance work and family life. With the majority of parents at work and most families having no full-time caretaker in the home, employers must recognize that their workers should not have to choose between being good workers and being good parents. It is women who continue to not only do the most caretaking, but who bear the brunt of the economic penalties of the workplace. Policy initiatives like paid sick days, paid family leave, increased access to flexible workplaces – without pay penalties – are all important steps in leveling the playing field between men and women on the job."[7]

On a global level the situation of women is often quite desperate. Elizabeth Palmberg of *Sojourners* magazine writes: "On the most basic level, about 70 per cent of the world's poorest people (those living on less than a dollar a day) are women or girls. About two-thirds of children who aren't able to go to primary school are girls. Although women are participating in paid labor at higher rates than in the past, their wages still lag far behind men's, and they have starkly uneven family responsibilities, often made worse by lack of access to family planning and child care. Although they work twice as many working hours as men, women receive only one-tenth of the world's income, and own less than a hundredth of the world's property. In some parts of the world, when a husband dies the household's land and possessions may be legally swallowed up by his extended family, leaving his widow and children destitute."[8]

Across the world, women have a triple burden. First, women are the ones who bear the greatest burdens and suffer the most consequences from the world's injustices and calamities. They are more likely than men to be the victims of poverty, of pandemic diseases, of war and other violent conflicts, and of global disasters. This is because of their greater vulnerability: they have less power in the structures of families and societies, and certain abuses are specifically targeted at them, like systematic rape in wartime and retribution arising from family codes and so-called honour cultures.

Second, despite their less powerful position, women still bear the lion's share of the burden of literally keeping things together. Sustaining day-to-day life, even survival in families, villages, neighbourhoods, and societies, still falls disproportionately on women – wives and mothers in particular. They are the ones most depended upon by everybody else. The strength of women across the globe who hold human life together in the most tenuous circumstances makes a lie of their common designation as "the weaker sex".

Third, while being the most vulnerable yet still regularly fulfilling their sustaining role, women must do so without the corresponding power and authority to change the facts that create the burdens in the first place. They become the glue that keeps things together, but have the least power to change the situations that tear things apart. Even when it is demonstrated, for example, that women often play a much more effective role in resolving conflicts then men do, they are passed over repeatedly for such roles.

Women are clearly not the weaker sex, but their "weaker" power in the structures of the world is a serious detriment, not only to women, but to us all.

In September 1995, the Fourth World Conference on Women met in Beijing. The conference called for new and strong commitments to international standards for promoting equality, development, and peace for and with all the women of the world. In its final declaration, the "Beijing Declaration", the governments assembled recognized "that the status of women has advanced in some important respects in the past decade but that progress has been uneven, inequalities between women and men have persisted and major obstacles remain, with serious consequences for the well-being of all people", and "that this situation is exacerbated by the increasing poverty that is affecting the lives of the majority of the world's people, in particular women and children, with origins in both the national and international domains". We are convinced, they said, that "women's empowerment and their full participation on the basis of equality in all spheres of society, including participation in the decision-making process and access to power, are fundamental for the achievement of equality, development, and peace".[9]

The conference adopted a Platform for Action as "an agenda for women's empowerment", with the purpose of "removing all the obstacles to women's active participation in all spheres of public and private life through a full and equal share in economic, social, cultural and political decision-making. This means that the principle of shared power and responsibility should be established between women and men at home, in the workplace and in the wider national and international communities. Equality between women and men is a matter of human rights and a condition for social justice and is also a necessary and fundamental prerequisite for equality, development and peace."[10]

Women are also the key to overcoming global poverty. As Palmberg writes, "Women aren't just at ground zero of the problem of poverty – they're also central to the solutions. In addition to being primary stakeholders in getting clean water (a task that takes about forty billion hours per year worldwide, according to the United Nations), women are usually responsible for caring for sick family members. They also take primary responsibility for raising children and for household nutrition."

Palmberg points out, too, that "studies have repeatedly shown that when women receive extra income, they spend it on family food and education at higher rates than men do. As Ritu Sharma of the Women's Edge Coalition, an advocacy group, puts it, 'Teach a man to fish, he eats. Teach a woman to fish, everybody eats.'... What would a well-conceived aid policy – one that recognized the vital role women have to play – look like? In part, it would be aware of the potential of thinking small. In the past decade, microcredit, the practice of giving modest loans to help individuals start small businesses, has finally begun to receive well-deserved attention (in fact, the U.N. proclaimed 2005 to be the International Year of Microcredit). By the end of 2003, different microcredit groups reported making loans to over fifty-four million people living in poverty, more than four-fifths of them women; the U.S. Agency for International Development is devoting $200 million to microcredit this fiscal year."[11] One of the best examples is the Grameen Bank, which along with its founder, Muhammad Yunus, won the 2006 Nobel Peace Prize for their work in fighting poverty through economic development. As of May 2007, the bank had 7.21 million borrowers, 97 per cent of whom were women.[12]

In 1994 my wife, Joy Carroll, was among the first women ordained as priests in the Church of England. Later she served as script consultant for a popular British comedy show called *The Vicar of Dibley*. The series was about the travails of a fictional woman vicar in the English countryside, a long way from the urban parishes in South London that Joy served for ten years. But the witty and entertaining comedy helped to humanize and commend the idea of women as priests to the British public, even according to many church officials.

I believe that institutionalizing the leadership role of women in religious communities goes a long way toward securing respect and equality for them in many other sectors. Pastors and priests are key community conveners, healers, service providers, and spokespeople. These are pivotal roles, and when filled by women they serve to advance the social position of other women, and of all those who have been left out or left behind. So it was disconcerting when Neela Banerjee of *The New York Times* reported that even in mainline denominations where the ordination of women has been resolved for decades, it was still very difficult and painfully rare to see a woman in the senior pastoral position in the large and leading churches. Many were still being relegated to "associate" and "assistant" pastor roles or had gone into other forms of ministry. It's a pattern that some call "the stained-glass ceiling", and it correlates to the invisible barriers in other sectors as well.[13] The article showed that a change in leadership within the religious community will not come easily, but come it will with more women in seminaries than ever before and more women feeling the call to ministry. That will change much more than our congregations.

A Teachable Moment?

In spring 2007, a media firestorm erupted over the comments of radio talk-show host Don Imus, an aging "shock jock" whose stock-in-trade included regular slights, insults, jokes, and attacks at the expense of countless people and groups because of their race, gender, or class. Imus clearly was not familiar with the biblical texts I quoted above. But one day Don Imus went too far, and seemed to cross a cultural line, when he referred to members of the Rutgers University women's basketball team as "nappy-headed hos". The young women athletes/scholars, some of them only eighteen years old, had had a Cinderella season, winning the hearts of America and becoming role models for a whole generation of young girls. And they had done nothing but show character and class when an old white man who liked to wear cowboy hats in his radio studio demeaned them with a racist and sexist insult for no apparent reason, other than his own meanness and stupidity.

The nation was outraged and a public discussion ensued, with a high-profile media scrutiny of the man and his show that ultimately led to his being fired. This time it wasn't just liberal civil rights groups that swayed the decision to let Imus go but also the advertisers who pulled their business from the show and the executives on the inside of CBS and MSNBC, especially women and African Americans who now hold key positions in broadcast journalism.

The question is whether the rightful verdict against Don Imus will be a teachable moment for the nation, a milestone and turning point when the nation will say "enough" to the profitable talk of division and hate. The jury is still out on that one as I write this chapter, and it is not yet clear whether the Imus incident will be relevant, or even remembered, by the time this book comes out. Is it now as you read the book over a year later? Or is it already a forgotten media blip?

I agree with all the people who said to me after the Imus flap that we must not have any double standards and need to be consistent in opposing all manner of demeaning hate talk and behaviour whether it's on the air, in the lyrics of music by young hip-hop artists of colour themselves, or even in backrooms, hallways, or candid closed-door conversations among people who have race, ethnicity, or gender in common. It's time that we all were responsible for what comes out of our mouths. As the Bible says, "The things that come out of the mouth come from the heart" (Matthew 15:18, NIV).

It's just not okay to talk that way, even in private, and it's not excusable even when it is partly a symptom of the self-hate far too prevalent in communities of colour themselves and a mirror image of the assaults directed at them. Since the Imus affair, more civil rights leaders are speaking against the ugly and vicious language that emanates from much of the enormously popular hip-hop world. For instance, Russell Simmons recently made a courageous call to the hip-hop industry to ban use of the N-word in its music. Culture, behaviour, standards of decency, the need for civility, and the moral compass of right and wrong do indeed matter, as black leaders such as C. Delores Tucker, Robert Franklin, Calvin Butts, Cornel West, Tavis Smiley, and many others have said for some time.

Respect

When it comes to equality and diversity, racism and sexism, I believe the underlying issue, and the most deeply felt pain, revolves around one word – *respect*. For people of faith, the meaning of respect goes much deeper than mere tolerance or the granting of human rights. Respect is rooted in the universal and essential human dignity that comes from all of us bearing the very image of God. And even deeper, from the love that we owe to one another because of how we have been loved by God. But on the street, the word that often comes up is "respect" as what is wanted and often not received. Respect is the thing we all want and need, and it is what is denied to people over and over again because of race, gender, and class. So many of the demands of protests, so much of the aggrieved voice in response to racism, and even the angry counterattack, is, down deep, a cry for respect. As Aretha Franklin once sang, "R-E-S-P-E-C-T, Find out what it means to me."

There is also a cycle of disrespect that works like this: the disrespect begins with the obvious injustice, as massive an offence as racial or sexual slavery, or the more subtle yet cruel forms of racial or gender discrimination. The pain of disrespect is felt and it hurts. Then the response begins. We are undeservedly blessed when the response is in the form of a Martin Luther King Jr. calling us all to forgiveness, reconciliation, nonviolence, and higher ground. But the more human and common response is to return the disrespect with more disrespect.

Sometimes it is visited upon members of one's own group, especially if the disrespect has been deeply internalized. How else do we explain the ugly racial and sexist language of too much (but not all) of contemporary urban hip-hop music and culture, or the black-on-black or brown-on-brown violence that has terrorized so many urban neighbourhoods? The disrespect is also played out in both verbal and physical attacks on other oppressed groups, which ultimately results in the tragic gang violence that plagues our cities – black-on-brown-on-Asian, and so on, often following learned patterns of disrespect: learned by being disrespected.

The disrespect also works itself out as payback against the dominant group. But the relative powerlessness of the oppressed group, the lack of direct and equal access to the dominant communities and their people, and the much stronger police protection of the majority culture (as opposed to the relative weak protection of minority groups) all limit the impact of the countermove of disrespect directed back to those who have disrespected them. So it takes more subtle forms. At shopping malls, it appears in the behaviours of minority youth working in the shops or cruising the territory with a characteristically adversarial posture and stance. The stereotypes, rooted in both perception and reality, are remarkably set now in the majority culture: the sullen, angry, resentful, and unhelpful African American youth; the happy young Hispanic housekeeper; or the bright, very-eager-to-please Asian youth. These stereotypes represent tapes in our imagination and psyche, helping us make mental shortcuts for interpreting people and the world around us. But these stereotypes and behaviours can be coping mechanisms that result from a disrespect that comes from being disrespected and can harden into prejudice and bigotry.

In the next part of the cycle of disrespect, those attitudes of disrespect come to define the minority group, and their worst behaviours are lifted up as normative. Other realities, such as the large number of young African Americans who are bright, hardworking, well behaved, and succeeding, are rarely lifted up – either in the media (which loves to play on the mass stereotypes) or in the imaginations of the majority. And, of course, disrespectful behaviours are also often self-destructive and self-defeating, like the attitude among too many urban and minority students that being smart in school is "acting white", a charge that many black leaders have desperately tried to counter.

Even the more acceptable behaviours of other minorities are also privately treated with disrespect – Asians being regarded as annoyingly "sucking up" or Latinos easily and invisibly taken for granted and said to love doing "grunt work". The slurs, jokes, and assaults (both verbal and physical) against women go on and on – with the kind of cultural acceptance that would never be allowed if they were directed toward any other group.

So disrespect breeds more disrespect in return, which is used to confirm the disrespect in the first place, which further increases the resentment and anger of the disrespected, and so on. All of this leads to deep and abiding group tensions and regular cultural collisions, which only take the wrong spark and the wrong time to erupt in major conflict. In America, the white majority remains on top with an increasingly racially diverse battleground at the bottom end of the society. The Oscar-winning movie *Crash* illustrates this vicious cycle in which our racial fears, distrust, biases, and stereotypes set off a dangerous chain reaction in society with dire consequences for everyone.

There is only one solution to the cycle of disrespect. That answer is ultimate respect, meaning the showing of respect for the human dignity of all created in the image of God – as an act of principle, and an act of faith. Respect for other people is not something they should be forced to earn, or to beg or fight for; it is owed to them by virtue of their very humanity. There is clearly a religious imperative to all this. We respect one another because God made us equal, views us as equal, and treats us as equal – and expects us to treat one another the same way. We get respect when we give respect. But only ultimate respect, not respect just in return for respect, will break through the cycle of disrespect. Breaking the cycle requires the reassertion of our absolute equality in the eyes of God.

I remember participating in several meetings to plan a series of "gang peace summits" during the mid-1990s. Often I was the only white person in the room with dozens of young African American and Latino youth. Every time a new "crew" from another city would walk into the room, I would get a look from the newcomers that would have killed me if looks could kill. They said, in effect, "Why is he here? What's a white man doing here in our territory, our discussion!?" I could see other eyes silently shooting back at them with another message like, "Okay, chill, hold up, just give him a chance, it's all right." And it always was after a day of talking together. I learned with the leaders and "defence ministers" of some of the country's biggest and toughest gangs that, in the end, we all pretty much need and want the same thing – just a little respect, a little kindness, and maybe even a little love.

Religious Pluralism

As a Christian, and an evangelical Christian at that, I want to say emphatically that America is not, and should not be, a "Christian nation". While it is clear that the founders of the nation had a high regard for religion and generally believed it made an essential contribution to the well-being of society, they decided to disentangle religion from the state and thereby create a new thing in the world. As for their own faith, many were religious and some were not; there were likely more "deists" than evangelical Christians among them (despite the historically groundless claim by some that the founders were mostly dedicated believers).

What we have come to call the separation of church and state is good for both the government and religion – that citizenship should have no religious tests, and that faith should not be implemented (or hindered) by the state. The path of Jesus, for example, could never be followed by the state, and the prophetic integrity and power of religion to hold governments accountable to higher values and better behaviour specifically depends on the faith community's political independence.

Neither should religion need the state's power to enforce its language and theology, which is why the "war against Christmas" discussion is finally so absurd. Does Jesus' message really depend on our being reminded to have a "Merry Christmas" just before we plunge into shopping malls and engage in orgies of holiday consumerism that run so directly contrary to his message? Are Wal-Mart and Target to be seen as critical places of theological and spiritual reflection?

On the other hand, does the cultural visibility of religious language and symbols in holiday seasons threaten the religious liberty of diverse believers (especially if all the pluralistic faith traditions of the nation can enjoy public display at the appropriate times in their religious calendars)? I don't think so. But it is a tactic of religious fundamentalism (in all our traditions) to try to make the state an enforcer of religious belief and practice, and it is always dangerous.

Does anybody really want to say that America has behaved in the world as a "Christian nation"? For the sake of Christian integrity, I hope not. It is far better to regard faith communities as essentially countercultural, calling us all to higher ground and challenging political and economic power when it becomes abusive of the religious values of compassion and justice. Only through its independence and separation from any state can religion exercise its vital prophetic role in every society.

As an orthodox Christian, I believe that Jesus was the Son of God. I believe the things that Jesus says about himself in the New Testament, and I affirm what the scriptures and church creeds say about Jesus being the Son of God. But that doesn't mean many of the things that Christians have too often concluded, nor does it justify many actions Christians have taken on the basis of our beliefs.

Jesus being the Son of God does not mean that Christians are better, more righteous, more moral, more blessed, more destined to win battles, or more suited to govern and decide political matters than non-Christians. Instead, believing that Jesus was the Son of God would better mean that people who claim to believe it ought to then live the way Jesus did and taught. On that one, many of us Christians (who believe the right way) are in serious trouble when it comes to the way we live. Those who believe that Jesus was the Son of God should be the most loving, compassionate, forgiving, welcoming, peaceful, and hungry-for-justice people around – just like Jesus, right? Well, it's not always exactly so.

I'll never forget hearing Billy Graham, the world's greatest evangelist, the last time he spoke at Harvard. He preached at Harvard's Memorial Church (to a huge crowd of students who had slept out all night just to get a seat), and then to the prestigious JFK Forum at the Kennedy School of Government the next night. After giving a statesmanlike address at the Kennedy School, he turned to the audience for questions. All the Christian triumphalists had shown up for their man and their night at Harvard. One young believer stood up and asked Dr. Graham, "Since Jesus said, 'I am the way, the truth and the life, and no man cometh to the Father but by me,' doesn't that mean people from other religions – Jews and the rest – are going to hell?" Billy replied, "I'm sure glad that God is the judge of people's hearts and not me! And I trust God to decide those questions justly and mercifully." The student was disappointed and pressed further, "Well, what do you think God will decide?" Graham demurred, "Well, God doesn't really ask my advice on those matters."

Another questioner started again, "Well, what about those who aren't even monotheists – like the Buddhists?" Graham replied, "You know, I've been to some Buddhist countries, and so many of the people I met seem to live more like Jesus than too many Christians I've seen." Now, Billy Graham would clearly answer the question "Is Jesus the Son of God?" in the strong affirmative. But the man who has arguably brought more people to Christ than anyone else in our time refused to join in Christian triumphalism. To answer yes to the question of belief is, at the same time, to admit our human failings, stand under judgment ourselves, and humbly seek to follow the one we say we believe in. That might open up a wonderful dialogue with those who believe other things.

In all the great religions today, a crucial battle is going on for the hearts and minds of the faithful. That battle is often between a fundamentalist version of a faith and its prophetic vision. It's between the kind of religion that promises easy certainty and the kind that prompts deeper reflection. One version attacks all those outside the circle of faith (or even outside their faction of the faith), while the other seeks a genuine dialogue without compromising its sacred ground. The conflicts between religions in today's world capture all the headlines, but the real struggle is the internal battle for the soul of each community of faith.

I love a word I discovered through Irshad Manji's book *The Trouble with Islam Today*. Manji speaks of the great need for *ijtihad* – independent thinking, personal reflection, self-criticism, self-examination, rigorous rethinking, renewal, reformation, and revival. She examines the basic religious conflict between those who look inward and try to root out both internal hypocrisy and religious dysfunction through *ijtihad* and those who externalize their anxieties, fears, and insecurities by pursing violent jihad against external enemies instead. This is the conflict between authentic faith and aggressive religion. We can hope and pray that this conflict over religious integrity will replace the prophesied "clash of civilizations".

The Commitment

Because racism, sexism, and class bias are both attitudinal and institutional, both personal and political responses are required. That means changing how we think and feel about people, but also changing how people are treated through societal structures, laws, and policies. Those need to be fleshed out in our families and communities, and in national politics.

First, on the personal and family level it is crucial what we model and how we lead by example. For one thing, it is important how a family talks about the subjects of equality and diversity – what we say about race, gender, and class distinctions. Language is important. What children hear from their parents is very formational in their lives. If they hear people who are different from them spoken of with respect and affirmation, they are much more likely to regard them in those ways. Diversity, like many other things, begins at home. What names are revered in a home, whose pictures are on the walls, what books are on the shelves, which films and music become part of a family's life, and which political and societal leaders are held up as role models – all these are very important.

In my son Luke's school, the third and fourth graders are each assigned a major figure from black history to research and report on. In the third grade, Luke was assigned Nelson Mandela, which delighted his parents. In his opening statement, Luke told his classmates this: "When I was just two weeks old, my parents took me out into the world for the first time. We went to the Harvard Yard, in Boston, to hear Nelson Mandela speak. He was eighty years old, and I was just two weeks old. So he was the oldest person there and I was the youngest. My dad and mom said they took me to hear Nelson Mandela so someday we could talk about him. This project has given us that chance."

Where we choose to live, to enroll our kids in school, to go to church, and to take them into the community are all critical choices that will dramatically affect our children's worldview and their experience with diversity. For my family, choosing a racially diverse public school has been an important choice, as well as remaining in a neighbourhood that is both culturally and economically mixed. Who our family's friends are, where and with whom we socialize, who our common houseguests are, and whom we choose to be role models and even godparents are also important decisions. Whom our children have their playdates with will colour their view of the world more than many other choices we make.

Having a mother who is a priest and a father who is also a pastor has helped to normalize our children's understanding of leadership in the church being shared between men and women. They have seen their mom in action as a priest – preaching, presiding over the Eucharist, and performing weddings and funerals, just as they have seen their dad do similar things and speak in a variety of religious as well as secular contexts. It would never occur to our two boys that there should be a limitation on the role of women in the church or society, because seeing their mom, and other women, serve in many leadership capacities has been a natural part of their life experience.

One of the reasons we chose our home church was the decision the congregation had made to try to be "the opposite of racism". We thought that was a deeper commitment than just to be "diverse" or even "antiracist". It means a commitment to try to create a communal life that seeks to transform racial attitudes, practices, and public policies, and to model a community life that counters the culture's conformity to racism. Scott Garber, the pastor of our Washington Community Fellowship, says:

> Racism does not disappear just because of the passage of time. Racism does not disappear just because we are sorry. Racism does not disappear just because we're "workin' hard". Racism doesn't disappear just because we denounce it. Racism doesn't disappear just because we change our laws. Racism doesn't disappear just because we compensate for its consequences. Racism doesn't disappear just because we build a memorial to Martin Luther King. Racism, like any other sinful condition that God desires to transform, will disappear when, and only when, it is replaced by its opposite.
>
> What is the opposite of racism? Well, racism involves attitudes of

superiority and inferiority. So, transformation means replacing those attitudes with equality and love and meekness and affirmation. And racism involves social systems characterized by stigmatization and oppression of those we perceive as different. So, instead, a just society must create a community defined by mutual submission and solidarity, protection and opportunity... At this juncture in the history of our nation God is looking for a model home for his transforming kingdom values – a staging ground for the opposite of racism. To prove that such a transformation is possible and to show what it looks like.[14]

To do that, the church will have to commit itself to both truth-telling and a direct engagement that goes far beyond just denouncing racism. Pastor Garber says we have to first be honest about what the role of the church has been and yet insist upon what that role now should be. He confesses, "Historically, despite some noble exceptions, the church has alternatively prostituted its theology to the institution of slavery, looked the other way during decades of discrimination, dragged its feet through the civil rights movement, ignored the problem once the external stimulus was removed, and finally settled for something resembling 'separate but equal' in church life. It's hard to be part of the problem and part of the solution to the problem at the same time. And, yet, God still desires to display his transforming power through the church." For that to happen, Garber says that the church must "turn the bright lights of righteousness on the sin of racism".

In addition to a central commitment to challenge racism in our personal and family life choices and in our communal and congregational lives, we must also make the crucial and often controversial commitments to overcome racism in the public institutions of our economic and political life. Our workplaces are critical arenas for establishing corporate commitments to the equality of opportunity and even affirmative action toward fair and diverse employment environments, and that includes our faith-based institutions as well. In politics, candidates' commitment to and track record for advancing racial justice should be central to their moral compass and to our electoral choices. A whole range of policies are involved here, from ensuring voting rights to pursuing economic fairness, from achieving educational opportunity for minority students to taking affirmative action in employment, from seeking restorative instead of punitive and discriminatory criminal justice and reforming immigration policies to redressing historical grievances and, ultimately, repenting of our racial sins.

Those who say or imply that we have made no racial progress in America are being disingenuous in ways that simply serve their own, often divisive agendas. They also disrespect all those who have fought, sacrificed, suffered, and even died to achieve the racial justice gains we now have. But our progress is very incomplete, especially concerning key issues such as educational and economic opportunity and stark racial disparities in our criminal justice system.

The idea that our racial sins are mostly behind us and that we have no systematic racism anymore is simply a denial of the truth that betrays a lack of serious relationship to communities of colour. From the prisoners who still face the double jeopardy of being black or brown and poor to the well-dressed black professionals who have such high dry-cleaning bills from all the times they have been spread-eagled and searched for drugs over the hoods of their cars when driving through suburban neighbourhoods – most people of colour in the United States can still tell personal stories of racial discrimination.

The question still for white Americans is: Are we listening? The true reality of any society is best understood, biblically speaking, not from the top but from the bottom. Where we are listening also becomes a critical question. The truth is that most Americans of colour are still forced to deal with realities that most white Americans choose to ignore or relegate to a distant past for which they are not responsible.

In facing the vast changes in U.S. population trends, someone must prepare the nation for living in a dramatically different cultural context, one in which diversity is the norm. I believe the faith community can play a critical leadership role in that process. It is a way to serve the nation, to heal its wounds, and to lead – not just by our words, but by our example. Racial reconciliation has been a central vocation of the Christian community from its beginning, and there is no better time than now to recover that mission. That commitment could change America's racial future.

8

LIFE AND DIGNITY
Critical Choices

I meet many interesting people on the road, and they teach me a lot. I learn what they really care about and what gives them hope. Recently, I met a woman who had an amazing story to tell. She began by saying that her daughter was graduating from Harvard and how proud she was. Because I teach part-time at Harvard, I figured she was making that connection. I smiled and told her that she should indeed be proud of her daughter and that I thought Harvard was a great school. But then she added, "I was a low-income woman at the time. And if I hadn't got food stamps and health care, I would have aborted my daughter. And now she's graduating from Harvard. [A tear now ran down her face, and mine.] I want you to tell people that if they want to prevent abortions, they need to support low-income women like me." She looked me straight in the eyes and was very clear in what she had to say to me. She had a message and wanted me to share it. So I do, whenever I get the chance.

Then God said, "Let us make humankind in our image, according to our likeness." ... So God created humankind in his image, in the image of God he created them; male and female he created them. (Genesis 1:26a, 27)

When I look at your heavens, the work of your fingers, the moon and the stars that you have established; what are human beings that you are mindful of them, mortals that you care for them? Yet you have made them a little lower than God, and crowned them with glory and honour. (Psalm 8:3–5)

The spirit of God has made me, and the breath of the Almighty gives me life. (Job 33:4)

Thus says God, the Lord, who created the heavens and stretched them out, who spread out the earth and what comes from it, who gives breath to the

people upon it and spirit to those who walk in it: I am the LORD, I have
called you in righteousness, I have taken you by the hand and kept you...
(Isaiah 42:5–6)

Here is the bottom line: human beings are created in the image of God,
and the breath of God gives us life. All our social, economic, and political
judgments should come from this basic foundation about the sanctity
and sacredness of human life. The God of the Bible is both creative and
relational. God is the creator, not the creation as some new spirituality
suggests, but God is profoundly related to all of creation, including every
plant and animal species. Yet human beings – male and female – are the
"crowning creation" of God's creative work. And God's relationship to
human beings is the most personal and intense of all God's creation.

The biblical images for God's relationship to us are very intimate indeed
– they include both a loving father and a mother hen who gathers and
protects her chicks. But after making us, God needed a rest. We human
beings would cause God both great joy and terrible pain in this most
intimate relationship – an experience we ourselves best know through the
parenting of our own children.

None of the biblical images of creation is more profound, however, than
the assertion that human beings are made "in the image of God". No other
of God's creatures and creations is given that distinction. What is at stake
in how we treat one another is nothing less than how we regard the image
of God in us. Therefore, how we treat others is an indication of how we
truly regard and, indeed, treat God.

The profound claim in Genesis that the image of God is in each and
every human being is a prefiguring of what Jesus would say when he told us
his standard for judgment: "As you have done to the least of these, you have
done to me." Jesus tells us that the way we treat our brothers and sisters
who are hungry, thirsty, naked, strangers to us, sick, or in prison is how
he will know if we love him. In fact, this text from Matthew 25 invites us
actually to see Jesus in the faces and lives of those who are most vulnerable.
Jesus himself is known for how well he treated the most marginal – the
poor, women, those of low reputation, members of despised races, the sick,
the dying, the "unclean", the criminals, and all the outcasts of society.

And this is the nub of the issue. It is always with "the least of these"
– the poorest, humblest, and most vulnerable of human beings – that we
will test our commitment to honouring the image of God in each and every
one of us. The most powerful, the wealthiest, the most beautiful, and
the most benefited of human beings are always the best treated. Indeed,

the best-regarded human beings, by human standards, are often treated like royalty. Human beings love to have "celebrities" and love to lavish benefits on them while enviously and vicariously enjoying the way they get to live. But the least-regarded human beings, by human standards, are subject to the worst treatment and abuse. The impoverished millions, the displaced, the sexually trafficked, the economically exploited, the refugees, the countless victims of natural and human-caused disasters, those who live their lives in the world's "camps" for the destitute, or those who meet untimely deaths because of great pandemic diseases, the prisoners, and, yes, the unborn children – all are easily forgotten by those who live in the world's mainstream culture. In fact, the pets of the best-regarded human beings are often better treated than the least-regarded human beings.

In contrast to our voyeuristic fascination with the "lives of the rich and famous", we don't want to see or even be reminded of the "lives of the poor and wretched". They just make us feel guilty, so we prefer to ignore their existence or deny that they have any claim on us – "it's not my fault!" But this is precisely the radical character of the assertion of *imago Dei*, the "image of God", in every human being. Our solidarity together is bound up with our creation as the enormously valuable and profoundly coequal children of God. The principle is this: how we treat the most vulnerable human beings is the best test of how much we value the image of God. It is a tough test indeed, and one that we fail every day.

The U.S. Conference of Catholic Bishops wrote: "Every human person is created in the image and likeness of God. Therefore, each person's life and dignity must be respected, whether that person is an innocent unborn child in a mother's womb, whether that person worked in the World Trade Center or a market in Baghdad, or even whether that person is a convicted criminal on death row. We believe that every human life is sacred from conception to natural death, that people are more important than things, and that the measure of every institution is whether it protects and respects the life and dignity of the human person. As the recent Vatican statement points out, 'The Church recognizes that while democracy is the best expression of the direct participation of citizens in political choices, it succeeds only to the extent that it is based on a correct understanding of the human person.'"[1]

In a highly significant and controversial 2007 "Evangelical Declaration Against Torture", this same principle of the sanctity of human life is asserted:

> We ground our commitment to human rights, including the rights of suspected terrorists, in the core Christian belief that human life is sacred.

Evangelicals join a vast array of other Christian groups and thinkers – Roman Catholics, mainline Protestants, Eastern Orthodox, and others – in a long history of reflection and activism on behalf of this critical yet threatened moral conviction.

The sanctity of life is the conviction that all human beings, in any and every state of consciousness or self-awareness, of any and every race, color, ethnicity, level of intelligence, religion, language, nationality, gender, character, behavior, physical ability/disability, potential, class, social status, etc., of any and every particular quality of relationship to the viewing subject, are to be perceived as sacred, as persons of equal and immeasurable worth and of inviolable dignity. Therefore they must be treated with the reverence and respect commensurate with this elevated moral status. This begins with a commitment to the preservation of their lives and protection of their basic rights... Rightly understood, the sanctity of life is a moral norm that both summarizes and transcends all other particular norms in Christian moral thought.[2]

The principle of life and dignity must therefore be applied to every place that human life is threatened, including abortion (but not just abortion), euthanasia, human trafficking, torture, genocide, capital punishment, and pandemic diseases, to name just a few. Indeed, most of the issues raised in this book are "life issues", including the great environmental threats, racism, poverty, and war.

The Third Rail of American Politics

Perhaps no issue has been more politicized and manipulated in America than abortion – on both sides. An astute political observer once said to me that abortion is "the third rail of American politics". Symbolic positions of "pro-life" and "pro-choice" have replaced the actual saving of unborn lives. Abortion, as a volatile and highly emotional issue, is used in every election cycle to galvanize highly partisan political bases in each party, then quickly forgotten when the winners begin to govern. Year after year, the number of abortions remains roughly the same, no matter which party is in power. The abortion rate actually declined a little during the Clinton administration, likely because of the improved status of low-income women, which is a consistent causal factor in diminishing the choice for abortion. But the abortion rate went up again in the Bush years, likely with the decreasing status of low-income women and families.

To suggest that the only issue at stake in the abortion debate is protecting the "choice" that women have in their reproductive rights is simply not enough. That is to neglect or even deny the existence of another life, a growing life, at stake in the decision. The long-term impact on women who, at the time of this most difficult decision, ignore the thought of that other life should make us all more sober about how morally and psychologically profound the "choice" really is. Many honest feminists, even if they would still protect the legal right to abortion, have been rethinking their position. Naomi Wolf, a brilliant feminist writer, began to feel the contradiction between how couples she knew on the Upper West Side of Manhattan treated their wanted pregnancies – with everything from Mozart and French lessons in the womb to designer nurseries and outfits for their "babies" – and how they treated their unwanted pregnancies, where the new life was reduced to "foetal tissue", "products of conception", or "material" to be quickly dispensed with. In a groundbreaking 1995 article in *The New Republic,* she wrote:

At its best, feminism defends its moral high ground by being simply faithful to the truth: to women's real-life experiences. But, to its own ethical and political detriment, the pro-choice movement has relinquished the moral frame around the issue of abortion. It has ceded the language of right and wrong to abortion foes. The movement's abandonment of what Americans have always, and rightly, demanded of their movements – an ethical core – and its reliance instead on a political rhetoric in which the foetus means nothing are proving fatal.

The effects of this abandonment can be measured in two ways. First of all, such a position causes us to lose political ground. By refusing to look at abortion within a moral framework, we lose the millions of Americans who want to support abortion as a legal right but still need to condemn it as a moral iniquity. Their ethical allegiances are then addressed by the pro-life movement, which is willing to speak about good and evil.

But we are also in danger of losing something more important than votes; we stand in jeopardy of losing what can only be called our souls. Clinging to a rhetoric about abortion in which there is no life and no death, we entangle our beliefs in a series of self-delusions, fibs, and evasions. And we risk becoming precisely what our critics charge us with being: callous, selfish, and casually destructive men and women who share a cheapened view of human life.[3]

More and more people on the "choice" side are now speaking of the "tragic" character of the decision for abortion. Hillary Clinton surprised many people in 2006 when she said: "I believe we can all recognize that abortion in many ways represents a sad, even tragic choice to many, many women."[4] It is the beginning of wisdom on the complicated questions of abortion to acknowledge that the choice for abortion is always tragic and often desperate.

But that insight should lead pro-life advocates to be incredibly sympathetic and compassionate toward women who are caught in that most tragic or desperate choice. The judgmentalism often found in the pro-life stance is too often unsympathetic to the very difficult position in which many women find themselves because of an unintended pregnancy. Women of all persuasions on this issue will often grimace at the ideological, unequivocal, and even arrogant pronouncements made by some men on the subject. Sometimes it can even feel like the most strident positions on this side are motivated by an urge to punish women for making the bad decisions that lead to unwanted pregnancies. The truth is that women are often still trapped in these most difficult choices because of the extremely unequal power differentials in their relationships to men and are biologically the ones most affected by the decision. It is no wonder that the rights, protections, and "autonomy" of women in the decision-making process are a vital concern for many.

Perhaps this is why the conversations among women with different views regarding the abortion decision are often much more helpful and illuminating than the diatribes that go back and forth between men. Women on both sides of the debate have sought to find common ground in their compassion for women, in seeking serious reductions in unwanted pregnancies, and in support for women with those unwanted pregnancies. A new position is emerging that defies old categories; it is called "feminists for life". Even for some pro-life scholars and activists, merely imposing legal sanctions and perhaps pushing desperate women again into the back alleys of terribly dangerous illegal abortions is not really a "pro-life" position. My religious and moral view is that abortion is wrong, even when the circumstances are wrapped up with great difficulties and inequities. My public-policy view has a strong bias toward protecting unborn life in every possible way, but without criminalizing abortion. How do we actually prevent unwanted pregnancies, protect unborn lives, support low-income women, offer compassionate alternatives to abortion, make adoption much more accessible and affordable, carefully fashion reasonable restrictions, and thus dramatically reduce the shamefully high abortion rate in America?

The Supreme Court's decision in the "partial-birth abortion" case in the summer of 2006 could be the start of a new direction. The decision, written by Justice Anthony Kennedy, "opened up a new phase in abortion jurisprudence – one in which abortion is largely permitted though disdained," according to Chris Gacek, senior fellow at the conservative Family Research Council. Gacek concluded that "Kennedy's view of abortion can be summarized as follows: Abortion is a regrettable but necessary evil that will be protected within well-defined boundaries."[5]

Some new and potentially significant efforts have also emerged in Congress, aimed at practically and substantially reducing the abortion rate in America. The measures proposed could make a real difference in changing the circumstances that make abortions more likely, rather than conforming to the usual political practice – on both the right and the left – of using the issue as a litmus test with nothing ever really happening to prevent more abortions. At the request of the bill's sponsors, I made the following supportive statement: "Sojourners applauds the recent introduction of two pieces of legislation in the House of Representatives aimed at dramatically reducing abortions in this country. We hope these two bills (the Abortion Reduction Act and the Pregnant Women Support Act) will help deepen the national conversation and lead to concrete action."

In the summer of 2007, the "Reducing the Need for Abortions Initiative" passed in the House of Representatives. Sponsored by members Rosa DeLauro (D-CT) and Tim Ryan (D-OH), the initiative contains preventive provisions that increase access to contraceptives and seek to reduce teen pregnancies, along with supportive provisions that assist women by ensuring they will receive help in raising a child. Congresswoman DeLauro pointed out: "We are offering policy solutions that promote life and support parents beyond the birth of their new child. We are affirming the need to prevent unintended pregnancies and to help women with the economic pressures that may lead them to choosing an abortion." Congressman Ryan added, "Whether you are pro-life like me or pro-choice like my friend Congresswoman DeLauro, the common ground we must build on is our serious desire to reduce the rate of abortions."[6]

The Los Angeles Times wrote that this common-ground position can appeal to a broad centre "who don't want to criminalize every abortion – yet are troubled by a culture that accepts 1.3 million terminations a year". The article cites Rev. Joel Hunter: "An evangelical megachurch pastor in Florida, Hunter says he's 'very strongly pro-life'. He's also disillusioned: The right has spent three decades on legislation and litigation, yet one in five pregnancies still ends in abortion. This fall, Hunter plans to urge his congregation of 10,000 to support politicians who work hard to reduce abortions – even if they don't share the goal of protecting every single one of the unborn. 'It's past time to reach out,' Hunter said. 'There's so much more that can be done without compromising our principles.' "[7]

Both pro-life and pro-choice legislators have worked on these new measures, and what could be most important is that political leaders, the media, women's groups, children's groups, medical experts, religious groups, and more might find an approach that can, hopefully, lower the alarming rate of abortion in our nation. That is a goal that leaders all along the political spectrum should be able to support.

It is crucial to create a "culture of life" that advances the dignity and equality of women, protects and defends the vulnerable unborn, and promotes a consistent and healthy sexual ethic, especially for teens and young adults. Promoting male sexual responsibility is essential to finding solutions to the abortion dilemma and should be a primary message that men are speaking to other men. Most Americans support approaches that reduce abortions, carefully incorporate reasonable restrictions, and promote policies that prevent unintended pregnancies while assuring adequate health care for women and reforming adoption and foster care so that they are more viable options for women who elect to carry their children to term. Supporting low-income women economically, with the long-term goal of women achieving economic parity with men, is absolutely key. There is no single solution for reducing abortions in America. Therefore, we need a strategy employing multiple approaches to effectively and dramatically lower our abortion rate.

House leaders and others working to reduce abortion deserve the support of their colleagues, the faith community, and other leaders in Washington for taking an important step toward preventing abortion and supporting pregnant women. For too long, too many people have been satisfied with only a contentious debate over simplified positions of "life" and "choice". A better approach is to foster more energy for and commitment to advancing a dialogue that aims for solutions. A constructive debate should include how best to prevent unwanted pregnancies and support pregnant women who find themselves in an unexpected and often very difficult and lonely situation.

There are, of course, differences of opinion regarding how to meet these goals. But we must advance the dialogue and create a moral framework for developing a reasonable, comprehensive strategy for making abortion truly rare in America and making healthy families the norm. Differences are welcomed in a positive discussion, but sustaining the discussion and moving toward solutions are critical.

The Power of Example

Sadly, it's rare for a church leader or a leader of most of our dominant institutions to demonstrate a spirituality that attracts millions of people around the world, particularly many young people. Thus the scene of huge crowds lining up to pass by the body of Pope John Paul II and attend his 2005 funeral in Rome was remarkable indeed. The enormous attraction to this pope went far beyond the circle of those who agree with all the positions of the Catholic church or even all the decisions of his papacy.

The ecumenical and interfaith attraction to John Paul II reflected his own practice of reaching out to more people in more faith traditions than any pope ever had before. He was the first pope (since Peter) to visit a synagogue and the first to visit a mosque. His March 2000 trip to Israel, with its moving visit to the Western Wall and the Holocaust memorial at Yad Vashem, said more against anti-Semitism than all the words he spoke. It changed the relationship between the church and Judaism.

As I watched the nonstop news coverage after the pope's death, I was struck by how many people – especially political leaders – wanted to claim the pontiff as their own, as someone who affirmed their causes and commitments. At the same time, they ignored the other things this pope said and did that directly challenged their own political decisions.

One of the great attractions of Pope John Paul II's spirituality was his consistency. At the core of Catholic social teaching is the idea of a "consistent ethic of life", an ethic that seeks to protect and defend human life and dignity wherever and whenever they are threatened. It is an ethic that challenges the selective moralities of both the political left and the political right.

Many conservatives pointed to the pope's clear teachings on abortion, euthanasia, and sexual morality, which are often contrary to the positions of liberals. But they seemed to forget his strong and passionate opposition to the war in Iraq, to capital punishment, and to the operations of the global economy that neglect the poor and deny human rights for millions. This pope helped bring down communism, but he was no uncritical capitalist, and he constantly lifted up a vision of economic justice.

Promoting a "culture of life" was the language of John Paul's papacy before it became the rhetoric of President George W. Bush, and its meaning for the pope went far beyond the narrow interpretations of the Republican party. Yes, Pope John Paul II certainly opposed most Democrats' views on abortion, but the White House did not get the photo op it wanted when the president visited the Vatican and the pope shook his finger disapprovingly at Bush over the U.S. war in Iraq.

A clear statement of the pope's beliefs appears in his final "State of the World" address, delivered to members of the diplomatic corps on January 10, 2005.[8] John Paul II identified four of what he called "the great challenges facing humanity today", These four were the causes to which he had dedicated his life.

First, the pope noted the challenge of life, and said: "Life is the first gift which God has given us, it is the first resource which [humankind] can enjoy. The Church is called to proclaim 'the Gospel of Life'. And the State has as its primary task precisely the safeguarding and promotion of human life." He went on to refer specifically to abortion and other issues at the beginning of life, and the social and cultural threats to the family.

Second is the challenge of food. He cited the dramatic statistics of millions of children dying from hunger and called for "a radical commitment to justice and a more attentive and determined display of solidarity. This is the good which can overcome the evil of hunger and unjust poverty."

He also raised the challenge of peace, decrying the wars and other armed conflicts around the world and the numberless innocent victims they claim. "I have spoken out countless times," said the pope, "… and I shall continue to do so, pointing out the paths to peace and urging that they be followed with courage and patience. The arrogance of power must be countered with reason, force with dialogue, pointed weapons with outstretched hands, evil with good."

Two years earlier, just before the Iraq war began, the pope had declared even more strongly, "War is not always inevitable. It is always a defeat for humanity… War is never just another means that one can choose to employ for settling differences between nations." In a tribute to the pope in *Time* magazine, James Carroll, *Boston Globe* columnist and author of *Constantine's Sword*, wrote that "John Paul II made the renunciation of coercive force the political centre of his pontificate."[9]

Finally, the pope raised the challenge of freedom. "Freedom is a great good, because only by freedom can human beings find fulfillment in a manner befitting their nature. Freedom is like light: It enables one to choose responsibly his proper goals and the right means of achieving them." Noting in particular the right to religious freedom, he said, "As long as human beings are alive, it will always be present and pressing."

Many legitimate concerns have been raised about the pope's internal church policies. His conservative opposition to married or women priests, his anticommunism that sometimes led to an overly harsh treatment of liberation theologians who were committed to the poor, his replacement of progressive bishops with far more conservative ones – all are a part of his legacy. But the world will long remember his consistency in defending human life and human dignity. It was deeply attractive, spiritually and morally, to people who long for public integrity, particularly to those of a new generation. And the life of John Paul II was a lesson in its truth and power for all of us.

Time for the New Abolitionists

In a 2007 book called *Not for Sale: The Return of the Global Slave Trade – and How We Can Fight It,* David Batstone turns a spotlight on one of the greatest moral scandals of our time. Many people believe that slavery ended with the Civil War, but a look at reality in the twenty-first century quickly reveals otherwise.

Batstone begins his book with this shocking statement: "Twenty-seven million slaves exist in our world today. Girls and boys, women and men of all ages are forced to toil in the rug looms of Nepal, sell their bodies in the brothels of Rome, break rocks in the quarries of Pakistan, and fight wars in the jungles of Africa. Go behind the façade in any major town or city in the world today and you are likely to find a thriving commerce in human beings."[10]

In poorer countries of the world, poverty and inequality create the conditions that lead to slavery. From destitute parents selling their children, to young rural women looking for work in the cities, to people being trapped in debt with no way out, the pool of potential slaves continues to grow. The International Labor Organization estimates that the work performed by trafficked individuals generates $32 billion a year, rivalling drug trafficking and the illegal arms trade for the top criminal activity on the planet, according to Batstone's research.

When one recalls the history of William Wilberforce and the abolitionist movement that rose up in eighteenth-century England to defeat the slave trade, vivid parallels come to mind. Indeed, a new abolitionist movement is rising up in our own day. Organizations such as the International Justice Mission, the Hagar Project, the Polaris Project, Shared Hope International, the Coalition to Abolish Slavery and Trafficking, and many others have been engaging in the same kind of activities that characterized the earlier antislavery movement – rescuing women and children from sexual slavery, helping those rescued to reestablish their lives through microeconomic development, educating a public that is largely unaware of the problem, challenging local and national political leaders in the offending countries who are passively and even actively complicit in the problem, and advocating for the political, legal, and structural changes that could end the horrible practices of modern sexual and economic slavery.

I met one of these emerging leaders and social entrepreneurs, a Swiss businessman and Christian named Pierre Tami, who went to Cambodia and began rescuing women and children caught up in sex trafficking. In twelve years, The Hagar Project, the Christian development organization he founded, has touched the lives of 100,000 women, many of whom have been freed from sexual slavery and have found new ways to live and work through a myriad of successful small businesses started by Hagar.

These new abolitionists have been converted on the issue of modern slavery, and they are now calling for our conversion. We can already see the beginnings of a new abolitionist movement: heroic individuals who are rescuing slaves and creating a modern-day underground railroad to carry them to freedom, and organizations that provide social services and legal advocacy for victims of human trafficking. *Not for Sale* tells the story of this new abolitionist movement. Batstone's final chapter, "Ending the Slave Trade in our Time", begins: "I believe in the power of individuals to change the world. Social movements take root and blossom when enough individuals take personal action." The chapter then offers creative ideas for becoming an abolitionist, from the personal level of assisting people liberated from slavery, to joining an antislavery organization (the book contains a listing of the major abolitionist organizations), to working to shape government policies. A new campaign is being created – the Not for Sale Campaign.

For God's Sake, Save Darfur

Beyond all the important things that we are doing, there is one thing that we must do now: stop the genocide in Darfur. For some time, the world has known the facts of Darfur: up to four hundred and fifty thousand people dead and nearly three million displaced; black citizens (mostly Muslims) of the western region of Sudan are being daily attacked, raped, and massacred by marauding militias armed and supported by the country's Arab-dominated government in Khartoum. But knowing the facts hasn't changed them on the ground. More die each week of murder, hunger, and disease, and the death toll could ultimately reach millions if the pillage of Darfur is not stopped.

In Washington, D.C., and in other cities around the country, tens of thousands of people have rallied to say "enough" to the horrible events that have been unfolding since 2003. This human crime and tragedy is bringing people together from across all our boundaries. Jewish families with their children stood together with evangelical Christians, African American church people with leaders from the Religious Right, Republicans with Democrats, Hollywood actors with conservative activists, and many students (for whom Darfur is becoming a rallying cry) with human rights advocates who see this as the paramount challenge of the moment. Speakers invoked the Holocaust, Cambodia, and Rwanda, repeatedly reminding us that we have often said "never again" only to let the same thing happen again and again.

Although the situation is complex, the crisis is rooted in long-standing grievances against African farmers who point to government neglect and ongoing conflict with primarily Arab herdsmen over land, water, and safety. That is why rebel groups are demanding formal representation in the Sudanese government to redress these grievances. The Sudanese government already has the land; it just wants to "cleanse" the land of its people. President Bush and Congress have named the destruction in Darfur as genocide, and the administration has tried to pressure the Sudanese government. But the world has been too slow, and all the efforts thus far have failed to stop the daily death and atrocities. The Sudanese government has continued to resist international pressure.

Nothing less than a strong multinational peacekeeping force is needed now to stop the raping and killing by the Janjaweed militias; to assure the delivery of critical food, medical, and humanitarian aid; and to provide the security necessary to make the critically needed political solution possible. In August 2006, the U.N. Security Council passed resolution 1706, authorizing an expanded multinational peacekeeping force of up to 17,000 military and 3,300 civilian police personnel to deploy to Darfur to relieve the understaffed, underfunded, and exhausted African Union peacekeeping force. This force of troops from several African countries, funded by U.N. member nations, including the United States, has been attempting to protect civilians in Darfur but has been largely unsuccessful. The Sudanese government has refused the additional peacekeepers, dismissing the U.N. resolution as an excuse for Western intervention. In part to answer that objection, the Arab League has offered to send a force of Arab and Muslim peacekeeping troops to the region, but yet again Khartoum has refused.

The Bush administration has been clear in its language about Darfur. In a speech to the U.N. General Assembly, President Bush said, "To the people of Darfur: You have suffered unspeakable violence, and my nation has called these atrocities what they are – genocide... The Security

Council has approved a resolution that would transform the African Union force into a blue-helmeted force that is larger and more robust... If the Sudanese government does not approve this peacekeeping force quickly, the United Nations must act. Your lives and the credibility of the United Nations is at stake."[11] On a trip to the Middle East, Secretary of State Rice said, "The international community does have a responsibility to protect the most vulnerable. What is going on in Darfur now cannot be tolerated."[12] Those are strong words, but they need to be followed by strong actions.

The U.N.-authorized multinational peacekeeping force has yet to be implemented because of the Khartoum regime's intransigence and the reluctance of other nations to offer troops against the opposition of a sovereign government. Tough economic sanctions are necessary to force the Sudanese government to comply with U.N. demands. On this issue, the U.S. government has called for many of the right things but has not applied the necessary pressure to accomplish them. Only a massive outpouring of public opinion could change that and force the United States to do whatever it takes to end the carnage in Darfur. As long as that does not happen, many more people will be savagely attacked and cruelly displaced.

In his last official news conference, outgoing U.N. secretary-general Kofi Annan said that more could be done in Darfur. "There are measures short of force that could be used," Annan said, including "political pressure, economic sanctions, isolation, and of course in the last resort, there is the use of force."[13] The Bush administration must quickly move from words to real actions. Maximum political and diplomatic pressure should be used at all possible points to force Sudan to accept additional peacekeepers. Key Security Council members, especially Russia and China, are obstructing U.N. action; the United States needs to increase its efforts to gain their cooperation. And additional actions should be taken against Sudan, including targeting sanctions against top government officials while enforcing existing sanctions.

After Bono spoke to the National Prayer Breakfast in 2006, he met with a handful of religious reporters. When the rock star and Africa advocate was asked why he was so interested in engaging religious people in his cause, he replied, "You have a bigger crowd than I do." He was right; we have the biggest crowd and one with political clout in Washington. It may now take the big crowd of the religious community to stop the genocide in Darfur. If the religious community would speak and act with one voice on Darfur, despite our many differences on so many other issues, we might persuade our government to do the right thing and make sure the right thing works.

So, when Americans opened their newspapers on October 18, 2006, many of them saw full-page ads by an unprecedented collection of twenty-four evangelical Christian leaders who were launching Evangelicals for Darfur. The ads, which ran in USA Today, The New York Times, The Washington Post, and a host of other national and regional newspapers, called on President Bush to use every resource and diplomatic tool available to him to get a U.N. peacekeeping force on the ground in Darfur. Articles about the campaign appeared in 167 publications. We urged President Bush to use his "personal leadership in supporting the deployment of a strong U.N.·peacekeeping force and multilateral economic sanctions". That campaign generated nearly six million impressions and the coverage of it, nearly eleven million. These ads were only the beginning of what we hoped could be a tipping point in the world's response to this horrible crisis. Evangelical Christian leaders had discovered a profound unity on the crisis in Darfur. Believing this is a time and an issue that transcends other political differences, a number of us began talking about how we could respond to this enormous moral challenge. Those conversations have led us to create Evangelicals for Darfur, an effort that brings together the voices of evangelical Christians to call for an end to the incredible suffering in Darfur.

We do not all agree on other issues, but we are united in the conviction that our faith compels us to do everything we possibly can to bring an end to the horror in Darfur. In crucial matters of life and death, there is no left or right, there is only right and wrong. When I spoke to Richard Land – a key Southern Baptist leader – about this effort, he said, "Jim, if people see evangelical leaders like you and me speaking together on this issue, it could light a fire in America and give the president the power to do what he would really like to do." We are acting on our faith, calling on President Bush to act on his faith and lead the effort to put a substantial peacekeeping force on the ground in Darfur – nothing else will save the people.

We have been able to speak with one voice for millions of evangelical Christians in our nation. Genocide is being committed against God's children and our response to that is a matter of faith, not politics. We have put aside other differences to heed God's call to act. This is not about Republicans or Democrats, conservatives or liberals, Christians or Muslims – this is about compassion and the commands of God.

I am deeply encouraged by the broad spectrum of Christians and other people of faith and good will that are speaking out on Darfur, and I truly believe this is one of those moments in our lives when what God requires of us couldn't be clearer. Like the Good Samaritan, we simply cannot pass by our suffering brothers and sisters on the side of the road. We called the effort Evangelicals for Darfur not to exclude any other denominations or faith groups, but to recognize the special impact that evangelical Christians – from across the political spectrum – can have on this crisis.

God commands us to "Rescue those being led away to death; hold back those staggering toward slaughter. If you say, 'But we knew nothing about this,' does not he who weighs the heart perceive it?" (Proverbs 24:11–12, NIV). We know about the slaughter of innocent people in Darfur, the world knows, and God knows. The people of Darfur have no other recourse. We must plead for their rescue. Our faith and our humanity demand it.

Who Would Jesus Torture?

Tragically, torture has become a political issue in the United States because of the ways the Bush administration has chosen to fight the "war on terror". Many people are shocked that we are even having this debate in America.

Even prominent Republicans challenged the administration's approach. Colin Powell, the first-term secretary of state, wrote to Senator John McCain, "The world is beginning to doubt the moral basis of our fight against terrorism." McCain and a few other courageous Republican senators opposed the proposal that the United States no longer abide by the Geneva Convention's prohibition against "outrages upon personal dignity", including "humiliating and degrading treatment" – a proposal that would allow Bush's secret CIA interrogators a free hand to ignore international law in dealing with terror suspects. The GOP senators argued that America should operate on higher ground, even if the terrorists don't, and worried that the administration's actions might put American servicemen and -women in grave jeopardy.

It was absolutely stunning that the president of the United States was advocating, as an operational American policy, what most of the world would regard as "torture". What happened at Abu Ghraib, at the Guantanamo prison camp, and at secret CIA interrogation chambers around the world put a deep moral stain on America. The Bush administration's war in Iraq and its conduct of its "war on terror" generated massive anti-American sentiment around the world – to the absolute glee of terrorists eager to recruit a new generation of angry murderers.

The statement on torture endorsed by the National Association of Evangelicals therefore became a political issue, and gave opponents of the use of torture a major boost. The "Evangelical Declaration Against Torture: Human Rights in an Age of Terror" begins:

From a Christian perspective, every human life is sacred. As evangelical Christians, recognition of this transcendent moral dignity is non-negotiable in every area of life, including our assessment of public policies. This commitment has been tested in the war on terror, as a public debate has occurred over the moral legitimacy of torture and of cruel, inhuman, and degrading treatment of detainees held by our nation in the current conflict. We write this declaration to affirm our support for detainee human rights and our opposition to any resort to torture.[14]

The evangelical statement includes sections on the scriptural grounding of and the ethical implications of human rights, and on international law and treaties regarding human rights. Drafted by a group of evangelical ethicists, theologians, and pastors, the statement is carefully researched and coherently argued. Its conclusion consists of four fundamental declarations: (1) We renounce the use of torture and cruel, inhuman, and degrading treatment by any branch of our government (or any other government) – even in the current circumstance of a war between the United States and various radical terrorist groups. (2) We call for the extension of basic human rights and procedural protections to all persons held in United States custody now or in the future, wherever and by whomever they are held. (3) We call for every agency of the United States government to join with the United States military and to state publicly its commitment to the terms of the Geneva Conventions related to the treatment of prisoners, especially Common Article 3. (4) We call for the legislative or judicial reversal of those executive and legislative provisions that violate the moral and legal standards articulated in this declaration.

A new Web site has been launched by Evangelicals for Human Rights. It seeks to "reaffirm the centrality of human rights as an unshakable biblical obligation fundamental to an evangelical Christian social and moral vision". The site provides resources for churches and organizations, current legislation on torture, and news developments.

"Human Life Is a Gift from God"

During Holy Week 2005, the U.S. Catholic bishops launched a new "Catholic Campaign to End the Use of the Death Penalty". Cardinal Theodore McCarrick opened a press conference by noting, "This holy week is the time Catholics and all Christians are reminded of how Christ died – as a criminal brutally executed." The church opposed the death penalty twenty-five years ago, but this new campaign, he said, "brings greater urgency and unity, increased energy and advocacy, and a renewed call to our people and to our leaders to end the use of the death penalty in our nation".[15]

I am against the death penalty in principle. We simply should not kill to show we are against killing. It's also possible to make a fatal mistake, as DNA testing has demonstrated. The death penalty is biased against the poor, who cannot afford adequate legal representation, and is used disproportionately along racial lines. Few white-collar killers sit on death row and fewer still are ever executed. Moreover, there is no evidence that the death penalty deters murder; it just satisfies the urge for revenge.

More deeply, as Cardinal McCarrick explained, "For us, ending the use of the death penalty is not simply about politics, it is about our faith. We believe human life is a gift from God that is not ours to take away... We cannot teach that killing is wrong by killing. We cannot defend life by taking life."

From 1996 through September 2007, 740 people have been executed in the United States.[16] At the end of 2006, 3,350 people were on death row. And although the Supreme Court has continued to narrow the scope of who is executed – prohibiting the execution of mentally retarded people and those who were juveniles when they committed their crime – executions continue.

The results of a poll of Catholics conducted by Zogby International were released in 2006.[17] John Zogby reported that "support for the use of the death penalty among American Catholics has plunged in the past few years". The poll showed that 48.5 per cent of Catholics supported the death penalty and 48.4 per cent opposed it. As recently as October 2003, an ABC/Washington Post poll had shown 62 per cent of Catholics in support and 34 per cent opposed. Zogby noted, "Of particular interest is the finding... that frequent attendees of Mass are less likely to support the death penalty. Traditionally, this group has been seen as among the most politically conservative cohort." And, unlike the general population, "the most popular reasons why Catholics oppose the death penalty are related to 'Thou shalt not kill' and 'respect for life'. They lead over such important concerns as poor legal representation among the condemned, the conviction and sentencing of some innocent people, and racially discriminatory practices on capital murder cases."

Also present at the news conference launching the Catholic Campaign were Bud Welch, whose daughter Julie was killed in the Oklahoma City bombing, and Kurt Bloodsworth, who spent nearly nine years in prison, including on death row, before being exonerated of a murder conviction through DNA testing. Welch eloquently concluded, "My conviction is simple: More violence is not what Julie would have wanted. More violence will not bring Julie back. More violence only makes our society more violent."[18]

The new Catholic Campaign will continue education within the church. A new Web site, www.ccedp.org, contains information on church teaching, facts about the death penalty, educational resources, and suggestions for action. The church also will act by continuing its advocacy in Congress and the courts.

I welcomed this new campaign, and I was pleased that the bishops have taken this strong and hopeful initiative. It is a new and important step in affirming the consistent ethic of life so strongly emphasized in Catholic social teaching. I affirm Cardinal McCarrick's words: "I've come to believe the death penalty hurts all of us, not just the one being executed. It diminishes and contradicts our respect for all human life and dignity... I hope I will see the day when the nation I love no longer relies on violence to confront violence. I pray I will see the day when we have given up the illusion that we can teach that killing is wrong by killing people."

More Revenge Than Justice

Ironically, the public execution of Saddam Hussein occasioned a worldwide conversation about capital punishment. Because the Iraqi dictator represented the worst kind of mass murderer, his execution provided a clear case for a fresh discussion of the moral and political consequences of the death penalty.

In the alarming video of the dictator's execution that travelled around the world, we looked into the darkness of the human soul in a society seemingly possessed by killing. Saddam's crimes were certainly deserving of punishment, but his execution turned into an abusive and offensive sectarian killing much like what is happening every day in an Iraq overcome by tribal violence. Even in the punishment of Iraq's greatest criminal, justice was put aside in favour of revenge.

The extreme example of Saddam's execution reveals more generally the problem with capital punishment. Justice does require punishment, but what message does state killing to punish killing finally send? Isn't capital punishment always more about revenge than justice? Wouldn't it be a more fitting punishment for the Timothy McVeighs and the Saddam Husseins of this world to be stripped of their wealth and power, forgotten in the public memory, and subjected to menial and meaningless manual labour, in obscurity, for the rest of their lives?

Religious leaders condemned the execution of Saddam. The Vatican repeated its commitment to a consistent ethic of life. Federico Lombardi, S.J., director of the Holy See Press Office, issued a statement titled "Tragic News", saying, "The execution of a capital sentence is always tragic news, a cause of sadness, even when the person is guilty of terrible crimes. The position of the Catholic Church against the death penalty has often been reiterated. The killing of the guilty is not the way to rebuild justice and reconcile society, rather there is a risk of nourishing the spirit of revenge and inciting fresh violence."[19]

In an interview on BBC the day before the execution, Archbishop of Canterbury Rowan Williams was asked whether he thought Hussein should be executed. He replied, "I'm not a believer in the death penalty as a general principle... I think that Saddam Hussein is manifestly someone who has committed grave crimes against his own people and grave breaches of international law. I think he deserves punishment, and sharp and unequivocal punishment; I don't think that he should be at liberty, but I would say of him what I have to say about anyone who's committed even the most appalling crimes in this country; that I believe the death penalty effectively says 'there is no room for change or repentance'."[20]

Saddam Hussein, like other murderers before him, was a violent and remorseless man. But by taking his life, we sink to his level. If we truly believe that all human life is created in God's image, then no matter how distorted that life may become, we do not have the right to take it. We simply should not kill to show we are against killing. That is indeed to prefer revenge over justice.

Catholic sister and death-penalty opponent Helen Prejean called Saddam's execution the "the greatest indignity of all". She said: "When Saddam Hussein and his aides Awad Hamed al-Bandar and Barzan Ibrahim were hanged, many were upset that the killings were not done with 'dignity'. They thought it unseemly and improper that some present at the execution hurled insults and taunted Hussein, or that his half-brother Ibrahim was decapitated in the process. That's like talking about icing without talking about the cake. Here's the cake: rendering Hussein or any human being defenceless and killing him. Imposing a violent death on a person is the greatest indignity of all; it makes name-calling or taunts pale in significance."

Sister Prejean quoted Pope John Paul II, who said during his 1999 visit to St. Louis: "A sign of hope is the increasing recognition that the dignity of human life must never be taken away, even in the case of someone who has done great evil." The pope renewed his call for the abolition of the death penalty, which, he said, "is both cruel and unnecessary".[21]

The response to Hussein's execution from Vatican officials was unequivocal in condemnation. "There is no doubt," said Cardinal Renato Martino, president of the Pontifical Council for Justice and Peace, "that Saddam was a ruthless dictator responsible for hundreds of deaths. But one does not compensate for one crime with another crime. The church proclaims that human life is to be protected from conception to natural death. The death penalty is not a natural death." Cardinal Martino said it was not morally licit for anyone, "not even the state," to kill another person.[22]

The Commitment

My favourite Catholic cardinal in recent years was Cardinal Joseph Bernardin from Chicago, who passed away in 1996. Perhaps more than anyone else, he pioneered the idea of "a consistent ethic of life", and it was he who coined the phrase "a seamless garment" to describe what the Christian response ought to be to every threat upon the life and dignity of others. Consistency is the commitment that should be asked of us in a cultural and political climate that is so often inconsistent and contradictory when it comes to the value of human life. Clearly, both the left and the right are quite selective when it comes to which lives and which issues they regard as most important. Nothing would clarify, and indeed elevate, politics as much as moral consistency. So consistency must become the moral touchstone for any serious ethic that would protect and safeguard human life and dignity.

Our scriptures tell us that life is sacred. Human life began with the breath of God and we are wonderfully created in God's image. The *imago Dei* is indeed the common ground of our shared humanity. Each and every one of us is to be respected, simply because of that common humanity as creations in God's image. That ethic begins on the personal level in the way we make our choices and in what we teach our children. All life and all lives must be important and valuable to us, and our children should learn that early and at home.

The "political correctness" of left and right should not shape the values and priorities of our congregations. Faith communities could lead by example in their local communities as to who and what is important. Signs in front of synagogues and churches to SAVE SOVIET JEWRY (in the 1970s and 1980s) and CALL TO CONSCIENCE: SAVE DARFUR (today) serve to remind local communities of the many lives so easily forgotten and made expendable. Religious congregations should be one place where moral consistency is given a higher value than political ideology and expediency.

The nation is hungry for the ethics of moral consistency to be applied to its political agenda. As we have said, actually saving unborn lives by dramatically reducing the nation's abortion rate with practical and compassionate policies and practices could help heal our fractious divides over abortion and locate our common ground. If I were an unborn child and wanted the support of the far right, it would be better for me to stay unborn as long as possible, because once I was born, I would be off its radar screen – no child care, no health care, nothing. Nor should I expect support from the far left, which speaks so much about human rights, because I won't have any until after my birth.

I have been encouraged by the statements of those from the conservative side of the debate who are now articulating a more consistent message. Rev. Joel Hunter, formerly the president-elect of the Christian Coalition and author of A New Kind of Conservative, has said, "My position is, unless we are caring as much for the vulnerable outside the womb as inside the womb, we're not carrying out the full message of Jesus."[23] Similarly, some on the left, such as Naomi Wolf, are also calling for a deeper moral ethic and consistency on the issues of life.

Correcting the injustices of the death penalty and setting a better example of how to punish those who commit the ultimate crime of taking another life could make us a more humane country. Applying our concern for the sanctity of human life to genocide in Darfur and the sexual trafficking of women and children around the world is also a movement toward consistency. The call is to consistency, and a more consistent political ethic would help us recover our moral consistency and integrity. Such consistency is crucial because there is nothing more basic than our commitment to life and dignity as the foundation of all other commitments.

Indeed, the consistent ethic of life could be a foundation for an expansive social and political ethic – one that has the capacity to challenge both the right and the left. All life is sacred, and all threats to human life and dignity are important and worthy of our attention. But such an ethic challenges politics to a test that it often fails – the test of consistency. In this matter, as in others, the faith community could lead the way.

9

FAMILY AND COMMUNITY
The False Choice

One night before dinner, my three-year-old son Jack asked to pray. So we all bowed our heads and waited for him to begin. When there was only silence, I looked up and saw him glancing around the table, and then he said, "We can't pray yet, there aren't enough people here." Joy and I now call it Jack's "prayer quorum," which reflects not only how often we have other people with us at the dinner table but also the connections our boys are making between family and community.

I believe Jack's connection is the one we all need to make to end the ideological war between "family" and "community." That's just the politics of left and right, and it's hurting our kids. Both sides in the political debate have it half right: the centrality of family on the conservative side and the importance of community on the liberal side. It's time to put the two together, where they belong, and end our false choices – for the sake of the kids who need their loving parents *and* the strong and supportive arms of a caring community.

> Honour your father and your mother, so that your days may be long in the land that the LORD your God is giving you. (Exodus 20:12)

> Then little children were being brought to him in order that he might lay his hands on them and pray. The disciples spoke sternly to those who brought them; but Jesus said, "Let the little children come to me, and do not stop them; for it is to such as these that the kingdom of heaven belongs." And he laid his hands on them and went on his way. (Matthew 19:13–15)

> Then his mother and his brothers came; and standing outside, they sent to him and called him. A crowd was sitting around him; and they said to him, "Your mother and your brothers and sisters are outside, asking for you." And he replied, "Who are my mother and my brothers?" And looking at those who sat around him, he said, "Here are my mother and my brothers! Whoever does the will of God is my brother and sister and mother." (Mark 3:31–35)

All who believed were together and had all things in common; they would sell their possessions and goods and distribute the proceeds to all, as any had need. Day by day, as they spent much time together in the temple, they broke bread at home and ate their food with glad and generous hearts, praising God and having the goodwill of all the people. And day by day the Lord added to their number those who were being saved. (Acts 2:44–47)

So then you are no longer strangers and aliens, but you are citizens with the saints and also members of the household of God, built upon the foundation of the apostles and prophets, with Christ Jesus himself as the cornerstone. (Ephesians 2:19–20)

These diverse biblical texts paint a rich texture of both family and community in the scriptures and in the life of the people of God. Mothers and fathers are absolutely central in the rearing of children. All the social science data (as well as our commonsense experience) shows that. Parents are indeed to be honoured and their "instruction" and "teaching" listened to (Proverbs 1:8). Most centrally, parents are to "Train children in the right way" (Proverbs 22:6). For people of faith, parenting is a central family issue, and the biblical focus on the well-being of children is abundantly clear. Jesus says, "Let the little children come to me, and do not stop them; for it is to such as these that the kingdom of heaven belongs." He even tells us that unless we all "become like children, you will never enter the kingdom of heaven" (Matthew 18:3). Children matter a lot to God – and not just our own children, but all of them. After all, they are all God's children. I often say the "God question" is "How are the children doing?" because children are clearly so important to God.

But Jesus also challenges the absoluteness of the natural family and its demands upon his disciples by asking "Who are my mother and my brothers?" Looking around at his disciples, he suggests to them that "Whoever does the will of God is my brother and sister and mother." The community of faith, along with the natural family, has great significance for believers. In the book of Acts, the communal reality of brothers and sisters in Christ is very strong indeed, much more so than in the life of the average congregation today.

What would a more biblical concept of family look like? If we examine the Old Testament, the families described are much more along the lines of what we would call the extended family. There would traditionally be a main household with children and various relatives, and adult children with their families would often live close by. Some displaced persons might also be taken in and become part of the extended family. This provided a much broader, cross-generational conception of family than does our contemporary nuclear family. The Bible speaks of extended families of upward of one hundred members. We are explicitly told that Abraham's extended family included sixty-six people. This does not mean that we can simply import these details into the contemporary period. But reflecting on these models helps us to see the inadequacy, compared to biblical concepts, of the individualism that is part and parcel of the contemporary "family values" debate. To return to more biblical living, we must begin again to think in much broader communal terms than we usually do in our culture. Our discussion needs to extend well beyond the boundaries of the typical family-values debate if we are to recapture a more Christian way of family and community life.

I believe that both Democrat Hillary Clinton and Republican Rick Santorum are right in their respective and (supposedly) competing books on this topic – Clinton's *It Takes a Village* and Santorum's *It Takes a Family*. It takes both a village and a family to raise children well, and there is no reason to make the false choice between the two. Don't just "focus on families"; also "focus on communities".

In a world in which globalization is now the accepted reality, justification, and ethic, the relationships that are closest to us in families and communities must become increasingly important. The vital integrity of marriage, the moral formation of parenting, and the interdependence of the people and families with whom we share common geographic space in the places we call neighbourhood and home may now be the most important things of all. We should, in fact, measure our personal and public choices by their impact on our families and our communities.

Parenting is a Countercultural Activity

The most important job in the world is still raising children, and that extends to all our children. Parenting in America has become a counter-cultural activity – both liberals and conservatives recognize this. As a parent one often feels at war with the popular culture these days. Since becoming a parent I have become much more sensitized to the continual assault on our children – especially from television, advertising, music, and movies in which materialism, hedonism, selfishness, aggressiveness, sexual imagery and messages, and violence are not only accepted but glorified. We instinctively want to protect our children from all the garbage – and that is an impulse that transcends left and right.

In a *Sojourners* article called "Taking Back Our Kids", Danny and

Polly Duncan Collum write: "'I never thought it would be this hard,' Polly said one night, standing by the kitchen counter on the verge of tears. 'I thought when I had children, I would have this great thing in common with everyone else. When my first child was born, I went out and bought a Disney video, because I thought that's what you do. Now I feel like I spend my whole life protecting my children from the culture. It shouldn't be this hard.'"[1]

"It shouldn't be this hard." That cry can be heard from parents outraged by an invasive, hyper-sexualized, greed-filled popular culture and from those struggling to find time for their children when both parents work full-time jobs. It can be heard from parents who have seen their children carried away to the Never Land of a materialistic and hedonistic youth culture created by and for advertisers.

With massive societal changes over the past several decades, parents are less and less able to focus their energy, time, and resources on raising their children. The Duncan Collums note that today 61 per cent of the mothers of children under age three are in the paid workforce. They haven't been replaced at home by a "new, sensitive army of at-home fathers", but rather by underpaid and often minimally trained daycare workers.

The combination of stagnating wages and the "plague of consumerism" that produces endless needs results in the necessity of more time for both parents in the workforce and less time with the kids at home. "These two facts created a double economic bind," the Duncan Collums write. In the past, "Wages were lower, but the economy needed American families to buy more stuff."

The loss of stay-at-home parents has had consequences. "Too little thought was given to the fate of children in all those two-income families," write the Duncan Collums. "But twenty years later the results began to appear. The traditional nuclear family of the 1950s was oppressive of women, but there were no school shootings, no epidemics of Attention Deficit Disorder and Type 2 diabetes. Teen suicide rates were half what they are today, and educational achievement was higher. These indicators of the declining well-being of children can be traced in part to the disappearance of traditional family life."

The feminist idea that women should have the right to participate in public life in any way they choose is correct, but many women are having second thoughts about the consequences of their choices. "Many American parents know in their guts that the way we are raising children does not make sense," the Duncan Collums write. "Of the mothers currently in the work force, only 16 per cent say they would choose to work full time if they felt they had the choice. If we were truly interested in the empowerment of women and the welfare of children, we would give the other 84 per cent that choice."

The most important character traits are best learned from parents. In good families, children receive structure, discipline, and emotional support. And religious families, of course, raise up their children in the context of their religious faith. Passing along such values is best accomplished when one parent, or both, have considerable time available to spend with their children. Nowadays, because so many jobs offer low pay and few or no benefits, it is difficult for even working families to afford to keep a parent at home. With both parents forced to be away from home so much of the time, it becomes a losing battle for those seeking to make the family – and not the market culture of individualism and consumerism – the primary shaper of children's values.

Society loses something, too, when so much of the primary care and nurture of children no longer comes from the family. Good families, as the Duncan Collums put it, "teach the core social values of solidarity, interdependence, and responsibility as the formational stuff of everyday life". When parents are forced to spend much of their time trying to bring in enough income to survive rather than in nurturing their children, "these values can get lost".

Conservative columnist George Will made a surprising statement about the economic ideology that runs our society, arguing that it has eroded our family and cultural stability. "Capitalism undermines traditional social structures and values," Will writes. "It is a relentless engine of change, a revolutionary inflamer of appetites, an enlarger of expectations, a diminisher of patience. It has taken its toll on those values and those institutions that conservatives hold most dear: family farms, local government, traditional craftsmanship, historic homes and buildings."

The Village

We want to teach our children that personal responsibility is very important because our individual decisions so clearly affect others and, of course, that social responsibility is also crucial because our destiny is so wrapped up with that of others. Trappist monk Thomas Merton once said, "In the end, it is the reality of personal relationships that saves everything." This relational ethic, as applied to our God, our children, our families, and our neighbours – just blocks away, or across the globe – may be the political value that counts the most.

I am a Little League baseball coach. We've had the same group of boys together since they were five-year-olds in T-ball. Over the three years together, the kids and their parents have become a real community. Because many of the boys go to the same school and play soccer and other sports together as well, my wife, Joy, often refers to this important network of relationships as "the village". We really do care about one another's children, and through constant playdates, playground afternoons, school activities, and, of course, baseball, we help in the raising of one another's kids.

I've been reading a book by Baltimore Orioles Hall of Famer Cal Ripken called *The Ripken Way: Parenting Young Athletes*. Ripken reports that most American kids are now leaving sports activities by the age of thirteen. The reason: pressure and stress – they don't find the sports fun anymore. The pressure to win, to be the best compared to others, can come from coaches, parents, themselves, and certainly the competitive culture in which we all live. But too much stress and pressure make sports no longer fun, and the kids quit. So all the advantages of sports – fitness, health, learning physical and mental skills, learning teamwork, discipline, and sportsmanship – are lost. Ripken also points out that he doesn't remember the win-loss records of his youth sports teams. What he remembers is when it was really fun, when he loved his teammates, when the coaches were nice (or not), and when they learned a lot. Ripken says the most important thing in youth sports is whether the kids have fun and really enjoy themselves.

I want the kids I coach to do their best; I want them to love the game; I want them to support each other and be good teammates. And I want them to win, but not by sacrificing other important values. They're just seven-, eight-, and nine-year-olds! Even our best players make mistakes, and the weakest players can often delightfully surprise us. So we will cheer for our teammates and for the other team when they make good plays, and we will enjoy winning when we do it right and lose gracefully and with good sportsmanship when we are outplayed. Parents can help instill those values in the players, and those values can last a lifetime, in and out of sports.

I told the parents that because there were other really good teams in the league, we were unlikely to win every game – and that it might be a good thing for the kids' character development if we did not win every game. It was our job as coaches and parents to help our kids learn life lessons, which is really what Little League is about.

Some of my coaching calls to our kids from the sidelines, or when I'm running the pitching machine that hurls the balls to them at home plate, could also be valuable lessons for life (I am told by the parents), like

"Pretend the ball is coming to you!" or "Look alive," or "Think about what you're going to do," or "Take a breath and relax," or "Wait for one you like," or "Let's see a smile up there."

My Little League experience has taught me much about the "village" and the importance of the "community". Yet my two young boys are absolutely clear who their core family is, who their mom and dad and brother are. The quality of our time together is central to Joy and me, and everything else takes second place to that. Every night when Luke and Jack say their prayers, they always begin the "God bless" part with "God bless Mom, Dad, and my brother, Luke (or Jack)." And then all their many cousins get their blessings, then all their friends, then "everybody that we love," and usually ending with "everybody and everything in the whole wide world" – although the other night Luke did deviate a bit after "God bless Mom and Dad and Jack... and Babe Ruth, Derek Jeter, A-Rod, Pudge Rodriquez, and Lou Gehrig." Baseball has indeed become central to our family's spirituality!

On a recent spring vacation, we had an adventure that is sure to become a family legend for us. One day Luke, Jack, and Joy were headed down to the ocean, and I would soon follow. But just as they were passing the swimming pool, a big gust of wind blew four-year-old Jack (who weighs only forty pounds) right into the deep end – into water way over his head. Joy had her back to the boys because she was putting towels and bags on some pool chairs. She heard the splash and quickly turned to see no Jack. In a flash, before any of the adults who saw Jack fall in could get off their poolside lounges, big brother Luke had plunged in. Being a strong swimmer, our eight-year-old pulled our four-year-old out of the deep water and handed him to his mother, who had rushed to the side of the pool. Everybody was very impressed, Luke was beaming, and Jack was very grateful. That night he prayed, "Thank you God that I didn't drown in the pool and that my brother is a superhero." Though they battle like any other siblings, they are very committed to each other and are always ready to defend the inner circle of family. Yet both of them also delight in the village life of our extended community.

Our children learn by what we do, and they listen to what we say. Joy sent me an e-mail one day when I was on the road. "The homeless addict woman came to the door again last night. Luke is less scared than he used to be as he understands more about her... that she lives in an abandoned house. We talked about the homeless and how sometimes they are mentally ill or addicts, etc. We talked about what the best ways are to help, etc. Last night I gave her a bag of fruit and food but no money, which she wanted, but she still went away thankful and felt cared for. Luke watched over me the whole time from the top of the stairs… He was glad we did it and said, 'Good, I'm glad she's okay,' and went back to bed."

Another time in the winter, the car stank of urine when Joy picked up the boys from school. She explained it was because she had picked up another homeless woman that very cold morning and taken her to a shelter. The next day Joy and the kids saw the same woman on the street wearing a warm coat and the boys were thankful for that.

We talk to the boys about sharing, about the money that we give away. For our family donations, Luke helped to choose a project that holds baseball and literacy programmes in the Dominican Republic, run by John McCarthy, "Coach Mac", who also runs Homerun Baseball Camp in Washington, D.C., one of Luke's favourite summer and winter activities. And we regard highly the importance of Luke and Jack going to a good D.C. public school. We couldn't pay for the diversity they experience with friends from all racial, economic, and religious backgrounds.

Though these are personal stories of my own family, I share them with you to make the connection between family and community. Both are central to the biblical narrative, both are crucial to the formation of young children, and both are essential to the health of any society.

Ending the War over "Family"

It's time for the ideological warfare of left and right to end when it comes to the issue of the family. I believe that most people on both sides of the debate really do care about their kids – and other people's, too. And the debate is killing us. The good news is that both sides are half right: family is indeed important, as conservatives say, and community is critical for us all, as many liberals contend. The debate exploded again recently on a television talk show I was on between opponents from the Religious Right and the left. I found myself pleading, "These are false choices!"

We need to come together across our ideological lines precisely because family and community are both in serious trouble – and, therefore, so are our children. It should be of great concern to everyone that the rate of marriage formation is in dangerous decline, and not just in poor urban communities. Divorce rates remain high, even in the faith community, which shows no difference in the alarming statistics. Marital infidelity is a widespread problem, and too many children are falling between the cracks in our broken family systems. At the same time, the day seems to be gone when we could count on neighbours to play a role in watching, monitoring, disciplining, and helping to raise all the children of the community.

Nuclear families feel pretty much on their own now, with more pressures than ever. Economic pressures and insecurity now force both parents to work in most families, with 70 per cent of all women in the workforce. Yet, in most families the mothers still bear the lion's share of the work necessary to sustain the household. Lack of health care benefits, affordable and available quality child care, and flexible workplace policies just increase the squeeze on many families and make life extremely difficult for single-parent families. In our exhaustion at the end of the day, Joy and I sometimes wonder how it is possible for single parents to both work and manage family life all by themselves, when it is hard enough with two people involved. Many single parents are literally heroes, while others are drowning in an overwhelming sea of responsibilities while their children have to make do as best they can.

Politicizing these problems just doesn't make sense. I remember a dialogue I had with leaders of Focus on the Family in Colorado Springs a few years ago. I told them I was completely with them in believing that the breakdown of the family is a major crisis in America, and that the reality of many children falling through the cracks of our shattered family systems is a great danger and tragedy. But then I said that I didn't think gay and lesbian people are the ones mostly responsible for all of this, and I asked why their group's focus was so largely on them. After a long discussion, they conceded that point and said they agreed that the breakdown of the family in America is attributable more to "heterosexual dysfunction than to homosexuals". So we have some common ground to build on there.

The support and strengthening of marriage could be a critical component to that common ground. Many couples these days don't see the point of marriage: tax structures can make it disadvantageous, commitment is a less and less valued cultural norm, and living together in patterns of serial monogamy is on the rise. That pattern of social instability is not good either for society or for the nurturing of children.

It is not a throwback to sexual Puritanism but a statement of sociological observation that infidelity, betrayal, broken relationships, and casual sex are undermining the health and integrity of our society. As Diana Butler Bass wrote in the God's Politics blog, "Sin Is Neither Republican nor Democratic" – sexual brokenness is not an issue that should be politicized. She wrote:

A couple weeks ago, I was having lunch with a neo-conservative Christian friend… and he made the off-handed comment that students in mainline Protestant seminaries were "more likely" to engage in premarital sexual activity than those in evangelical seminaries – that sexual misconduct occurs more among liberals than conservatives.

"Sexual morality or immorality is NOT linked to either theology or politics," I argued back. "Sexuality is part of human nature. Whether left or right, all Christians struggle to be faithful people and live out our commitments to chastity or monogamy. Human sexuality isn't a liberal-conservative thing."

He laughed, realizing, of course, that every Christian theologian from St. Paul and St. Augustine forward has pretty much said the same thing.

Making sexuality a political issue, as much of the Religious Right has done, distracts from a host of other issues, such as poverty, war, and environmental concerns. But it also obscures the fact that Christians agree (as my friend and I do) on many things regarding this intimate part of our lives. We agree that sexuality is a gift from God, that love and commitment are foundational to sexual expression, that marriage is the best vessel for human sexuality, and that authenticity, honesty, fidelity, and mutual regard form the basis of Christian sexual relationships. Sex is, theologically, an ultimate expression of self-giving and surrender, qualities that resemble those in Christian spirituality. As the medieval mystics taught, humanity sexuality is a metaphor for our relationship with God...

We also know, as the Christian tradition teaches, that all of this is hard. Sexuality is difficult because it is potentially holy and potentially sinful at the same time. In the midst of this powerful mystery, we are merely human. And none of these things – honesty, holiness, fidelity, or mutual regard – come easily to us... Thus, to politicize sexuality divides us at the very point at which we are united – our shared human nature and our shared quests to live in faith-filled grace.[2]

If we cease the politicizing that merely obscures the real issues, we can focus our attention on the things that really do affect so enormously the health and integrity of marriage and family. For example, divorce. In the interest of full disclosure, I want to say that I had a brief and unsuccessful first marriage. We both knew we didn't have an adequate foundation to have children and so we didn't. When it comes to the problems of keeping marriages together, I have been purged of all feelings of self-righteousness by my own painful experience. The opportunity for a second chance at marriage and finally having the gift of family with Joy, Luke, and Jack has become the greatest blessing of my life. I was, in the words (and echoing the experience) of C. S. Lewis, surprised by Joy. Marriage and family are gifts of God, but they are impossible to sustain without the grace of God.

Although divorce is the greatest disrupter to marriage and children today, it is often an unspoken issue in the heated cultural debates over family values. Divorce rates seem to be declining for college-educated couples with higher incomes, but are much higher for lower-income families. What does that tell us about the importance of security and stability for successful family life? When will we understand that goals such as universal health care, affordable housing, and living-wage incomes are pro-marriage and family programmes?

We really need to focus on the health and strength of marriage, and all the attention given to gay marriage has been a distraction from that. Since the divorce rate is arguably a much greater threat to family and children than is gay marriage, why is divorce much more acceptable to many religious conservatives than gay marriage is? Perhaps because most religious people have close relationships with those who have been divorced, but they don't think they know any gay people. Yet we all know that Jesus spoke much more clearly about divorce than he did about gay marriage.

Sometimes we seem to confuse the social purposes of marriage with our culture's characteristic individualism and even narcissism. Marriage has been institutionally established by the state to provide a structure and environment in which to raise, protect, and nurture children, much more than to ensure our personal happiness and fulfillment. Therefore, wouldn't challenging the ease of no-fault divorce where children are involved be a cause to consider for conservative religious people, rather than having such a singular focus on stopping gay marriage?

I support civil rights for gay and lesbian people and equal protection under the law for same-sex couples. That, for me, is a justice issue. Many Christians, and I include myself, prefer the solution of "civil unions" from the state, and even spiritual "blessings" for gay couples (from congregations prepared to offer them), rather than altering the church's sacrament of marriage as between a man and a woman, but those differences should not be fundamentally divisive. Gay marriage should not be the primary battleground in the fight for the health and stability of marriage and family in our society. In a pluralistic democracy, we should support civil and human rights for all our citizens, regardless of our different theological and biblical interpretations of the complicated and thorny issues surrounding homosexuality. New evidence and understanding around those issues could cause any of us to alter our views. But we should find common ground by supporting concrete practices and practical policies that strengthen families and nurture all our children.

A Pro-Family Agenda

"Call to Renewal", the antipoverty coalition I convene, recently became
involved in the highly politicized debate over the reauthorization of welfare
reform. We represented Christian churches and organizations across the
political spectrum who were united in their commitment to overcoming
poverty. We were one of the very few voices in the debate (along with the
U.S. Conference of Catholic Bishops) who called both for programmes
that would strengthen marriage and family and for increased funding for
child care. Over and over, the conservative side of the debate endorsed the
family-support programmes while the liberal side focused mostly on more
child-care support, and both sides fought the other's agenda.

In fact, after our policy director testified at a congressional hearing,
our conservative friends came up and thanked him for our support of
the marriage-formation proposals but wondered why we wanted more
government funding for child care. Our liberal friends were grateful for our
support of the child-care increases but wondered why we had to get into
all that marriage talk. Neither side understood that both are important and
necessary.

It was quite extraordinary to behold our weekly meetings with top Senate
staff members (the ones responsible for writing the actual legislation) from
both sides of the aisle. Very few of their senators could see this ideological
split as the false choice it was. That political divide was partly why a good
bill could never be passed in both houses of Congress, a bill that balanced
the many factors that go into how a family succeeds in escaping poverty.

It's time for our political leaders to propose a real pro-family agenda, which
I believe neither political party now has. The Democrats have not talked
nearly enough about the problems for marriages and families today, and
the Republicans mostly just have an anti-gay-marriage policy. Neither
side has anything like a comprehensive pro-family agenda, and we need
one desperately. Such an agenda would have to address all the issues that
are putting enormous pressures on families today, including the lack of
living family wages, adequate health care, affordable housing, and child
care. We need to explore more flexible workplace policies, which have
supported the role of parenting in "secular" European countries far more
generously than have American corporate and governmental policies. We
also need to remove the "marriage penalty" and other tax barriers that
make marriage financially more difficult. We need to provide incentives
for family wealth accumulation, make home ownership accessible for
lower-income families, support moms and dads as they try to ensure

quality education at all levels for their children, and find effective ways (short of censorship) to deal with the moral pollution that attacks the minds and hearts of the younger generation. Whoever might advance such a comprehensive pro-family agenda would win votes from both liberal and conservative parents.

If we are to seek a deeper and richer sense of family in America, people on both sides of the political divide must wake up to the valid points being raised by the other side. We must move beyond false dichotomies and sound-bite rebuttals to serious dialogue on what are clear contributors to the many problems that families face. Both economic and sociocultural factors make a difference. We must look for ways to lift families out of poverty, but also look for ways to stem the high divorce rate in America. We must accept responsibility as a society to make sure that working families do not get trapped in poverty because of unjust wage or hiring practices, but we must also work to elevate our attention to the damage done by a society that uses sex to sell just about everything. We must realize the importance of good parenting skills and take the necessary steps to ensure that adequate opportunities exist for all. In other words, we need to come together to put forward a bipartisan agenda that deals with all these problems and not just one side or the other.

The Commitment

Ultimately, both family and community are very personal things that we best learn about by watching, joining, participating, and experiencing – more so than by reading books, hearing lectures, or being hectored by sermonic diatribes on family values. Seeing and doing was how I learned, and that's because I had two of the best teachers anyone could have. My parents were experts in building family and making the connection to community. They would never have thought of themselves that way, but both of them became mentors to legions of people who testify to what Jim and Phyllis Wallis taught them about marriage, family, community, and, most of all, the faith that makes those things possible.

More than five hundred people came to my mother's memorial service. My mother battled cancer until her seventy-fifth birthday – the day her youngest granddaughter came into the world; she uttered her last words with the new baby in her arms in the hospital bed, "I'm happy; I'm very happy." There were two things my mother always told me to do: First, if there is any child that nobody is playing with – you play with that child. Second, if there is a bully picking on people – you stand up to him. Those principles have shaped my understanding of community in many ways.

Seven years later, while I was writing this book, my father died suddenly. I will always be profoundly grateful for his legacy: his children, grandchildren, and the countless other people whose lives he touched will be blessed forever. From the most important to the little child, all were special to my father. Many people, in and out of the family, have told us our dad was their "mentor", "partner", "teacher", or like a "father" or "grandfather" to them or their kids – "He made me/us feel like a part of his family." Someone said to me, "Your family must have felt jealous – so many of us had a piece of your family, your mom and dad." No, they always had plenty of love for us, and amazed us with their love for others. My father and mother were truly my teachers, and no people ever taught or showed me more about the vital connection between family and community. (If you would like to read the eulogy that I gave at my father's funeral service, you can find it in the appendix.)

At a personal level, the best thing we can do for family is to honour our own commitments to our spouses and our children. Are our wives, husbands, and kids important enough to alter our schedules and change our priorities? Since family and community are indeed the ties that bind and hold, they must occupy one of the highest places in each of our lives. Parenting in particular is both the hardest and the most important job any of us could have. Our children and their well-being must be a compass that helps guide all our other choices.

The moral imperative to treat other people's children with similar regard is of uppermost importance in a world where pandemic disease, grinding poverty, and family disintegration have made child abandonment a global epidemic. Jesus' words in the King James Version of the famous text "Suffer the little children" have taken on a whole new meaning in our day of AIDS orphans, child prostitutes, boy soldiers, and babies caught in urban crossfires. And the only antidote to child abandonment is adult recommitment.

That's true on both the personal level and the congregational level. All our families can expand to make room for those who have been left out and who need to be at a family table, and congregations can play major roles in the support, care, and even adoption of lonely and needy children. Governments should indeed pursue policies that don't penalize marriages, but rather offer incentives for parents and supports for family success. But there are clearly limits to how effectively governments can nurture family commitments, which will more likely happen in the institutions of civil society, including in our congregations and local communities.

Congregations can also offer important formation in providing premarriage and postmarriage counselling.

Let's all commit to no longer politicizing and polarizing our conversations around family. There is indeed common ground to be established here, especially among parents across the political spectrum. Our children are too important to be pawns in our partisan games. If the well-being of families and communities were used to guide our public life, our political policies would be fundamentally reshaped. It's time to call all political parties to a genuinely pro-family agenda – and hold them accountable to it.

NONVIOLENT REALISM
Resolving Our Conflicts

My dad, Jim Wallis Sr., came to visit us often. He was well into his eighties during the last trips before he died, but he still did pretty well, travelling on his own to see his two grandsons in Washington, D.C. I remember one typically wonderful grandpa week – going to see Luke's second-grade class and Jack's new preschool, watching Little League practice and the big Saturday game, checking out the new Sojourners office, and eating some special Mexican meals.

On Luke's personal sharing day at school, he brought his grandpa to "share". When Luke told his classmates that his grandpa had been in the Navy during World War II, one kid asked who won the war. When they heard that we did, the class started cheering. Of course, at this age they have no idea what war really is.

Later in the week, my dad and I went to the World War II Memorial, then about two years old. He liked seeing the names of all the Pacific islands he remembered as the junior engineering officer on a destroyer-minesweeper. His ship had been scheduled for the invasion of Japan, and high casualty rates were expected. Like many others, my father believed that the atomic bomb saved his life and made our family possible. His new bride, waiting at home, might otherwise have become a young widow.

The memorial includes a comfortable stone bench in the shade, where we sat and talked for a long time about those war years, his school days, and my parents' first months and years of marriage, which were so dramatically affected by the war. Amazingly, my father was commissioned in the Navy, graduated from the University of Michigan, and got married all on the same day! The Navy was in a hurry to get fresh officers into the last days of the Pacific conflict, which ended only months after he was deployed. He became part of the mop-up operation after the Japanese surrender.

My father recalled the visit he made to Hiroshima, just weeks after the world's first nuclear explosion in warfare had been detonated there. He was part of a two-man team, surveying the impact of the bomb on major structures such as factories. The devastation, he told me, was like nothing he had ever seen or imagined. He described how the nuclear explosion had sucked out all the air in the area, and when it rushed back in everything was flattened, even huge factories.

He admitted that he had not been sympathetic to the Japanese after they had attacked Pearl Harbor in Hawaii, and especially after they and their German allies had killed so many of his friends. Along with many of his fellow soldiers, he felt that they deserved the atomic bomb – though at the time, he said, few of them fully understood what it was.

But then he saw Hiroshima. As the two young Americans walked through the flattened rubble, they passed a small pile of bricks that had been fashioned into a makeshift shelter. Suddenly, a little girl appeared from behind a wall. My father remembered her as about five years old, with dirty tattered clothes falling off her body. As far as they could tell, she was all alone with no one to take care of her.

As he talked about the child, he seemed to remember her vividly, as if it were yesterday. He recalled the feelings that welled up inside him: she was just a little child; none of this was her fault. They knew she would die soon, if only from exposure to all the radiation. My dad, an eighty-two-year-old war veteran, began to cry as he remembered a day more than sixty years before.

"That's war," he said, "and that's why I hate it." He still believes that we had to defend ourselves from a direct attack in World War II. But why did they drop the bombs on civilian targets, he asked, cities with little military significance? They could have dropped them on a deserted island to make the point.

My dad opposed every war since then and was especially upset about the war in Iraq. "They just lied about it, and it was totally unnecessary," he said, as his tears turned to anger.

My father was part of what former NBC anchor Tom Brokaw named the "greatest generation", and I know two little boys who, after a week's visit, thought he was the greatest grandpa. But my dad didn't like the direction his country had taken since his generation retired. He often shook his head while he watched CNN. "How do they get away with it?" he would ask me on the phone.

Sitting with him at the memorial, I was moved to see how this war veteran had so turned against war and still felt the emotions that senseless suffering brings. Most of those who run our wars now are not veterans of any war and seldom comment on the deaths that occur every day. I wonder what would happen to them if a five-year-old girl came out from behind the rubble of war to stop them in their tracks. But most of them never get close enough to the rubble to see her.

"But as for you who forsake the LORD and forget my holy mountain, who spread a table for Fortune and fill bowls of mixed wine for Destiny, I will destine you for the sword, and you will all bend down for the slaughter; for I called but you did not answer, I spoke but you did not listen. You did evil in my sight and chose what displeases me."

Therefore this is what the Sovereign LORD says: "My servants will eat, but you will go hungry; my servants will drink, but you will go thirsty; my servants will rejoice, but you will be put to shame. My servants will sing out of the joy of their hearts, but you will cry out from anguish of heart and wail in brokenness of spirit. You will leave your name to my chosen ones as a curse; the Sovereign LORD will put you to death, but to his servants he will give another name. Whoever invokes a blessing in the land will do so by the God of truth; he who takes an oath in the land will swear by the God of truth. For the past troubles will be forgotten and hidden from my eyes.

"Behold, I will create new heavens and a new earth. The former things will not be remembered, nor will they come to mind. But be glad and rejoice forever in what I will create, for I will create Jerusalem to be a delight and its people a joy. I will rejoice over Jerusalem and take delight in my people; the sound of weeping and of crying will be heard in it no more.

"Never again will there be in it an infant who lives but a few days, or an old man who does not live out his years; he who dies at a hundred will be thought a mere youth; he who fails to reach a hundred will be considered accursed. They will build houses and dwell in them; they will plant vineyards and eat their fruit. No longer will they build houses and others live in them, or plant and others eat. For as the days of a tree, so will be the days of my people; my chosen ones will long enjoy the works of their hands.

"They will not toil in vain or bear children doomed to misfortune; for they will be a people blessed by the LORD, they and their descendants with them. Before they call I will answer; while they are still speaking I will hear. The wolf and the lamb will feed together, and the lion will eat straw like the ox, but dust will be the serpent's food. They will neither harm nor destroy on all my holy mountain," says the LORD. (Isaiah 65:11–25, NIV)

The prophet Isaiah paints a starkly vivid picture of what God wants and doesn't want, what God accepts and won't accept, and what God is already creating. This is clearly not just a prophecy of heaven but one for the future of the earth that is already coming into being. The text speaks of God's vision for human relations and institutional practices, about good and evil, and about conflict and violence.

Those who aren't cooperating, aren't listening, and aren't responding to God's call will have some very harsh things in store for them. For those "who spread a table for Fortune… I will destine you for the sword, and you will all bend down for the slaughter; for I called but you did not answer, I spoke but you did not listen. You did evil in my sight and chose what displeases me." Many who believe they are the masters of history have turned from what God has in mind. What they can look forward to, according to Isaiah, is a future of hunger, thirst, despair, broken hearts, crushed spirits, and having their names reduced to curse words.

On the other hand, God is creating something new that will be characterized by justice, joy, and hope and invites us to join in. Children will no longer suffer early and untimely deaths or adults shortened life spans. People will be able to live in the houses they build and not have them taken by others, eat what they plant and not have it stolen by others, enjoy the work of their hands and not have their labour exploited by others. They will no longer suffer the heartache of losing their children to calamitous events and circumstances, but with their offspring will enjoy long and blessed lives. The result of this change for social justice will be peace: old enemies will comfortably eat together, the more powerful will no longer intimidate the less powerful, and there will be no more hurting or killing anywhere on God's holy mountain. Now that's a vision for global security.

The clear implication of the Isaiah text is that peace and security will be the fruit of dramatic change in social and economic relationships. The text suggests that ending conflict and killing must be preceded, or at least accompanied, by the progress of justice. Those who now benefit the most from things the way they are, and "spread a table for Fortune", will be in serious trouble for ignoring what God wants and doing what God deplores, while those who now suffer most will have their fortunes reversed. It is very similar to the vision of the prophet Micah, whom I often call my favourite prophet of national security.

> In days to come the mountain of the LORD's house shall be established as the highest of the mountains, and shall be raised up above the hills. Peoples shall stream to it, and many nations shall come and say: "Come, let us go up to the mountain of the LORD, to the house of the God of Jacob; that he may teach us his ways and that we may walk in his paths." For out of Zion shall go forth instruction, and the word of the LORD from Jerusalem. He shall judge between many peoples, and shall arbitrate between strong nations far

away; they shall beat their swords into plowshares, and their spears into
pruning hooks; nation shall not lift up sword against nation, neither shall
they learn war any more; but they shall all sit under their own vines and
under their own fig trees, and no one shall make them afraid; for the mouth
of the LORD of hosts has spoken. For all the peoples walk, each in the name
of its god, but we will walk in the name of the LORD our God forever and
ever. (Micah 4:1–5)

Here again, the claim is that the reduction of violence (and we could
add terrorism) – beating swords into plowshares, spears into pruning hooks,
and learning war no more – will come about only when people have "their
own vines and fig trees" and no one can make them afraid anymore. Until
people have a little patch of their own, a piece of the planet, a chance
for security, a stake in the world, they will always be subject to fear and
vulnerable to violence. In other words, our security is dependent on other
people's security, more than it is on how many swords we have. This is a
simple proposition and a regular theme of the prophets, but it is almost
unimaginable to us as a basis for foreign policy. I would contend that the
prophet's vision is neither utopian nor idealistic but rather both pragmatic
and practical – the demonstrable core of realism in today's modern world.
Swords alone cannot bring security; we need plowshares. The mountain
isn't safe for anybody, even those who own the tables of fortune, as long as
so many others live lives of utter insecurity.

But we are sceptical of the prophet's vision. I can't help recalling Woody
Allen's comment on Isaiah's vision: "The lion will lay down with the lamb,
but the lamb won't get much sleep!" The operational rule of America's
current foreign policy leaders comes from neither Isaiah nor Micah but
from the ancient Romans: *Oderint dum metuant* – "Let them hate, so
long as they fear." Today's Pax Americana is based on principles from an
earlier Pax Romana. Only American military supremacy, only U.S. global
hegemony, only pre-emptive strikes, only a state of permanent war against
communists, terrorists, or some other legion of barbarians will keep us and
our way of life safe.

The early Christians questioned that logic and were a serious threat to
that way of thinking. Their allegiance was to a new kingdom of God whose
leader blessed the "peacemakers" and admonished them, scandalously,
to "love their enemies". Have modern American Christians substituted
the peace of Rome and America for the peace of Christ? Rev. Rich
Nathan, pastor of The Vineyard church in Columbus, Ohio, says, "Many
evangelicals are now saying, 'How did it come to be that we who claim

to follow the Prince of Peace are stauncher advocates of war than any other demographic group in America?' Even those of us who do not come from a pacifist tradition, but rather a just war tradition, have begun to ask, 'How can some of our most recent wars be considered just?' You know, St. Augustine, the father of the just war tradition, said that Christians may, on occasion, legitimately go to war. But we always do so with great reluctance and with tears."[1]

As I read the Isaiah and Micah texts and look at today's world, I see two competing visions of globalization and security. If we merely set the global table for "fortune", we had better be prepared to do what is "evil in [God's] sight", to be both hated and feared, and to look forward to the ultimate consequences of that choice: despair, destitution, shame, and, ultimately, death, according to the prophecies of Isaiah. Remember Rome's mighty fall?

If we instead seek to cooperate with God's creative vision of social justice, common security, and the peaceful resolution of conflicts, our future looks much better. This is not a utopian vision; it's about what works and doesn't work in the world, and about those realities to which we will finally be held accountable. It involves the practical choices we make regarding the direction of globalization and the shape of our security. It's time to redefine what "realism" is, and that begins by questioning the moral and political logic of modern warfare.

The Rubble of War

I was shedding my own tears as I listened to Celeste Zappala in the National Cathedral on the night of March 16, 2007, during the Christian Peace Witness that marked the fourth anniversary of the war in Iraq. That day brought the worst weather I had ever seen for an evening service and planned candlelight procession to the White House, where a nonviolent prayer vigil was to take place. An ice storm was predicted and had already hit to the north, preventing many from getting into Washington. Buses full of Christians had to turn back in Pennsylvania, Virginia, and Ohio. Flights were cancelled around the country, cars stranded, and people in the nation's capital warned to stay inside. But amazingly, the cathedral began to fill anyway, until it was packed with three thousand people, with an overflow crowd of six hundred watching the proceedings on a big screen at New York Avenue Presbyterian Church. This Christian witness had struck a chord and served a need for believers to express their deep faith convictions, not merely to protest the war.

Celeste Zappala is the mother of a fallen soldier in Iraq, and she told the throng what it meant to lose her son.

My son, Sgt. Sherwood Baker, was killed in Baghdad on April 26, 2004. I am here tonight as a witness to the true cost of this war… Three thousand, two hundred and three American families. We are all part of the ever-growing, sad fellowship of families who have met their worst fear when they opened their front door.

"Are you Sherwood Baker's mother?" said the man with medals on his chest on the rainy night that death came to my door. "Yes, I am the mother" – of my sweet and noble son who always made me laugh, who was there if you needed help, and who more people than I could ever have imagined called their best friend – "Yes," I said, and fell to the ground, while somewhere outside of myself I heard someone screaming and screaming.[2]

That night at the National Cathedral, Zappala recounted the costs of war. What happens, she asked, to "the souls of soldiers who have picked up their friends in pieces, or fearfully fired into a moving car – to discover a shattered Iraqi family a moment later?" She talked about the many victims, on two continents. "An Iraqi mother searches a morgue for the familiar curve of the hand of her child beneath a pale sheet; an American father watches his son beheaded on videotape; an Iraqi child wakes up in a shabby hospital in excruciating pain and without his arm; an American girl writes letters to her dead soldier father; a young vet wraps a garden hose around his neck and leaps away from the nightmares that beset him." And she recited the tragic numbers: "1,950 U.S. kids lost a parent; 25,000 wounded and struggling through the V.A. system; scores and scores of suicides, 500,000 and more dead Iraqis; 2 million refugees…"

"Each one of us are witnesses to this war and to our own complicity in it," Zappala said at the cathedral. "When were we silent and should have spoken, whose eyes would we not meet to face the truth? Now we are prostrate at this altar, begging, 'Lord, help us. War is our failure to love you, and peace is your command. Peace is not the easy way out, its creation is the most confounding – the hardest – thing we can do. Help us.'"

Both my father and Celeste knew the pain of war and the complications of peace. "Help us." Peace is indeed confounding us. While violence threatens to engulf us through the menace of terrorism, weapons of mass destruction, seemingly irresolvable regional conflicts, and apparently endless wars that rob us of our resources and our young people, the world remains hungry for a better way to solve our inevitable conflicts.

Turning away from the real threats and the realities of powerful evils in our world isn't the answer, but responding to them in better and more effective ways may be. How do we defeat the monsters in our world without becoming monsters ourselves, and how do we protect ourselves and keep our families safe without compromising our most important values and democratic principles? How do we move beyond the old arguments of pacifism versus just wars to a new ethic and to practise the art of conflict resolution? And how do we teach people, especially a new generation, the critical skills for creating nonviolent alternatives to our chronic violence? It isn't easy, but the failures of our present course make the learning of those skills absolutely necessary.

What would it mean to "love our enemies" when they are trying to kill us, and how might we become the "peacemakers" whom Jesus called "the children of God"? And, finally, how do we think more globally and not just in terms of narrow national interests? What is the promise of strengthening the institutions of international law as a better alternative to the unilateral action of nation-states in situations of conflict? These are the hard questions we must address, perhaps in ways we have never done before.

The Power of a Bad Example

The war in Iraq may well turn out to be the best example of how not to confront a serious threat, how not to deal with evil, how not to defeat terrorism, how not to find security, how not to foster democracy, how not to seek peace – and, for people of faith, how not to honour God and follow Christ. All these things – confronting threats, dealing with evil, defeating terrorism, finding security, fostering democracy, seeking peace, and, of course, obeying God and following Christ – are worth doing and are necessary for us as both citizens and believers. But the disastrous failure of the Iraq war offers us a tragic object lesson in how not to do them. It could teach us instead that peace, as well as all the other goals, is much more complicated.

Those who have died in Iraq may not have perished in vain if we can finally learn the lessons of our failure there. Rev. Raphael G. Warnock, senior pastor of Atlanta's Ebenezer Baptist Church, also spoke at the National Cathedral service and reframed the most common media and political question about the war. "On both sides of the aisle," Warnock said, "the controlling concern is that America may lose the war, and so the question being asked is, 'What are we going to do to keep from losing the war?' I submit that as people of faith, we must reframe the question and help others to understand that the danger confronting America is not that we may lose the war. The real danger is that America may well lose its soul."[3]

While Fox News loves to press that question with every war critic, it is indeed the wrong question. The war in Iraq cannot be won, should never have been fought in the first place, makes everything it promised to solve even worse, and continues to be pursued at the cost of America's soul. Let's get specific.

The war was justified by faulty intelligence that was manipulated and misrepresented to make the case for a war that Bush administration officials had already decided to fight on ideological grounds. There were, of course, no weapons of mass destruction after all. When half truths, exaggerations, and outright lies justify war, it produces a deep crisis of confidence. How much will the world ever trust what America says again after the deception of the war in Iraq?

Then came the "shock and awe", and if any doubted how quickly American military firepower could defeat an adversary, they were now quite convinced. But few talked about the human costs that were only beginning for the Iraqi people. Military success doesn't speak much of "collateral damage", but the videos of it were quickly available on Middle East television and Web sites across the globe, and the moral high ground that America had occupied after the September 11 attacks was soon tragically lost.

Arrogance soon turned to incompetence, and many very bad decisions were made. Even while the president proudly declared "Mission Accomplished", dressed in a flak jacket and standing on the deck of an aircraft carrier, the insurgency had begun and would prove how much easier it is to wage a war than to establish a peace. When only military solutions are sought, the political causes of conflict will soon come to the surface, as they did when Iraq's historical factions began to rise up in enmity against both the American occupation and one another. The emerging revelations of massive corruption in the occupation's rebuilding plans, symbolized by Vice President Cheney's former Halliburton company and its notorious no-bid contracts, further undermined the entire American project in the eyes of the world.

The war to "liberate" Iraq had now become a "civil war" (although it would take four years for Pentagon officials to say those words), one that placed American soldiers in highly dangerous situations as the liberators became the targets of an increasingly sophisticated and lethal insurgency. Inevitably, a few fearful and angry American occupiers descended into atrocities against the civilian population; and a lack of respect for human rights and the conventions of war, at the highest levels of command, resulted in the horrible humiliation and torture of Iraqi prisoners at Abu Ghraib. The photographs of this abuse became the recruiting posters for a whole new generation of angry Islamic terrorists. The allegations of torture at Guantanamo and at secret sites around the world added more shame and made the American boast of establishing democracy in the Middle East seem a sham.

Yet the war went on and on and the bloody insurgency seemed to get worse with each passing month. Young American lives were being lost every day, and the soldiers' stories were being heard in the media back home, including the grief of their parents, wives, husbands, and children. Along with a death toll in the thousands, the number of servicemen and -women injured, maimed, and permanently disabled has climbed into the tens of thousands. The subsequent revelations of the ill treatment and abandonment of those disabled veterans after they returned home became a national scandal.

Sadly, records of Iraqi deaths and injuries were never carefully kept, but almost every family in Iraq could tell stories of casualties, which reached into the hundreds of thousands. Two million Iraqis fled their dangerous country, more than a million more were displaced internally, and basic services were yet to be restored four years after the American invasion.

Four years into the war, a majority of Americans believed the war "wasn't worth it", and their ballots in the 2006 election were a clear public referendum on the failed Iraq war. But President Bush soldiered on, promising new troop surges and rejecting political solutions and plans, from older and wiser American foreign policy veterans, for responsible withdrawal. Without the moral or political imagination to seek a different course, the administration continued doggedly to pursue the old course, with more American and Iraqi lives lost every day. Nobody seemed to ask the question, Are our children safer or less safe because of the war in Iraq? Everyone knew the answer. A classified National Intelligence Estimate (NIE) prepared by sixteen U.S. intelligence agencies, which came to light in September 2006, warned that the war on Iraq had increased, not lessened, the threat from terrorism and has spawned a "new generation of Islamic radicalism".[4] A July 2007 NIE warned that al-Qaeda's association with the insurgency in Iraq has helped it "energize the broader Sunni extremist community, raise resources, and to recruit and indoctrinate operatives, including for Homeland attacks".[5]

The administration's consistent tactic has been to attack its critics' integrity, motives, and patriotism. Vice President Dick Cheney took the low-road approach of attacking critics of the war as "appeasers", accusing them of giving aid and comfort to terrorists. Then Republican House majority leader John Boehner showed just how low politicians can go by saying, "I listen to my Democrat friends, and I wonder if they're more interested in protecting the terrorists than in protecting the American people."[6] One of the first casualties of the war in Iraq was honest and civil debate about the direction of our foreign policy and what brings us true security.

The president still delivers speeches in which he equates his war in Iraq with the war on terror, despite widespread public opinion that the Iraq war is both a failure and a distraction from the real battles against terrorism. He becomes "theologian-in-chief", using stark imagery of good and evil and language about the "clash of civilizations" to defend his apocalyptic mission. Despite all the evidence of failure, the president becomes ever more self-confident, declaring, "I've never been more convinced that the decisions I made are the right decisions."[7]

In fall 2006, Bush met in the Oval Office with a group of conservative journalists and linked the war in Iraq to his faith and to what he saw as the possibility of a "Third Great Awakening" tied to the war against terrorism. He invoked Abraham Lincoln and the Second Great Awakening, the nineteenth-century movement that connected conversion to Christian faith with the battle to abolish slavery. Commenting on how impressed he was that so many people he'd met at presidential rope lines said they were praying for him, he then remarked, "A lot of people in America see this as a confrontation between good and evil, including me."[8] But, as in many things, Bush got the facts wrong.

The Second Great Awakening came quite a few years before Lincoln, and Abraham Lincoln stands out among presidents as one who called for national humility and repentance, not self-righteousness and triumphalism. In his Second Inaugural Address, Lincoln drew no easy lines of good and evil but said that both sides in the Civil War stood under the judgment of God. "Both read the same Bible and pray to the same God, and each invokes His aid against the other," Lincoln said. "That of neither has been answered fully. The Almighty has His own purposes." Bush's constant rhetoric of "the evildoers" arrayed against the absolute goodness of America, with no hint of self-reflection on how U.S. policies have contributed to global resentments and conflicts, is hardly Lincolnesque.

Bush sees his war on terrorism as "the decisive ideological struggle of the 21st century, and the calling of our generation". According to him, the war in Iraq is not a mistake but a "war that will set the course for this new century – and determine the destiny of millions across the world". It was clear that no course changes were being contemplated, because the president believed that "the safety of America depends on the outcome of the battle in the streets of Baghdad".[9]

The threat of terrorism is very real, but it is clear that the war on Iraq was not the answer. Bush's complete self-confidence is tied to his theology – "we go forward with trust in that spirit, confidence in our purpose, and faith in a loving God who made us to be free". Rich Lowry, editor of the conservative *National Review,* reported, "Bush's faith in the rightness of his strategy in the broader war is deep-seated – it is, indeed, a product of faith."[10]

But a God who warns us not to trust in military might and who judges the rich and powerful most of all, and a Saviour who challenges his disciples not just to see the log in their adversary's eye but also the one in their own, seems quite foreign to the faith of George W. Bush. I don't doubt the president's personal faith, but Bush's bad theology (they are evil and we are good) is the foundation for his bad foreign policy and reveals an alarming lack of capacity for self-examination. Bush's belief (unlike Lincoln's) that God is on his side poses a real threat to the safety of our children and to the peace and security of the world. A foreign journalist recently asked me if I regarded George Bush as "my brother in Christ". I said, "George Bush is my brother in Christ, but he is also the most dangerous president in American history."

Marching Orders

The amazing crowd of believers in the National Cathedral on that March night in 2007 night showed that we might be learning the lessons of Iraq. It also showed that our opposition to this war was not just political but had become, for many, a matter of faith. Those three thousand people marched out into the cold Washington night, with one thousand more joining them at Lafayette Park across from the White House. My role as the last speaker was to issue the call to faith and action and to suggest that turning our nation away from the war in Iraq must now be a work of faith. I told those gathered that evening:

> Four years ago today, my son Jack was born – two days before the war began. I always know how long this awful war has gone on. The war in Iraq is personal for me. It's personal for you too, or you wouldn't be here tonight, especially in this weather. It's personal for the families and loved ones of the

more than 3,200 American soldiers who have lost the precious gift of life. They are so young to die, and it is so unnecessary. When I look at my son and celebrate his birthday, I think of all the children whose fathers or mothers won't be coming back from the war to celebrate theirs.

It's personal for the tens of thousands of service men and women who have lost their limbs or their mental and emotional health, and who now feel abandoned and mistreated. It's personal for all the Iraqis who have lost their loved ones, as many as hundreds of thousands. And when I look at my son, I think of all the Iraqi children who will never celebrate another birthday. This isn't just political; it's personal for millions of us now. And for all of us here tonight, the war in Iraq is actually more than personal – it has become a matter of faith.

By our deepest convictions about Christian standards and teaching, the war in Iraq was not just a well-intended mistake or only mismanaged. This war, from a Christian point of view, is morally wrong – and was from the very start. It cannot be justified with either the teaching of Jesus Christ or the criteria of St. Augustine's just war. It simply doesn't pass either test. This war is not just an offense against the young Americans who have made the ultimate sacrifice or just to the Iraqis who have paid such a horrible price. This war is not only an offence to the poor at home and around the world who have paid the price of misdirected resources and priorities. This war is also an offence against God.

And so we are here tonight, very simply and resolutely, to begin to end the war in Iraq. But not by anger, though we are angry; not just by politics, though it will take political courage. But by faith, because we are people of faith. This service and procession are not just another political protest, but an act of faith, an act of prayer, an act of nonviolent witness. Politics led us into this war, and politics is unlikely to save us by itself.

I believe it will take faith to end this war. It will take prayer to end it. It will take a mobilization of the faith community to end it – to change the political climate, to change the wind. It will take a revolution of love to end it. Because this endless war in Iraq is based ultimately on fear; and Jesus says that only perfect love will cast out fear. We say, as people of faith, as followers of Jesus, that the deep fear that has paralyzed the conscience of this nation, which has caused us to become the kind of people that we are not called to be, that has allowed us to tolerate violations of our most basic values, and that has perpetuated an endless cycle of violence and counter-violence must be exorcised as the demon it is – this fear must be cast out!

And to cast out that fear, we must act in faith, in prayer, in love, and in hope – so we might help to heal the fears that keep this war going. Tonight we march not in belligerence, or to attack individuals (even those leaders directly responsible for the war), or to use human suffering for partisan political purposes. Rather, we process to the White House tonight as an act of faith, believing that only faith can save us now.

Ironically, this war has often been cloaked in the name and symbols of our faith, confused American imperial designs with God's purposes, and tragically discredited Christian faith around the world, having so tied it to flawed American behaviour and agendas. Millions of people around the world sadly believe this is a Christian war. So as people of faith, let us say tonight to our brothers and sisters around the world, and as clearly as we can: America is not the hope of the earth and the light of the world – Jesus Christ is! And it is his way that we follow, and not the flawed path of our nation's leaders who prosecute this war. As an evangelical Christian, I must say that the war in Iraq has hindered the cause of Christ and, in this season of Lent, we must repent of this war!

My son Luke marched out of the cathedral with me, carrying a candle, and then walked with the thousands of others all those 3.5 miles to the White House where more than 220 of us Christians were arrested for praying on the White House sidewalk. (I told Luke he was still too young for that!) Would we learn the lessons of Iraq in time for him to see some different choices for America's future, for his future!

A Better Way

The good news is that many voices are calling for change, for a deeper vision of global security and a more holistic view of how to confront the genuine threats in our world – a better way. A few years ago I had a conversation with Tim Cross, a major general in the British army. I had been preaching in the U.K. about the clear differences between the vision of Micah for national security and the strategies of the neoconservative leaders who were running American foreign policy. I said we had to choose one or the other. Cross wanted to have coffee after my speech. Having just returned from Iraq, where he was in charge of the British occupation, the general said to me, "Micah is right and Rumsfeld [then the U.S. secretary of defense] is wrong." Tim Cross has taught me much about the view from the ground in the midst of conflict, and how a solely military approach simply doesn't work.

British prime minister Gordon Brown has clearly linked the struggle for social and economic justice with the battle against terrorism and the pursuit of global security. In a 2007 speech in Bangalore, India, then-Chancellor Brown laid out the clear moral and political choices we face in the kind of globalization we seek.[11] He said that cooperating to reform international institutions "can ensure that globalization works to ensure prosperity and opportunity not just for some people but all people". The struggle against "global terrorism in a new era of global insecurities" includes "the battle for hearts and minds that can and will ensure security and justice for all".

Future Prime Minister Brown spoke of an "emerging new world order" that will come about by "recognizing our essential interdependence… by matching the necessary embrace of openness, free trade, and flexibility with an offer to every individual of education", and "by building an alliance for economic and social justice and environmental care". And then he went deeper, saying:

> But the new world order that I suggest is one that has to be founded on values – on liberty under the law, the dignity of every individual, participatory and accountable democracies – and this will require a new deal between rich and poor people – and that the benefits of globalization will be open not just to some but to all. There are those who define the next stage of globalization as an inevitable growth in insecurity and inequality. But this depends on the decisions we make. Properly managed globalization has the potential to make the world a fairer and safer place, breaking down boundaries and uniting people.

Brown quoted a name familiar to his audience: "In the words of one of your greatest leaders, indeed one of the world's greatest leaders, Mahatma Gandhi: 'Whenever you are in doubt apply the following test. Recall the face of the poorest and the weakest person whom you may have seen, and ask yourself if the step you contemplate is going to be of any use to them … then,' he said, 'you will find your doubts melt away.'"

In his remarks, Brown said that four things are essential for the battle against terrorism: (1) We must do all we can with counterinsurgency strategies to expose and isolate murderous extremists who practise terrorist violence. (2) We should back the moderates who are championing reform. (3) We must address real, justifiable grievances, most urgently acting to put the Middle East road map back on track. (4) It is the power of argument, debate, and dialogue that will win the cultural fight against extremism. Brown concluded with the words of Gandhi: "We must be the change we wish to see."

In June of 2007, Gordon Brown became the prime minister of the U.K.

In a speech in which he laid out the values that would govern his leadership vision, Brown said:

> Our foreign policy in years ahead will reflect the truth that to isolate and defeat terrorist extremism now involves more than military force – it is also a struggle of ideas and ideals that in the coming years will be waged and won for hearts and minds here at home and round the world. And an essential contribution to this will be what becomes daily more urgent – a Middle East settlement upholding a two state solution, that protects the security of Israel and the legitimate enduring desire for a Palestinian state...
>
> Because we all want to address the roots of injustice, I can tell you today that we will strengthen and enhance the work of the department of international development and align aid, debt relief and trade policies to wage an unremitting battle against the poverty, illiteracy, disease and environmental degradation that it has fallen to our generation to eradicate.[12]

In a similar vein, Robert Wright, a senior fellow at the New America Foundation, calls for a new "progressive realism". It is essential, Wright says, that the United States pay attention to what happens in other countries, in part because authoritarian regimes can bring unrest to large regions of the world and serve as cauldrons of violence and terrorism. Wright sees globalization as inevitable but says groups such as the World Trade Organization and other bodies of regional and global governance must be given the authority to address both labour and environmental issues.

For Wright, arms control is the only alternative to simply invading every nation that might be on the way to producing nuclear weapons. He explains that outside inspections, on all parties concerned, are essential to prevent cheating in arms-control agreements, and that such inspections – and other constraints on America's behaviour – serve U.S. national interest when they also constrain other nations. And the same principle applies to other international issues, from global warming ("we'll cut carbon dioxide emissions if you will") to war ("we'll refrain from it if you will"). Ignoring this principle in the case of Iraq has had serious consequences, including a weakening of international standards against military invasions not justified by imminent threats and a diminution of the U.N.'s authority as an arms inspector. The U.S. invasion of Iraq sent the unfortunate message to the nations of the world that permitting weapons inspections provides no protection against being invaded. This certainly will not make it any easier to oppose the nuclear programmes of Iran and North Korea without the use of force.

Ironically, the foreign policy approach taken by the Bush administration is perhaps the *least* likely to result in genuine democracy around the world. Military invasions and U.S.-backed coups proved to be not only ineffective in democracy building, but actually counterproductive when compared with "more indigenous, more culturally authentic paths to democracy", as Wright puts it – and have made America less secure, not safer. Moreover, the administration's go-it-alone approach as the world's sole superpower means that the United States must shoulder the lion's share of the costs of war – working through multinational organizations and supporting international law will actually save our country money.

The costs, however, go well beyond dollars and cents, and even beyond the high price paid in casualties and death. American intervention around the world not only helps to provide recruits to terrorist organizations today, but it also lays the groundwork for increasing anti-American violence in the days and years to come. Quite simply, the fact that our own "domestic security depends increasingly on popular sentiment abroad makes it important for America to be seen as a good global citizen – respecting international laws and norms and sensing the needs of neighbors," Wright explains. The "war on terror" can be more effectively waged by other, nonmilitary means; for example, the U.S. response to the 2004 tsunami in southern Asia helped improve the image of America in Indonesia, the world's largest Muslim country, and elsewhere around the world.

Wright argues that the increasing economic interdependence of the world will help to make war less attractive, and even encourage a "humanitarian" approach. "Progressive realists," he writes, "see that America can best flourish if others flourish – if African states cohere, if the world's Muslims feel they benefit from the world order, if personal and environmental health are nurtured, if economic inequities abroad are muted so that young democracies can be stable and strong. More and more, doing well means doing good."

This sounds like Isaiah and Micah, doesn't it? Robert Wright cuts to the heart of the matter when he concludes that the "immersion in the perspective of the other is sometimes called 'moral imagination', and it is hard. Understanding why some people hate America, and why terrorists kill, is challenging not just intellectually but emotionally. Yet it is crucial and has been lacking in President Bush." Thankfully, there is a growing desire among Americans – and a very real need – for the United States to begin regaining the respect around the world that the Bush administration has squandered.

It is indeed our "moral imagination" that illuminates our view of the world. And it is indeed time to transcend the current view of American power – that it's just we versus they, good guys and bad guys, and that only military solutions will suffice. Is there a better way? Can we find effective ways to cope with emergencies and catastrophes such as Darfur through authorized and competent international interventions? Can we deal with rogue regimes and dictators such as Saddam Hussein through a universally accepted international criminal court?

Most of the world's economic and political conflicts are already and routinely resolved through peaceful means. How do we extend the circle of nonviolent solutions? What forms of carrots and sticks (incentives and sanctions) can be used internationally to change bad behavior of nation-states and their rulers? How can we teach the skills of conflict resolution to a new generation and make peacekeeping both respected and effective? And finally, how could international law become a real alternative to the limits and problems of superpower hegemony?

At Davos in early 2007, Tony Blair, then the British prime minister, spoke about how the complications and limits of politics, on the international level, were preventing a solution in Darfur while people continued to be raped, killed, and displaced. "We need proper, well-constructed means of conflict resolution and peace-keeping," Blair said. "Hundreds of thousands die or live lives of unbelievable risk and misery because we cannot assemble a proper peace agreement, properly enforced, with the full weight of the international community behind it." The real problem, Blair said, is "the absence of a sustained international focus, with the capacity to keep at it, report back credibly, and trigger action if nothing happens".

Blair concluded by emphasizing the very concrete aspects of peacemaking: "If we are to intervene successfully, we have to have the capability to do so. Therefore a key and new part of our international dialogue must now be strengthening the instruments and institutions, those between governments but also those within broader civic society, that can build capacity. We need new networks, new relationships between countries and between people which mobilize the practical means of bringing change into being."[13]

Lessons Learned

Just before he retired from his position as secretary-general of the United Nations, Kofi Annan wrote an op-ed piece for *The Washington Post* titled "What I've Learned".[14] He named five lessons that sound as if they could have come right out of Isaiah or Micah.

First, Annan argued, security is not something that an individual nation can accomplish on its own, apart from relationship with other countries. "Against such threats as nuclear proliferation, climate change, global pandemics, or terrorists operating from safe havens in failed states, no nation can make itself secure by seeking supremacy over all others," Annan wrote. Our responsibility for mutual security in the world "includes our shared responsibility to protect people from genocide, war crimes, ethnic cleansing, and crimes against humanity".

Second, the secretary-general said that the same principle applies to the economic connections among the world's people. "It is not realistic to think that some people can go on deriving great benefits from globalization while billions of others are left in, or thrown into, abject poverty," he said. "We have to give all our fellow human beings at least a chance to share in our prosperity."

Third, human rights and the rule of law must be the basis of both security and shared prosperity, according to Annan. "If our communities are to live in peace we must stress also what unites us: our common humanity and the need for our human dignity and rights to be protected by law."

Annan's fourth lesson is that governments must be accountable for their actions, not only at home but in the international arena as well. Such accountability is currently applied in very unequal ways. "As things stand, poor and weak states are easily held to account, because they need foreign aid," Annan wrote. "But large and powerful states, whose actions have the greatest impact on others, can be constrained only by their own people." That fact means that people and organizations in the "powerful states", such as the United States, have what he called a "special responsibility" to hold their nations accountable for their actions around the world.

The secretary-general's final lesson acknowledged that countries can hold each other accountable only through multinational institutions, including the U.N., and that these institutions "must be organized in a fair and democratic way, giving the poor and the weak some influence over the actions of the rich and the strong". For example, Annan said, developing countries should have a stronger voice in international financial institutions, "whose decisions can mean life or death for their people".

The departing U.N. secretary-general concluded in the American paper with a word to Americans. "More than ever, Americans, like the rest of humanity, need a functioning global system. Experience has shown, time and again, that the system works poorly when the United States remains aloof but it functions much better when there is farsighted U.S. leadership.

That gives American leaders of today and tomorrow a great responsibility. The American people must see that they live up to it."

Nonviolent Realism

Having debated the ethics of war for decades, Christians who seek effective means to combat terrorism sense that their traditional pacifist and just war positions both have limitations. A pacifism that refuses to recognize the reality of evil and stands above responding to the terrible violence of terrorism and genocide is not morally acceptable. And a pacifism that simply objects to war but has no alternative answer to the real threats of violence – whether sponsored by international networks of terror or by states – isn't very helpful. Nor is classical just war doctrine helpful when it simply offers endless scrutiny of the criteria for waging war, then usually ends up justifying wars rather than actually preventing any. Just war thinking has few answers to new forms of violence that are less vulnerable to traditional war-fighting methods.

When it comes to the problem of evil, we have been torn between two inadequate alternatives. One, which we will call liberal pacifism, often underestimates the realities of evil in our world, suggesting that the problems of violence merely derive from misunderstanding and miscommunication. Although those problems surely exist, they do not explain all the conflicts in our world today, some of which come from genuine threats and deliberate and determined evil. One of the worst forms of this option is the ascribing of evil only to the United States and the explaining away of other nations' destructive behavior by merely blaming the American superpower for prompting most of the bad things that happen.

The other response, which we will call conservative combat, often makes two fundamental mistakes. While recognizing the reality of evil, conservative combatants ascribe it only to our adversaries – they are evil and we are good – and aren't able to engage in critical self-reflection about the evil that also lies within us, which is a fundamental theological and spiritual mistake. The other miscalculation the conservative combatants often make is in believing that evil can easily be destroyed by military power. Often, though, the narrow military strategy of directly and aggressively combating evil can, inadvertently, result in its further spread or escalation, sparking a downward spiral of violence and counterviolence, and leading to a legion of unintended consequences. Evil is not always easily and quickly "smashed". Rather, it must sometimes be simply constrained or contained, surrounded and defused, undermined from within rather than from without, and patiently resisted and uprooted until the evil is eventually overcome. We can call that option nonviolent realism.

In contrast to liberal pacifists – who can dangerously minimize the evil in human nature – are some of the most realistic practitioners of serious conflict resolution based solidly in the biblical tradition. Examples include people such as John Paul Lederach and David Cortright from the Kroc Institute for International Peace Studies at the University of Notre Dame and Glen Stassen from Fuller Theological Seminary, people whose creative and effective strategies come out of Mennonite, Catholic, and evangelical traditions. Stassen and New Testament scholar Walter Wink have shown that the strategy of nonviolent realism was behind many of Jesus' instructions to his disciples, including his directive to "turn the other cheek" and to "go the extra mile" – actions meant to undermine the moral authority of the Roman occupiers.[15]

David Cortright, a research fellow at the Joan B. Kroc Institute for International Peace Studies at the University of Notre Dame and president of the Fourth Freedom Forum, talks about nonviolent realism – he uses the term "pragmatic pacifism" – in his new book *Building Peace*. Nonviolent realism, in his view, bridges the gap between traditional pacifism and the just-war tradition. "Pragmatic pacifism can be understood as a continuum of perspectives, beginning on one end with absolute rejection of any use of military force and extending across a range of options that allow for some limited use of force under specific conditions," Cortright explains. "The presumption is always against the use of force and in favor of settling differences without violence, but reality dictates that some uses of force may be necessary at times to assure justice and prevent the greater violence that often results when aggression is unconstrained."[16]

A limited and focused use of force, administered within the rule of law, is very different from aggressive, indiscriminate warfare. The former, akin to police power, as Mennonite theologian John Howard Yoder explains, is "subject to legal and moral constraints and is ethically superior to war". Distinctions matter, as Cortright puts it, and "a world of difference exists between unilateral, unprovoked military aggression and multilateral peace operations to protect civilian populations".

In fact, some analysts believe that developing more fully the concepts behind nonviolent realism might even contribute to eliminating war altogether. Gerald Schlabach, a professor of theology at the University of St. Thomas in St. Paul, Minnesota, asks in his new book *Just Policing, Not War,* "Is policing different enough from war that something more like policing (humanitarian military intervention) could possibly constitute a practice for abolishing war?"[17]

When it comes to war, I hear Christians regularly appeal to Romans 13 as if it gives carte blanche to any government that decides to go to war. But the text does nothing of the kind! Yes, we are to be "subject to the governing authorities". But the "rulers are not a terror to good conduct, but to bad" (Romans 13:3). They are the "servant of God to execute wrath on the wrongdoer". Clearly, the role of the state is to protect the innocent and punish the wrongdoers.

This passage is about policing a society and enforcing the rule of law – to protect everyone, especially the most vulnerable. The use of force, within proper boundaries, is appropriately given to the state for that task. How does this justify any war that a government decides to fight? Indeed, there is a basis in the text for a new concept of international policing and international law enforcement. What is most extraordinary are the verses in Romans 12 that immediately precede the famous Romans 13 passage:

> Bless those who persecute you; bless and do not curse them. Rejoice with those who rejoice, weep with those who weep. Live in harmony with one another; do not be haughty, but associate with the lowly; do not claim to be wiser than you are. Do not repay anyone evil for evil, but take thought for what is noble in the sight of all. If it is possible, so far as it depends on you, live peaceably with all. Beloved, never avenge yourselves, but leave room for the wrath of God; for it is written, "Vengeance is mine, I will repay, says the Lord." No, "if your enemies are hungry, feed them; if they are thirsty, give them something to drink; for by doing this you will heap burning coals on their heads." Do not be overcome by evil, but overcome evil with good. (Romans 12:14–21)

Here is a clear alternative to violence in response to our enemies, and an admonition to live in harmony with others and not to repay evil with evil. Don't "avenge" yourself, says Paul, but leave vengeance to God. A strategy is suggested here for how to confound and even defeat your enemies without killing them. Paul isn't saying just to be nice to your enemies. He's suggesting that doing the unexpected – feeding your enemies, for example – will confound their perceptions of you and perhaps their propaganda about you; it might really throw their plans and purposes off, and be like heaping "burning coals on their heads". This admonition, which directly precedes Romans 13, is hardly a call to war, but rather a smart plan of nonviolent direct action.

In discussions of foreign policy, clearly there are those who don't take evil seriously enough and whose counsel of pacifism often seems naïve. A biblical view of the human condition must take evil very seriously. Our experience in the last hundred years with Nazism, communism, imperialism, and terrorism are all painful confirmations.

The question is not whether evil is real, but rather how to confront and overcome it. In our war on terrorism, the challenge is how to combat evil without becoming evil ourselves. To fail to see the face of evil on September 11, 2001, is to be suffering from some kind of postmodern relativism. But to say "they are evil" and "we are good" is simply bad theology. It totally ignores the wisdom of Jesus, who encourages us not to see the speck in our neighbour's eye while ignoring the log in our own. That insight is crucial not only for personal relationships, but also for sound foreign policy.

Few people have known the reality of evil more than Soviet dissident Aleksandr Solzhenitsyn. In *The Gulag Archipelago,* Solzhenitsyn writes that the experience of being held for years in the Soviet prison system helped him understand that evil is not just outside of ourselves and good within. "[I]t was only when I lay there on rotting prison straw that I sensed within myself the first strivings of good," Solzhenitsyn writes. "Gradually it was disclosed to me that the line separating good and evil passes not through states, nor between classes, nor between political parties either – but right through every human heart – and then all human hearts. This line shifts. Inside us, it oscillates with the years. And even within hearts overwhelmed by evil, one small bridgehead of good is retained. And even in the best of all hearts, there remains... an un-uprooted small corner of evil."[18]

Similarly, the American theologian Reinhold Niebuhr, known for his "Christian realism", had this to say about the problem of evil: "The worst evils in the world are not done by evil people, but by good people who do not know they are not doing good."[19] If we are honest, each of us has that same struggle, as certainly every nation does. So who wins the battle of good versus evil – in our hearts and in the world of nations?

In an April 2007 *New York Times* opinion piece called "An Easter Sermon",[20] Robert Wright examined Jesus' admonitions about how to treat our enemies for what they have to teach us about political strategy. He argued that it would greatly change things if George Bush, who once named Jesus as his favourite philosopher, could match "the Bible's strategic savvy". Jesus taught us to "love your enemies and pray for those who persecute you". The point of the kindness is to "heap coals of fire" on your enemies' heads, as in the Romans 12 passage quoted above. The sense of the "coals of fire" reference, Wright says, "seems to be that undeserved kindness awakens the remorse and hence conversion of the enemies". In reality it doesn't always work that way, but it is demonstrably true that responding to our enemies with love rather than hatred can undermine their cause.

Wright suggests that the apostle Paul's ideas might be applied to the fight against terrorism in our context today, but he starts by pointing out that "Mr. Bush is more in the shoes of the Roman emperor than of Paul." But even though the tables are turned, we can still learn a lesson from Paul's logic: "Great powers, by mindlessly indulging retributive impulses, can give fuel to small but growing religious movements. If you want to deprive jihadists of ammunition, make it hard for them to persuade others to hate us."

How about overcoming evil with good? Is that just Christian pacifist talk or is it also good strategy? Fighting evil with evil, as recent events show, just fuels the fire – a powerful example is found in the photos depicting torture at Abu Ghraib, which helped recruit a new generation of al-Qaeda operatives. The main threats from terrorists are their ideas and their attitudes, and the way to counter the "virus of hatred" is with a countervailing way of acting – hence the power of "overcoming evil with good".

Finally, Wright argues that the key to good foreign policy may be "viral marketing", something he says both the early Christians and today's terrorists are good at. "One of the few things Usama bin Laden has in common with the Jesus of the Gospels is belief in the power of viral marketing. The ultimate in viral marketing was Jesus' ultimate sacrifice. Deemed a threat to the social order, he was crucified under Roman auspices. But the Romans forgot one thing: If you face a small but growing movement that threatens the imperial order, you shouldn't attack the men in ways that help the memes [the ideas they seek to get across]." The lesson, according to Wright, is clear: "Mr. Bush says his favourite philosopher is Jesus. One way to show it would be to spend less time repeating the mistake of the Romans and more time heeding the wisdom of Christ."

The Commitment

Conflict resolution, as they say, begins in the home. How we talk about other people and nations, especially how we talk about our "enemies", is crucial in shaping the worldview of our children. We must teach the "moral imagination" to understand how others who are different from us might think and feel – and why that may be essential for avoiding the next war.

One day my son Jack came home and, naming one of his friends at school, said, "He doesn't know the meaning of peace; he bit me on the playground." I asked, "What is the meaning of peace, Jack?" And he replied, "It means you don't hurt people." At his preschool, run by Quakers, Jack is taught to use words instead of hitting when there is a conflict between the children. He told me about "The Angry Rules: It's okay to be angry, but DON'T hurt others, don't hurt yourself, don't hurt property, DO talk about it." When he tells me the things he is learning, I often wish some of our Washington foreign policy elites could spend a day in his classroom. Sure, geopolitics is a bit more complicated than conflict on Quaker playgrounds, but there are principles that we desperately need to apply. And what our children see and hear us doing in relation to our conflicts will likely affect how they handle theirs.

Indeed, the arts of conflict resolution are becoming a serious course of study at an increasing number of the best educational institutions around the world. Local congregations and other community forums could and should become new laboratories for the teaching of those critical arts. I am not a utopian when it comes to human nature; I believe that human conflicts are inevitable. The big question is how we will handle them, whether they will be allowed to spin out of control, creating ever wider and deeper circles of costly conflict and horrible violence. Teaching and practising the arts of conflict resolution must become a communal curriculum.

Finally, it is time to put aside the assumption that war is the most effective response to evil. It is time to subject the methodology of war to the same scrutiny that its alternatives have received. Modern warfare, with all its unpredictability, costly consequences, and collateral damage, is increasingly failing to accomplish the purposes advertised by the war-makers. When it comes to whether or not to go to war, the burden of proof must no longer rest on those who do not want to begin violent conflicts, but on those who do. Is war, before every other method has been attempted, really the best or only course of action? Our commitment must be to ensure that these hard questions are always asked, that the case for war is thoroughly scrutinized, and that the nonviolent alternatives are completely explored.

Nonviolent alternatives to warfare are often harshly judged by those who invoke the canons of effectiveness, realism, and expected outcomes. It's time to evaluate war by the same criteria. With Iraq as our most recent and egregious example, war often fails to solve the problems it is intended to address. In the case of Iraq, the option of war has arguably made even worse everything it portended to solve. Other alternatives might have produced a far better result. They include a preference for international rather than pre-emptive solutions, the use of international law more than military force, a many-faceted response of carrots and sticks, and a robust peacekeeping force with the authority and capacity to enforce the demands of the international community – yes, including the use of force, but strictly targeted rather than indiscriminate force. In the Christian tradition, war has always been suspect at the point of moral and theological principles. It is only fair to demand that the methodology of war also submit to vigorous examination of whether it is really even effective, and that other methods receive consideration and development.

For example, the creation of a much stronger international court could be central to resolving many conflicts in the world today. War criminals could be indicted for their crimes, and international warrants issued for their arrest. Bringing the full weight of international opinion to bear against criminal behaviour would be much more effective if there were legal and institutional mechanisms for doing so. The international community could then isolate the perpetrators and undermine their power without attacking their people.

To enforce these judgments, we would need a well-trained and sufficiently funded international police force. It should be an *international* force, including personnel from both the region in question and other countries. If lightly armed, or even unarmed, a police force would bring necessary attention to the problem, but not the military force that can escalate conflict into crisis. And if world opinion and the authority of a court were behind such a force, criminals and dictators would be hesitant to attack it.

It is time for us to explore more seriously the alternatives to war – not just because modern warfare fails to meet ethical standards, but also because it is failing to resolve the genuine threats of evil in our time. We must find a better way.

There is another step that at least some among us will be called to take. That is the power of a good example. We need to begin to experiment with nonviolence as a strategy, not only for protest and civil disobedience, but for the resolution of the world's most difficult conflicts. As in war making, peacemaking will have its casualties, and the commitment required for the courageous strategies of conflict resolution is quite high. Already, small groups such as the Christian Peacemaker Teams have been doing such nonviolent experiments in some of the world's most dangerous places, by placing violence-reduction teams in crisis situations. This group "embraces the vision of unarmed intervention waged by committed peacemakers ready to risk injury and death in bold attempts to transform lethal conflict through the nonviolent power of God's truth and love". Some have already paid for such efforts with their lives. Tom Fox, a member of the Christian Peacemaker Teams, was taken captive in Iraq in 2005 and later killed by his captors. At a memorial service held in Washington, D.C., a fellow Christian peacemaker said of Fox, "He believed in following Christ's call to love God and love your neighbor and your enemy as yourself."

In many ways, the world depends on just that commitment.

I I

INTEGRITY AND ACCOUNTABILITY

Doing the Right Thing and the Question of Leadership

One evening an old Cherokee told his grandson about a battle that goes on inside people. He said, "My son, the battle is between two 'wolves' inside us all. One is Evil. It is anger, envy, jealousy, sorrow, regret, greed, arrogance, self-pity, guilt, resentment, inferiority, lies, false pride, superiority, and ego. The other is Good. It is joy, peace, love, hope, serenity, humility, kindness, benevolence, empathy, generosity, truth, compassion, and faith." The grandson thought about it for a minute and then asked his grandfather: "Which wolf wins?" The old Cherokee simply replied, "The one you feed."

I do not understand my own actions. For I do not do what I want, but I do the very thing I hate. Now if I do what I do not want, I agree that the law is good. But in fact it is no longer I that do it, but sin that dwells within me. For I know that nothing good dwells within me, that is, in my flesh. I can will what is right, but I cannot do it. For I do not do the good I want, but the evil I do not want is what I do. Now if I do what I do not want, it is no longer I that do it, but sin that dwells within me. So I find it to be a law that when I want to do what is good, evil lies close at hand. For I delight in the law of God in my inmost self, but I see in my members another law at war with the law of my mind, making me captive to the law of sin that dwells in my members. Wretched man that I am! Who will rescue me from this body of death? Thanks be to God through Jesus Christ our Lord! So then, with my mind I am a slave to the law of God, but with my flesh I am a slave to the law of sin. (Romans 7:15–25)

Whoever walks in integrity walks securely, but whoever follows perverse ways will be found out. (Proverbs 10:9)

The integrity of the upright guides them, but the crookedness of the treacherous destroys them. (Proverbs 11:3)

The wicked are overthrown by their evildoing, but the righteous find a refuge in their integrity. (Proverbs 14:32)

The word *integrity* was the most-looked-up word in dictionaries in the year 2005.[1] (The dictionary defines it as "Firm adherence to a code of, especially, moral... values.") What does that tell us? The hunger for integrity – both public and personal – grows ever deeper in our postmodern world of moral relativism. Corruption in government is a growing concern across the political spectrum; in fact it was named the leading issue in exit polls taken after the 2006 midterm elections.

In a political culture awash with scandals, rolling back the corporate capture of government, giving up pork for a better political diet, securing both electoral and lobbying reform, and taming the special interests that now literally write our laws on the floor of Congress – all would be good places to start the process of renewing democracy. As the flawed voting procedures of recent elections have painfully demonstrated, even our elections are not safeguarded.

We must be concerned about the process of politics and not just the content – the pressures and temptations of fund-raising for our elected officials, campaign finance reform, civic and business practices, and truth-telling in both business and politics. And we must address the huge responsibility of the media in all of this.

The corruption in personal behaviour and relationships is also eroding the health and well-being of our society. Faithfulness in marriage, responsibility in raising the next generation, diligence in work, honesty in finances, loyalty in friendship, and generosity with neighbours are all threads that either bind our body politic together or make us unravel. We must pay close attention to both the public and private sides of the "politics of integrity".

The Capital of Corruption

After the 2006 elections, the nation and world watched the new Congress to see if changes in power would bring real changes in both approach and results. Just as in 1974, when President Gerald Ford called our nation to healing, Congress had a chance to begin to overcome the cynicism about government that has become so widespread, to combat the extreme partisan warfare that has so polarized and paralyzed our nation's public life, to renew the concept of the common good over individual gain and special-interest control, and to think and act boldly and creatively on the biggest issues our nation faces. The public rightly wondered, will Congress rise to the challenge?

In the past few years, corruption has been one of the primary issues motivating voters to seek change. The nation needs to see its political leadership make serious reforms in congressional ethics, the starting point for policy debates. Will changes be cosmetic or substantial? Americans are hungry for a new tone and new ways of practically meeting real needs. Honesty and transparency are moral values, too, according to the voters, and these two virtues must now set the stage for improving everything from our political discourse to our reputation in the world.

People across America want a better political process, one that restores core democratic principles. We cannot produce the change our country needs to help those who are hurting without changing a system corrupted by money. This will require a comprehensive package of reforms that starts with a ban on lobbyist gifts and paid travel and goes on to strengthen inadequate disclosure requirements around earmarks. Broader campaign finance reform, electoral reform, and ethics reform will be critical for restoring integrity to our democratic system. Congress still refuses to resolve the scandal of pork-barrel spending and the ability of special-interest money to determine policy decisions.

In recent years, three Republican members of Congress were indicted because of financial and political scandals, and two have been imprisoned. Randy "Duke" Cunningham (R-CA) was convicted of conspiracy to commit bribery, fraud, and tax evasion and is currently serving an eight-year sentence. Robert Ney (R-OH) pled guilty to conspiracy to defraud the United States and is serving a thirty-month sentence. A former House majority leader, Tom DeLay, was indicted on charges of conspiracy to violate campaign finance laws and resigned his congressional seat. A Democratic member of Congress, William Jefferson (D-LA), was discovered to have $90,000 in cash, allegedly from bribery payments, divided among various frozen-food containers in his freezer. He has been indicted, but so far remains in office. Another Republican member of Congress, Mark Foley (R-FL), chairman of the Congressional Caucus on Missing and Exploited Children, was caught sending salacious e-mails and engaging in predatory behavior toward teenage male congressional pages.

When a party has been in power too long, just staying in power becomes more important than truth-telling, which was also true when Democrats controlled both houses of Congress. As conservative Richard Viguerie candidly wrote in *The Washington Times,* "The Republicans have become what they beheld in this town when the Democrats were in control – presiders over a culture of corruption, only it far exceeds what they complained about with the Democrats."[2]

The immediate response of many Democrats to Republican scandals is to jump on the news for partisan gain. And of course, many Republicans leap on scandals involving Democratic members of Congress for their partisan gain. But the roots of this crisis go far deeper than partisanship. Diana Butler Bass wrote on the God's Politics blog that "we know that sin is not the exclusive possession of any political party. The darkness that stalks us is neither Republican nor Democratic. It is part of the human condition."[3]

We need political leaders, of both parties, who believe in the importance of integrity, humility, honesty, and a commitment to the common good – and are willing to challenge their own party's desire for power at the expense of moral principle. And we need a pledge by all of us to make fundamental changes in our culture and support political leaders who will work for those changes.

Political leaders aren't the only ones who have fallen; some of the biggest scandals in recent days have involved religious leaders. All the scandals remind us again of the basics – that we are all sinners and utterly dependent on the grace of God. The failures of leaders, and our own failures, call us to remember why we all need that grace. We should also remember the need for humility and forgiveness in response to such painful revelations. Some critics of religion say the scandals in the faith community show that all Christians and their leaders are hypocrites. That is not true, but it does remind us that all Christians, and their leaders, are sinners with their own "darkness", in deep need of the light of Christ. "None are righteous, no not one," wrote the apostle Paul, and we perhaps should be reminded by these tragic circumstances not to expect so much of leaders – who are every bit as human and fallible as those they lead, and every bit as dependent on God's grace.

In a high-profile religious sex scandal, former National Association of Evangelicals president Ted Haggard confessed his "sexual immorality" to his home congregation. A particularly insightful comment came in his letter of confession: "The public person I was wasn't a lie; it was just incomplete." That's true of most, if not all, leaders. Haggard's letter also contained a warning for public leaders: "When I stopped communicating about my problems, the darkness increased and finally dominated me. As a result, I did things that were contrary to everything I believe." Haggard and his family are paying a high price for his behaviour, and he himself said he should be "disciplined and corrected". In every tragic situation like this, there are redemptive possibilities. In his letter, Haggard asks his congregation to "demonstrate the incredible grace that is available to all of us."[4]

As a parent, I grimace watching the news of each developing scandal in the nation's capital, just miles from my living room. Sadly, I am not surprised. My kids are growing up in a culture that has lost its way – a poisonous society in which sex and money permeate our news, television shows, movies, advertising; almost the entire popular culture. When political power is thrown into the mix, the latest scandal is never a shock.

Money, Sex, and Power

One of the central problems for a leader is the need to learn self-control, especially in the three classic areas of money, sex, and power. We live in a society driven by greed and materialism, where the mere possession of money (regardless of how it was accumulated) is one of the most important measures of success, influence, and power. We also live in a sex-saturated culture of alluring images, illusions, and symbols, one in which personal attractiveness is a much-sought-after goal. And we are captivated by power, often the kind of power that is almost entirely egocentric. Just having power has become an end in itself; we seldom ask how or for what that power is going to be used.

It's no wonder that the early Christian monastics focused on money, sex, and power as the primary battlegrounds of the spiritual life. Their answers to these three were poverty, chastity, and obedience. What might those commitments look like today?

Wes Granberg-Michaelson is a longtime friend and was once managing editor of *Sojourners* magazine. Wes is a denominational church leader (the Reformed Church in America) and was formerly on the staff of U.S. Senator Mark Hatfield. He indeed knows leadership "inside out". In his book *Leadership from Inside Out*,[5] he examines the problem and what the monastic commitments might mean in our day and age.

> Three human needs have the capacity to destroy any leader: money, sex, and power. It is no wonder that even early monastic communities established three vows for those called to religious leadership: poverty, chastity, and obedience. These vows were, of course, severe protective measures to guard against the potentially fatal compulsion of these three needs. But they did underscore the crucial importance of controlling those needs that otherwise

can totally control us – money, sex, and power. Individuals whose lives are controlled by the unbridled quest for any one of these eventually will find their effectiveness as leaders put in jeopardy and may be likely as well to damage the institution they were called to serve.

These ancient monastic commitments have contemporary equivalents, writes Granberg-Michaelson.

Obviously, vows of poverty, chastity, and obedience are not the only safeguards for dealing with the temptations of money, sex, and power in our lives. Since the Reformation of Martin Luther and John Calvin in the sixteenth century, the church has stressed faithful stewardship, covenantal love, and self-giving service as healthy responses to these human realities, with the emphasis placed on controlling, directing, and redeeming the needs for money, sex, and power rather than denying them.

The Reformation tradition stressed that money, sex, and power are not evil in and of themselves but rather are a part of God's good creation. The issue is how they are used. Yet all three are indeed mortal dangers to our souls, and we are naïve if we think we are immune to their destructive power. Granberg-Michaelson writes, "Of course they have potential for good." But he adds, "Money, sex, and power have a subtle but persistent ability, especially in contemporary society, to cloud our judgment, to corrode our values, and to capture our will, in the end, leading us to behave in ways that are flagrantly irresponsible." When it comes to finding leaders we can trust, he says:

We should look for individuals who have demonstrated the inner capacity to deal creatively and responsibly with money, sex, and power in their lives… For centuries men and women have followed paths and practices that transform these three needs into joyous gifts rather than destructive compulsions. Leaders who can be trusted to guide the evolution of institutions into the future will be those who lead well-examined lives, who have recovered spiritual practices that liberate them from the power of compulsions and free their energy for outward service.

Robert Parham of the Baptist Center for Ethics has also written about the scandals plaguing the nation's politics in light of the three monastic categories and says, "Money, sex, and power have a moral toxicity when mixed and misused." He quotes author Richard Foster: "These issues seem inseparably intertwined. Money manifests itself in power. Sex is used to acquire both money and power. And power is often called 'the best aphrodisiac'." Parham warns against excusing bad personal behaviour or minimizing its importance in public life, and counsels against the idea that since "everybody is doing it" it must be all right.

Parham agrees with Foster, who argues for modern equivalents for the monk's poverty, chastity, and obedience. Foster writes that money, sex, and power, from a biblical perspective, have both their dark and light sides, and he suggests three practices today that would respond to the classic temptations – namely, the practices of simplicity, fidelity, and service.[6]

Feeding the Wolves

Our culture is in the business of feeding the wolves – unfortunately, mostly the bad ones. In fact, some have observed that modern advertising directly appeals to (and feeds) what have historically been known as the seven deadly sins – pride, greed, envy, anger, lust, gluttony, and sloth.

Gandhi incorporated a version of the deadly sins in his instructions to his young disciples in the ashrams of India. Gandhi's seven deadly social sins are politics without principle, wealth without work, commerce without morality, pleasure without conscience, education without character, science without humanity, and worship without sacrifice. Gandhi's list of sins resonates deeply with people's experience today and diagnoses accurately our modern moral morass.

What are we feeding – the evil or the good? Are we focusing our minds and hearts on destructive habits or are we nurturing and reinforcing the virtues? Whatever occupies our thoughts and gets our attention will shape our choices and, therefore, our lives. Values must be reinforced by habit, by discipline, and even by ritual if they are to have real power in our lives. We must always keep in mind that the consumer culture is also actively reinforcing its values – often in direct contradiction to the values of our faith or conscience.

Most of us still believe that we think our way into new ways of living, but the truth is that we live our way into new ways of thinking. The former is indeed what we learn in school and are taught in most of the other settings of our lives. But I don't think that reflects genuine reality. We need to focus on our habits, choices, disciplines, and decisions, rather than just on our thoughts. What are we feeding?

We have inherited a particularly Greek way of understanding the truth – that we simply master a body of material and then repeat it back on cue or merely implement the things we have learned. In contrast, the Hebrew way of understanding suggests that we really don't know the truth until it has affected our lives in some way. For the Greeks and for most of us, thinking precedes living; but for the Hebrews, living was meant to change thinking. The latter is both more biblical and more revealing of how most of us really do learn and change.

The Question of Leadership

What we look for in ourselves and in our leaders comes back to the issue of integrity – saying what we mean and doing what we say. Integrity is what people most long for in their leaders and in their own lives. At some level, at some time in our lives, most of us will provide "leadership" in some circle of people or activities – in our workplace, in our congregation, in civic organizations, in community activities, in political action, or in our own families as husbands and wives, fathers and mothers. Perhaps the leadership we demonstrate as parents is the most important of all. Parents are the chief example of moral authority and integrity for their children, either for good or ill, and the principal role models for the young. Questions of leadership are not just for the elites; they affect us all.

The alternative to bad leadership must not become no leadership; it should rather be good leadership. As obvious as that point should be, the massive and very public failures of so many leaders, who have misused or abused their authority in almost every sector of our society – political, civil, business, and even religious – has helped create a powerful antileadership culture. The popular bumper sticker QUESTION AUTHORITY says it all in its encapsulation of the cultural antagonism toward leadership. But without leadership – good leadership – we are in serious trouble. Leadership can appeal to our best or worst values and instincts, take us backward or move us forward, further divide us or bring us together to accomplish important things. Without leadership we are unlikely to act together to fulfill our best impulses and values.

There are many fine books these days about leadership skills and techniques, particularly from the business world. But while knowledge is important to the development of good leadership, wisdom is even more crucial. We need to learn not just the skills of leadership, but also the spirituality of leadership. We will learn the latter less from books than from people who are effective leaders. Good leaders need good mentors, and mentoring may be the most important thing a good leader can do to raise up the next generation.

Leadership comes with action. Whether it is leading a meeting or an organization, drawing diverse people together or helping them clarify a unified message, resolving conflicts or offering a prophetic word when one is necessary, we lead by action. But we cannot be effective leaders unless we are always seeking to develop our own moral and spiritual integrity.

We need nothing less than a new ethic of leadership in today's climate of corruption. Encouraging others to mistrust leadership may be a crucial corrective, but what we really need is a deeper social quest for a genuinely trustworthy leadership. Accepting our vulnerabilities rather than denying them is central to good leadership, as is the formation of character as a lifelong pursuit. We need a style of leadership based not only on talent but also on integrity.

Leaders must learn how to identify values, build integrity, and sustain vision, says Granberg-Michaelson. He stresses that listening for one's calling is essential for good leadership, as is a self-definition that is not just about the work. Freedom from inner needs requires a spiritual self-awareness that can save us (and others around us) from our unresolved issues. Don't try to be a well-rounded leader, says Granberg-Michaelson, but rather know your own gifts and strengths well enough to match them with what your co-workers can bring. In the end, it is better to understand yourself than to force the others around you to keep trying to figure you out! And self-knowledge requires a spiritual journey.

Leaders can change organizational cultures, instill new values, and get people to decide how they will decide things, not just what they will decide. Good leadership should not focus solely on the "techniques" of effective leadership but also on how to see the "big picture" and "cast the vision". But, Granberg-Michaelson says, "Vision without strategy is like faith without works." There is no best leadership style, as some would suggest; different styles of leadership are called for in different situations, at different stages in an organization's life, or even at different periods of a leader's life.

The challenge of organizational growth is enormous, and even more so is what Granberg-Michaelson calls the "arduous journey of transformation" for leaders. "Charisma alone in a leader is not enough, for inspiring people is not the same as leading them," he says. I will testify to the fact that leadership often feels, as Wes says, like "driving by faith". His book is full of good driving lessons for leaders. But what he and all the most insightful authors on leadership tell us is that leadership is vitally connected to spirituality.

The Personal and the Public

Some say that leaders should be judged only on the basis of their policies, that personal moral failures, although regrettable, are not really relevant to their jobs. Those who focus incessantly on personal morality often end up looking like the Pharisees who were ready to stone the woman taken in adultery (John 8:1–11). But what can we learn from the Washington-produced dramas of the combustible mix of sex, money, and power? What lasting wisdom about leadership is left after the curtain is drawn and the individual morality plays go off the air? How can the nation's moral scandals become "teachable moments" on the nature of leadership that the country can reflect upon? We quickly learn that these are not left or right issues, and that they have little to do with either side's political agenda.

First, effective public leadership cannot be severed from the trustworthiness of personal character. Ethics and integrity do matter, and not just superficially. Leaders need to be believed. They have to engender trust not only in their policies but also in their judgment. They must create a climate of faithfulness to shared commitments among colleagues and supporters. Thus, leadership derives credibility from example, and not simply from pronouncements. In times of crisis, people follow courage rather than charm.

"Successful" leadership has sometimes meant skillfully segregating public policy from personal integrity. But morality in politics is not defined solely by the pragmatic effectiveness of policies. Conversely, morality cannot exclusively be seen in terms of personal moral behavior that turns a blind eye to the sins of social injustice. A firewall between the personal and public dimensions of our lives is a secular fiction, and it is dangerous to both people and politics. Faith nurtures a healthy congruity between one's inner and outer lives. Its understanding of sin and vision of wholeness weave together the social and the personal. Any discerning ethic of leadership does the same.

Second, a poll-driven politics lacks a moral foundation and vision. Political leaders should not trust their pollsters more than they trust their pastors. Some leaders have the moral and political authority to shape, and even change, public opinion. For that, a moral compass is needed – a compass whose needle points toward where we, as a society, should be heading, rather than simply toward the next election. Too many politicians today try to govern by engaging in perpetual campaigns. As a result, their overriding principle becomes satisfying 51 per cent of the voters rather than serving a compelling moral and political vision for our society. Style is not more important than substance; despite the commercial slogan, image isn't everything.

While on a horseback-riding trek with my family in Colorado, I got an insight about leadership. I was focused on my two young boys riding horses for the first time, as the expert high-school horsewomen gave us instructions. They said to watch carefully where we were going. "Don't the horses do that?" I asked. "Well, actually, horses don't look ahead very well," one of them replied. "They just keep looking from side to side and have little forward-looking vision." *Wow*, I thought, as the revelation hit me. *We've got all kinds of political leaders just like that in Washington, D.C.!*

Third, sexual ethics are important. One doesn't have to be prudish or puritanical to worry about a sexual ethic based on the consumer model. The commodification of sexuality in the media for purposes of advertising and entertainment, and its degradation in exploitative or manipulative relationships, is indeed a sin because such an ethic can be so abusive and destructive of the human spirit. A real ethical choice today is between a sexuality that is merely recreational and one that is covenantal. Sexuality is meant to be enormously enjoyable and fulfilling, but because of how fragmenting or integrating sexual intimacy can be for human beings, the context of the relationship and the commitment or lack of commitment it contains are of obvious significance.

Are *Sex in the City* and *Desperate Housewives* our reigning cultural paradigms now when it comes to sexuality? Or is the reconnection of sexual intimacy with commitment a future worth fighting for? That's the question I hear most often from young people, and, perhaps surprising to some, many are moving back (or forward) to waiting for the committed intimacy of marriage rather than settling for the now-normative cultural pattern of serial sexual dating.

Value-free sexual ethics have had devastating consequences for our society, especially for the young, and most brutally for the poor. Leaders don't create the nation's declining sexual ethics, but it's tragic when their actions merely reveal and help support them.

The question "What's more important, a leader's personal morality or his or her public policy?" may be the wrong one. The more important issue may be the connection between the personal and the public. The idea that public leadership can be partitioned off from personal integrity is a dangerous illusion. The fact that several past political leaders have gotten away with doing so hardly establishes a reliable pattern of leadership for the future. Old styles of leadership are now passing, and new models are already in formation.

The information revolution has subverted our systems of hierarchical authority, transforming our institutions and the imperatives of leadership. The task of leaders today is to articulate vision, build trust, and create an open climate of integrity that facilitates decisions. Anyone who wants to be a leader in the twenty-first century needs to sustain values, nurture community, and clarify our common mission. That is equally true for a pastor, a principal, a president, or a pope.

In the end, leaders lead by behaviour and not just by skill. In any institution, people yearn for leadership that is morally seamless. Yes, they want imaginative and effective policies. But they also desire leaders whose examples walk their talk. A healthier blend of talent and character is needed to shape our next generation of leaders.

That coherence is quite different from the futile quest for "perfect" leaders. Those of us who seek to embed our lives in religious faith know full well the tenacity of selfish, sinful behaviour. The power, adulation, and pressure inherent in positions of leadership make leaders even more likely to fall victim to their own vulnerabilities – whether it is pride, promiscuity, or political prostitution. Because of this reality, leaders in particular need to undertake the difficult task of self-examination. That's why leaders bear a particular responsibility to nurture their private souls and not just their public personas.

We all have flaws, as Jesus was quick to point out to those who would have stoned the adulterous woman. But we don't get past our flaws by denying them and trying to manage the public fallout. In his or her heart, every leader knows that this denial is – in the words of Jesus – the path to destruction.

Mature leaders are those who not only rely on their strengths but also learn how to deal consciously with their weaknesses. In some safe and secure place, they bring their brokenness into the light and turn toward inner coherence. Thus they guard themselves against the disintegration of their inward life that could finally result in outward paralysis. Dealing with flaws and weaknesses is important for anyone, but especially for those who have responsibility for others.

In the future, we need leaders with the ability to navigate the troubled waters of their inner lives as well as the turbulent seas of public discourse. If institutions and societies are ultimately shaped by both the personal and the public ethics of their leaders, the concept of "spiritual formation" should become increasingly important as a component of the education needed for leadership development. Ultimately, personal integrity is vital to public trust.

Leadership instills vision, values, trust, mission, and community. These rest upon the habits of the heart. Perhaps the main question to ask about leaders concerns the trustworthiness of their moral compass, upon which all their judgments depend. Effective leadership is finally sustained not just by what people say but by who they are.

The Commitment

The commitment for this chapter is less about what we do than about how we do it. It is to conduct our lives, make our choices, follow our vocations, and raise our children with a central dedication to integrity always in mind. It means that anything worth doing begins at home or, as they say in my neighbourhood, "It's not enough to talk the talk; you've got to walk the talk."

This commitment requires us not to separate our personal values and public choices; it compels us to reconnect our inner lives with their outward expression. As my friends at Washington, D.C.'s Church of the Saviour remind us, the "inward journey" is vitally connected to the "outward journey".

It means to answer the classical temptations to money, sex, and power with simplicity, fidelity, and service. It recognizes that we're all leaders in one circle or another but requires that the cultural models of dominance be replaced by what Robert Greenleaf calls "servant leaders".

And it means not to rely too much on ourselves, but rather to trust in radical grace. Our accomplishments can be fleeting, but integrity survives. Finally, it means, surrounded by so many options, that the best and safest course is to just do the right thing.

Ultimately, integrity can save and change the world.

WHAT'S ACCEPTABLE,
WHAT'S POSSIBLE

Notes to the Next Generation

I was in Minneapolis and, after speaking, was signing books. I looked up from the table and saw that a little girl was next in line. "How old are you?" I asked. "I'm eleven," she said. I stopped the line; I wanted to know what she thought of what she had just heard. I asked her what she got from tonight. "Well... I think we are just going to have to change the world!" "And who is going to do that?" I asked her with a smile. "I think people like me!" she replied. I told her story the next night in Tacoma, Washington, halfway across the country. Sure enough, in the book-signing line afterward there was another little girl. She grinned at me and just said, "Nine!" So I told both their stories the next night in Seattle. There in line at the book-signing table was the littlest girl of all. When she approached the table, she said, "I think I'm the youngest so far. I'm eight." Even though she was very young, I couldn't help asking this child what had made sense to her that night. She paused thoughtfully for a moment and then answered, "When you talked about that silent tsunami that is killing so many children every day because of poverty – children like me... I was just sitting there and started to think to myself, If I'm a Christian, I better do something about that." She was in the third grade. The next week, back in my class at Harvard, I told my students about the three little girls. "If some of you want to help lead this new movement for social change," I said, "you'd better get moving because a whole new generation is coming up fast behind you!"

I see many signs of change from a new generation. Almost every week now, I'm talking to fourteen-year-olds about faith, politics, and how to change the world. Those three little girls really touched me, and I believe there is a great deal of both wisdom and hope in what they have to say to us.

First, the kids believe the world needs to be changed. The truth is that the rest of us do, too. The most consistent poll in America is the one regularly reporting that most Americans think their country is moving in the wrong direction. We're not happy with things as they are. But people also express very low approval ratings for the politicians in Washington, who are perceived to be part of the problem. And they don't think much better of the media, who always bring us the bad news. The public is also weary of so-called religious leaders who have become politically divisive and partisan, seeming to want to ram their theology down people's throats. All that adds up to both cynicism and apathy – which people justify by concluding that nothing can be changed. Resignation is more prominent than inspiration among many Americans.

But not with these young girls – they have decided the world needs to change. I found the kids very refreshing. We must never give up on change, because the hope for it literally keeps us alive. It's time to believe in change again, to dare to dream new possibilities. And the little children may lead us.

Second, the young people are often very specific about what needs to change. Talking with them after speaking events, I have learned that certain facts about the world strike them as just plain wrong. They aren't just complaining; rather, they are learning about things that are unacceptable to them – simply unacceptable. And that is always how change begins; when things we have long accepted are no longer acceptable, often first to a new generation that can't understand why we have accepted those things for so long. Again, the children's refusal to accept what the rest of the world does is very refreshing.

Third, the kids I speak with connect their desire to change the world directly with their faith – "If I am a Christian, I better do something about that." Their spirituality, even at this young age, has sensitized them to injustice and given them a sense of responsibility for it. Faith is a motivator; it inspires them to think they ought to try to make a difference. These are simple commitments, but ones that historically have led to change. Perhaps their childlike and simple faith will inspire ours.

There is a story I often tell in commencement speeches, about a very different group of "graduates" from the ones I usually address. Once I was invited to speak, not for the commencement at a great university or seminary, but to the inmates at Sing Sing Prison in upstate New York. The invitation letter came from the prisoners themselves, and it sounded like a good idea. So I wrote back asking when they wanted me to come. In his return letter, the young Sing Sing inmate replied, "Well, we're free most nights! We're kind of a captive audience here." Arrangements were made, and the prison officials were very generous in giving us a room deep in the bowels of that infamous prison facility – just me and about eighty guys for four hours.

I will never forget what one of those young prisoners said to me that night. "Jim, all of us at Sing Sing are from only about five neighbourhoods in New York City," he said. "It's like a train. You get on the train when you are about nine or ten years old. And the train ends up here at Sing Sing."

But this young prisoner had experienced a spiritual conversion. Now he and many of his fellow inmates were students, too, studying in a unique programme of the New York Theological Seminary to obtain a Certificate of Theological Studies – behind the walls of the prison. They graduated when their sentences were up! Here's what that young man at Sing Sing told me he was planning to do upon his graduation: "When I get out, I'm going to go back and stop that train." Two years later, I was in New York City speaking to a "town meeting" on ending poverty, and guess who was up front helping to lead the meeting? Two of the young men from Sing Sing were now back home trying to stop the train, and one was the youth minister of a black church in Harlem. Now that is exactly the kind of moral decision we desperately need today from the graduates of Sing Sing and all our major universities.

Each new generation has a chance to alter two basic definitions of reality in our world – what is acceptable and what is possible. If we are from the religious community, there is a third chance – also to shape what we mean by the word *faith*.

First, what is acceptable? There are always great inhumanities that we inflict upon one another in this world, great injustices that cry out to God for redress, and great gaps in our moral recognition of them. When the really big offences are finally corrected, finally changed, it is usually because something has happened to change our perception of the moral issues at stake.

That something is this: the moral contradiction we have long lived with is no longer acceptable to us. What we had accepted, or ignored, or denied, finally gets our attention, and we decide that we just cannot and will not live with it any longer. But until that happens, the injustice and misery continue.

It often takes a new generation to make that decision – that something people have long tolerated just won't be tolerated anymore. So I ask students and young people these questions: What are you going to no longer accept in our world? What will you refuse to tolerate, now that you will soon be making the decisions that matter?

Will it be acceptable to you that three billion people in our world today – half of God's children – live on less than $2 a day, that more than one billion live on less than $1 a day, that the gap between the life expectancy in the rich places and the poor places in our world is now forty years – meaning that death has become a "social disease" – or that thirty thousand more children will die globally, today, from needless, senseless, and utterly preventable poverty and disease? Many people don't know those facts or, if they are vaguely aware of them, have never given them a second thought.

That's the way it usually is. We have "easy" explanations for why poverty or some other calamity exists, for why it can't be changed – all of which make us feel better about ourselves – or we are just more concerned with lots of other things. We really don't have to care. So we tolerate the injustice and just keep looking the other way.

But then something changes. Something gets our attention, something goes deeper than it has before and hooks us in the places we call the heart, the soul, the spirit. And once we've crossed over to really seeing, hearing, touching, smelling, and tasting the injustice, we can never look back. It is now unacceptable to us. What we see now offends us, offends our understanding of the sanctity and dignity of life, offends our notions of fairness and justice, offends our most basic values; it violates our idea of the common good and starts to tug at our deepest places. We cross the line of unacceptability. We become intolerant of the injustice.

But just changing our notion of what is unacceptable isn't enough; we must also change our perception of what is possible.

I believe that the real battle, the big struggle of our times, is the fundamental choice between cynicism and hope. On the road, it's what I always call "the big choice". The choice between cynicism and hope is ultimately a spiritual choice, but one that has enormous political consequences. I always say that hope is not a feeling, it is a decision. And the decision for hope is based upon what you believe at the deepest levels – whatever we call faith. You choose hope, not as a naïve wish, but with your eyes wide open to the reality of the world – just like the cynics who have not made the decision for hope.

I believe it will take a new generation to reach the "tipping point" in the struggle to eliminate the world's most extreme poverty or alter our course of environmental degradation. At the beginning of a new century and millennium, I see a new generation of young activists coming of age and talking about globalization, climate change, HIV/AIDS, and reducing global poverty.

I am also convinced that global poverty reduction, for example, will not be accomplished without a spiritual engine, that history is best changed by social movements with a spiritual foundation. That's what has always made the difference in the Great Awakenings of the past – remember the examples of the abolition of slavery, women's suffrage, and civil rights. This will be no different.

Many of you who have gotten this far in the book are from that new generation. You are bright, gifted, and committed. There are probably many people who tell you that you have great potential, and they are right.

In that regard, I would encourage each of you to think about your vocation more than just your career. There is a difference. From the outside, those two tracks may look very much alike, but asking the vocational question rather than just considering your career options will take you much deeper. The key is to ask why you might take one path instead of another. It's about choosing to do something for deeper reasons than merely because you can, or because your background has steered you in a certain direction. The key is to ask who you really are and who you want to become. It is to ask what you believe you are supposed to do with your life.

Whether you are religious or not, I would invite you to consider your calling, more than just the many opportunities presented to you. That means connecting your best talents and skills to your truest and deepest values, making sure your mind is in sync with your soul as you plot your next steps. Don't just go where you're directed or invited, but rather where your own moral compass leads you. And don't accept other people's notions of what is possible or realistic; dare to dream things, and don't be afraid to take risks.

You do have great potential, but that potential will be most fulfilled if you follow the leanings of conscience and the language of the heart more than just the dictates of the market, whether economic or political. Those in power want our smartest young people just to manage the systems of the world. But what a waste of real talent! Rather than merely fitting into systems, ask how you can change them. You're both smart enough and talented enough to do that. That's your greatest potential.

Ask where your gifts intersect with the groaning needs of the world – right there is your vocation. The antidote to cynicism is not optimism, but action. And action is finally born out of hope. Try to remember that. The key is to believe that the world can be changed, because it is only that belief that ever changes the world. And if not us, who will believe it? If not you, then who?

What is really possible? Hebrews 11:1 says: "Now faith is the substance of things hoped for, the conviction of things not seen." My best paraphrase of that is still this: Hope is believing in spite of the evidence, and then watching the evidence change. Or, as Jesus said, "All things can be done for the one who believes" (Mark 9:23).

It is absolutely vital to make the connection between spirituality and social justice. In affluent societies, the quest for spirituality can easily lead to narcissism, with spiritual well-being becoming just another commodity to consume. Walls of books in our largest bookstores promise us the secrets of how to become spiritually aware, sensitive, balanced, whole, deep, successful, and even prosperous – for a price, of course. That's why I believe the path to genuine spirituality, especially in wealthy nations, must be disciplined by the struggle for justice. Being accountable to the facts of injustice and the need to change them is the only way for the spiritual life to have real authenticity. Without a commitment to justice, the search for spirituality can easily become self-serving.

On the other hand, the battle for justice, without the deep roots of spirituality, can quickly lead to burnout, despair, anger, and even violence. Facing or living with the realities of injustice and oppression can be overwhelming, even crushing to the human spirit. Unless our spirits are regularly nourished by spiritual practices and resources, the activist journey can easily lead to exhaustion. To be a social activist for the long term, you must also become a spiritual contemplative. And to be a contemplative with integrity, you must also engage the world where it needs to be changed.

Learn about people like Archbishop Desmond Tutu, who helped lead the fight to end apartheid in South Africa, and how central prayer was to him. In his compilation *An African Prayer Book,* Tutu wrote about prayer, "Saint Julian of Norwich says prayer 'is yearning, beseeching, and beholding'. We are made for God, we yearn to be filled with the fullness of God, and so we come asking the one who is always eager to give."[1]

Reflect upon the work of Trappist monk Thomas Merton, who lived a contemplative life in the Kentucky hills surrounding Gethsemane Monastery but guided many activists in the social struggles of his time. Merton insisted that the life of prayer cannot be removed from the problems of the world, explaining in his *Conjectures of a Guilty Bystander* that "the whole illusion of a separate holy existence is a dream". In *No Man is an Island,* Merton emphasized the connection between action and contemplation, saying that "action is charity looking outward to other [people] and contemplation is charity drawn inward to its own divine source. Action is the stream and contemplation is the spring." For Merton, meaningful activity in the world required that it be based on an experience of God in prayerful solitude. As he wrote in *Contemplation in a World of*

Action, "Without the deep root of wisdom and contemplation, Christian action would have no meaning and no purpose."[2]

Revolutionary Prayer

I pray, but there are many misunderstandings about prayer. For many, prayer is talking to God, sometimes with a great list of requests and needs – sort of like a child's Christmas list mailed to Santa Claus.

But at least for me, prayer is more often becoming a time of listening rather than talking. There is so much noise in our world and our lives (much of our own making); prayer becomes a quiet space that enables us to stop talking long enough to see what God might be trying to say to us. The disciplines of prayer, silence, and contemplation as practised by the monastics and mystics are precisely that – stopping the noise, slowing down, and becoming still so that God can break through all our activity and noise to speak to us. Prayer serves to put all parts of our lives in God's presence, reminding us of how holy our humanity really is.

And also for us, prayer is the act of reclaiming our identity as the children of God; it declares who we are and to whom we belong. The action of prayer places us outside the realm of the powers and principalities. As prayer declares our true identity, it destroys our false identities. In prayer we act upon who we really are, and thus prayer has the effect of diminishing the illusions that have controlled us and of helping us remember what is true. Prayer allows us to step out of our traps and find ourselves again in God.

Contemplative writer and priest Henri Nouwen once shared with our early Sojourners community that the desert fathers regarded prayer as an act of "unhooking" from the harness of the world's securities. Such prayer may be the only action powerful enough to free us from our spiritual bondage to consumption, money, or power, and even ideas and causes that often control our behaviour.

Only those who have truly found their identity in God can resist the violent tugs and pulls of the false values offered by the world. By re-establishing our security in God, prayer becomes an effective weapon in resisting the world's false securities.

Prayer changes our frame of reference; it is not merely a preparation for action. Rather, prayer must be understood as an action in itself, a potent political weapon to be used in spiritual warfare against the most powerful forces of the world. Prayer is not undertaken in place of other actions but is the foundation for all the other actions we take.

I recall the way Archbishop Tutu would pray in South Africa during the apartheid era. His prayers constantly affirmed God's power over the claims of the state – that God's power was a threat to the state's power. And prayer, in recognizing God's authority over the evil powers, moves us beyond opposition to affirmation and beyond resistance to celebration. Thus, prayer and the results of prayer can be the most revolutionary of acts. The powers that be in this world are aware of this. That is why they consider those who pray in this way to be a threat.

Humility is a Difficult Virtue

Humility is a difficult virtue for those who are called to a prophetic vocation – people like us. Humility is difficult for people who think they are, or want to be, "radical Christians". Humility is difficult when you're always calling other people – the church, the nation, and the world – to stop doing the things you think are wrong and start doing the things you think are right. Humility is difficult for the bearers of radical messages. When we're always calling other people to repent and change, it's not always easy to hear that message for ourselves.

There is a real tension between humility and the prophetic vocation. Most prophetic Christians I have known – present company included – are not very good at humility. We are always making judgments of others – church leaders, political leaders, majority cultures – but are not often good at applying the judgment to ourselves. Even when the prophetic judgments we are making are necessary, they seldom lead us to humility. After all, we are the ones who know how other people are supposed to change. We are the ones with the answers. We are the ones who are doing it right.

How do we preach like Amos – "Let justice roll down like waters, and righteousness like an ever-flowing stream!" – without becoming self-righteous ourselves? Perhaps Micah had it right: "What does the LORD require of you but to do justice, and to love kindness, and to walk humbly with your God?"

We are perhaps especially prone to turn our righteous judgments on each other, at those close at hand, even within our own community – and that can be especially destructive. When that happens, if the truth be told, radical Christian communities are not always pleasant places to be. When the prophetic indignation we offer daily to the world is turned toward those who happen to be within judging, glaring, or shouting distance of us, when we decide that they, too, have fallen short of our ideals – look out!

Let me be human and honest enough to say that leaders in church, state, and certainly faith-inspired organizations should always be held accountable, but being a leader in a prophetic Christian community is often a very hard place to be. Just look at the qualities necessary for the prophetic vocation: the capacity to speak clearly, strongly, boldly, decisively, distinctively, and of course, visibly. I would say, from my experience, that none of those qualities leads directly to humility. Likewise, the call to be and offer an alternative reality, community, vision, lifestyle, and so on, requires an energy and confidence that, again, do not necessarily make us prone to humility.

So what can save us? The same thing that saves everybody else: the grace of God. Grace is the logic of a loving God. There is nothing we can do to earn it, win it, or deserve it. Grace is simply a gift, not a reward. We can receive it only by faith, not through good works. As familiar as that is to us, we have great difficulty coming to terms with the meaning and reality of grace. We seem to find innumerable ways to deny the grace that is the gift of God's love for us. Either we abuse it and make grace self-serving, or we dismiss its reality altogether by acting to establish our own righteousness. In twisting God's purposes to suit our own or in striving to justify ourselves through our own efforts, we have, in fact, denied the grace of God. In so doing, we have denied ourselves the ability simply to rest in that grace, to be changed and used by God's love.

Grace saves the prophetic vocation. The knowledge and experience of grace can ease the seriousness with which we tend to take ourselves. Grace can restore our humility, our sense of humour, our ability to laugh at ourselves. All are regularly needed by prophets. Only sinners make good prophets.

Under the Cross

I will always remember the opportunity I had to speak to forty-five thousand Lutheran teenagers in San Antonio's Alamo Dome in the summer of 2006. It was the Youth Gathering of the Evangelical Lutheran Church in America that takes place every three years. I spoke to twenty thousand fourteen- to eighteen-year-olds one Friday morning and to twenty-five thousand the next.

It is an enormous affair put on by volunteer Lutheran laypeople who, in their regular jobs, produce things like the Super Bowl! The staging, the lighting, the symbols, and the excited crowd make the atmosphere simply electric. Lutherans love symbols, and as I entered the area to speak, I had to pass directly under a huge lighted cross that stretched several hundred feet into the air and onto a stage that was itself in the shape of a cross. The dramatic imagery made me adjust my remarks on the spot.

I told the Lutheran young people not to make the mistake of simply thinking that Christianity was either about the things we shouldn't do or about just being nice. That kind of religion could never hold their loyalty or demand their allegiance – and it shouldn't. Rather, I asked their generation to help clear up the confusion about religion in America and around the world. I pointed to the huge cross over our heads that lighted the Alamo Dome. Christianity without the cross, I said, is very confusing indeed. What is the cross? It is simply the place where Jesus took on himself all the suffering and pain of the world – then redeemed it, conquered it, and triumphed over it.

To encounter the cross today, I told these young people eager to explode out into the world, we will have to embrace the suffering and pain of our world. In fact, that is the most likely place we will find Jesus again. For an affluent country and a comfortable church, the pain of a suffering world may be the only dependable place to discover Jesus afresh. That cross is where Jesus stands again today, ready to redeem the suffering and pain – and he welcomes us to join him there. I invited a new generation of young Christians to clear up the confusion about the meaning of Christianity by finding Jesus again in a suffering world. Go to those places, and you will find Jesus.

Indeed, for a whole generation, this is becoming the path to conversion. I see it everywhere I go. I remember being at Azusa Pacific University, a Christian college in Southern California. They told me that a short three years before, only about thirty of their three thousand students were engaged in some kind of volunteer service. But that number had climbed to fifteen hundred – half the student body – and the school was being transformed. Young Azusa students were now engaged in tutoring and mentoring "at risk" kids in tough urban neighbourhoods just blocks away from their university, places where most had never been before and hardly knew existed. By working with Habitat for Humanity, they were getting to know poor families who were about to get new homes. And they had met children who lived on garbage dumps in the slums of Tijuana just a few miles – but another world away – from their comfortable campus.

The young director of the volunteer programme told me that at first the students felt betrayed. "Why didn't anybody tell me about this? I had no idea so many people were poor in this country, and just a few miles from our campus! And that there are children who are forced to live that way in Mexico and how many other places?" He said the students sometimes start to question their simple and comfortable faith and to doubt all they have been taught. Their worldview, their theology, and their politics all get turned upside down.

But eventually, he said, their faith kicks in and takes them deeper. Now their newfound or rediscovered faith begins to change everything else about their lives – their view of the world, their aspirations and dreams, their plans for the future. "I don't have to tell them what to think and feel," he said. "I just put them in the middle of poverty and human suffering, and eventually their faith takes over. I've learned to trust that."

I've learned to trust that, too. That's why I strongly recommend that young people spend at least a year in some kind of voluntary service programme immediately after college, or at some other point if they are not going to college. Some of the faith-based programmes are the very best.

People are signing up – at U2 concerts, at the Sojourners Web site, at our events, which feel like the old revivals must have felt. Many are signing up with their lives in service projects and placements all around the world. But we're asking for more than just taking an "urban plunge" for a few hours, a few weeks, or even a year. We're calling a new generation to build their vocations around lives committed to social justice. I'm not asking a new generation to join politics, but to join a movement to change politics.

I invited the young Lutherans at the Alamo Dome to make the pilgrimage to the other side, to the suffering places of humanity, to the cross, to discover Jesus again. I told them, "It converted me, and it will convert you, too."

Sure enough, the new wave of student activism I see rising up around the country is much more prevalent at evangelical Christian colleges, at Catholic Jesuit universities, and among the religious student groups at secular universities; these are often the ones leading student efforts on homelessness, HIV/AIDS, Darfur, and Iraq.

Even at typically liberal schools with a progressive history, student activism is often being generated by students of faith. In my own student days, many of us had to leave the religion of our childhood to engage in student activism. But this time around, the activism of a new generation seems to be much more faith-inspired, and I believe we have some exciting days ahead.

A Commission

In his inaugural speech, Nelson Mandela, the first president of a free South Africa, told his people and the world:

We understand it still that there is no easy road to freedom.

We know it well that none of us acting alone can achieve success.

We must therefore act together as a united people, for national reconciliation, for nation building, for the birth of a new world.

Let there be justice for all.

Let there be peace for all.

Let there be work, bread, water and salt for all.

Let each know that for each the body, the mind and the soul have been freed to fulfill themselves.

Never, never and never again shall it be that this beautiful land will again experience the oppression of one by another and suffer the indignity of being the skunk of the world.

Let freedom reign.[3]

The world is waiting to see what this generation is going to do. The children whose lives are in the balance are waiting for you to act on their behalf. Your own future children are already waiting to see what kind of world you will give them. The church is waiting for you to change our direction. Most of all, Jesus is waiting for you, waiting where he lives amid the sufferings of humanity, waiting for you to join him there. Are you ready? We need you now. This is your time and your moment. Don't let it pass you by.

So my advice is to take care of your faith, take care of each other, take care of your hope, and stay with the vision.

And my commission to a new generation is this:

No longer accept the unacceptable.

Change what is believed to be possible.

And always make the choice for hope.

EPILOGUE

Red Letter Christians and Justice Revivals: Coming to a City Near You

---

When I went to Nashville on a book tour I didn't do a lecture: I did a concert! Ashley Cleveland, Buddy Miller, Emmylou Harris, and Jars of Clay all played and sang, and I preached. We sold out the historic Belcourt Theatre twice in one night and had a lot of fun. While in Nashville, I did one interview that was particularly memorable. "I'm a secular Jewish country-music songwriter and disc jockey," my interviewer on a local radio station said. "But I love your stuff and have been following your book tour." He told me he loved my "riffs" and would like to spend an evening together just to get lines for some new music. "You're a songwriter's dream." Then he told me he believed we were starting a new movement but had noticed that we didn't have a name for it. "I've got an idea for you," he said. "I think you should call yourselves The Red Letter Christians. You know those Bibles that highlight the words of Jesus in red letters? I love the red letter stuff. The rest I could do without."

The truth is that there are many people who like the "red letter stuff", and, like my interviewer in Nashville, they may not even be Christians. Try it yourself sometime. Go out on the street or to your school or workplace and take a poll. Ask people what they think Jesus stood for. I've done it and the results are usually the same. You're likely to hear things like "he hung out with poor people and sinners", or "he was compassionate", or "he stood for love", or "he was for peace". Then ask them what they think Christians or the churches stand for. Sadly, but dependably, you're likely to hear some very different things. And if you throw in the word *evangelical,* it can get pretty nasty.

We have a problem. Most people have the idea that Christians and the church are supposed to stand for the same things that Jesus did. What a crazy thought! And when we don't stand for the things Jesus did, people become confused and disillusioned. Like I say, it's a problem.

When Jesus tells us that he will regard the way we treat the hungry, the homeless, the immigrant, the poor family, the sick, or the prisoner as if we were treating him that way, it likely means he wouldn't think ignoring them is good domestic policy. Or when he tells us "love your enemies" and "blessed are the peacemakers", it might be hard to persuade him to join "wars against terrorism" with so much "collateral damage" to civilians or to expect him to approve of the torture of our enemies.

Yes, Jesus is a problem – for the Wall Street traders, the Madison Avenue advertisers, the media moguls of Times Square, the Hollywood stars whose limos cruise the Sunset Strip, the K Street lobbyists, and the powerful people on Pennsylvania Avenue who strive to maintain American imperial power. But Jesus is also a problem for many churches on Main Street that have substituted the values of the culture for the teachings of Jesus.

Yet for millions of people, religious or not, Jesus remains the most compelling figure in the world today. The church may not be much more credible than the stockbrokers, the advertisers, the media, the special interests, or the politicians, but Jesus still stands far above the rest of the crowd. Somehow, Jesus has survived the church and all of us who name his name but too often forget most of what he said.

In *The Secret Message of Jesus,* Brian McLaren suggests that Jesus' real message has almost been kept a secret in the churches themselves and has been utterly disguised by many of our television evangelists who preach a conservative American religion across the world, giving a very different impression of Christianity than Jesus taught.

But the good news is that "the secret" is getting out. In our time the message of Jesus is breaking through again, drawing an alienated generation raised in the churches back to Jesus and attracting many outside the religious community to a Jesus they never heard about from the churches. Perhaps because our culture and politics have gone so far off course, with values so contrary to Jesus' message, more and more people intuitively recognize that his vision of God's kingdom – a new world of compassion, justice, integrity, and peace – is the good news for which they've been searching and waiting.

A fellowship of Christian authors, speakers, and activists have come together as the "Red Letter Christians".[1] We haven't formed a new organization, we're not from any one church or tradition, and we have no particular political agenda. We affirm the authority of the whole Bible, not just the "red stuff". But we believe that the "red letters" of Jesus need to be focused on again. We feel a real calling together, in this historical moment, to bring back the distinctive message of Jesus for our time, for our world, and for the critical issues we face today. We are preachers and writers, and the group is expanding rapidly.

Meanwhile, the landscape of religion, society, and politics in America is being transformed. As I crisscross the country, I feel a new momentum and even the beginnings of a movement – a great awakening. Perhaps the greatest sign of hope is the emergence of a generation of young people eager to rediscover Jesus and take their faith into the world. The Christianity of private piety, affluent conformity, partisan two-issue politics, and "God Bless [only] America" has compromised the witness of the church while putting many younger Christians to sleep. Defining faith mostly by the things we won't do does not create a compelling style of life. And a generation of young people is hungry for an agenda worthy of its commitment, its energy, and its gifts.

The Passing of Jerry Falwell

The death of Jerry Falwell in May 2007 signalled the passing of an era. I watched much of the cable television coverage on Jerry Falwell's death and legacy. I did a lot of grimacing, in response to the uncritical adulations of his allies (who passed over the divisive character of much of Falwell's rhetoric) and also to the ugly vitriol from some of Falwell's enemies (who attacked both his character and his faith). There were even some who attacked all people of faith, because of Jerry Falwell. On the day of his death, I offered a brief statement, which read:

> I was saddened to learn that Rev. Jerry Falwell passed away this morning at age 73. Rev. Falwell and I met many times over the years, as the media often paired us as debate partners on issues of faith and politics. I respected his passionate commitment to his beliefs, and our shared commitment to bringing moral debate to the public square, although we didn't agree on many things. At this time, however, what matters most is our prayers for comfort and peace for his family and friends.

Jerry Falwell, in his own way, did help teach Christians that their faith should express itself in the public square, and I am grateful for that, even if the positions he took were often at great variance with my own. I spent much of my early Christian life fighting the privatizing of faith, characterized by the withdrawal of any concern for the world (so as not to be "worldly") and an exclusive focus on private matters. If God so loved the world, God must care a great deal about what happens to it and in it. Falwell agreed with that, and he blew the trumpet that awakened fundamentalist Christians to engage the world with their faith and moral values. And that commitment is a good thing. Falwell and I debated often about how faith

EPILOGUE 247

should influence public life and about what the great moral issues of our time really are.

Many conservative Christians are now also embracing a broader agenda as a matter of faith and moral imperative. A survey conducted by the Pew Forum on Religion and Public Life in February 2007 and reported in *The Washington Post* found that "younger evangelicals are more likely than their parents to worry about environmental issues; 59 per cent of those under 30 said the United States was 'losing ground' on pollution, compared with 37 per cent of those over 30."[2] A May 2007 *New York Times* article on "the new breed of evangelicals" declared, "The evangelical Christian movement, which has been pivotal in reshaping the country's political landscape since the 1980s, has shifted in potentially momentous ways in recent years, broadening its agenda and exposing new fissures." It went on to say that "the new breed of evangelical leaders... are more likely to speak out about more liberal causes like AIDS, Darfur, poverty, and global warming than controversial social issues like abortion and same-sex marriage".[3]

It would have been nice to hear that Jerry Falwell, too, had moved to embrace a broader agenda than just abortion and homosexuality. Rev. Falwell, who was admittedly racist during the civil rights movement, in later years was honoured by the Lynchburg NAACP for his turnabout on the issue of race, showing the famous founder of the Religious Right's capacity to grow and change. But recently on television I saw the pain on the face of gay Christian Mel White, who lamented that despite the efforts of himself and others, Falwell never moderated his strong and often inflammatory language (even if maintaining his religious convictions) against gay and lesbian people. They still feel the most wounded by the fundamentalist minister's statements; that healing has yet to be done.

Ralph Reed said that Jerry Falwell presided over the "marriage ceremony" between religious fundamentalists and the Republican party. David Kuo, former special assistant to President George W. Bush, wrote, "It is ironic and a bit sad that the man who stood on the sidelines during the civil rights movement – saying pastors needed to preach Jesus, not politics – became the leading person marketing Jesus for political ends in the '70s, '80s, and '90s, and that he will be remembered not as a great spiritual leader but a powerful political one. But that was the choice he made over and over again. Falwell's Moral Majority became synonymous with Christianity in America, so that today, many people confuse the particular political stance of the Christian Right with the message of Jesus Christ."

Falwell, Kuo wrote, "helped define Jesus for much of America today, and his definition does not do justice to the Jesus of the gospels. When people hear the word 'Christian', too often they think not of Jesus and his teachings but of Jerry Falwell and his politics. I know of a lot of Christians who don't like to refer to themselves as 'Christians' because they are afraid of the Falwellian association."[4]

The Religious Right's political partisanship is still a concern for many, and should be a warning for the relationship of any so-called religious left with the Democrats. But perhaps in the overly partisan mistakes that Jerry Falwell made – and actually pioneered – we can all be instructed in how to forge a faith that is principled but not ideological, political but not partisan, engaged but not used. That's how the Catholic bishops put it, and it is a better guide than the direction we received from the Moral Majority.

Falwell proclaimed a public faith, not a private one. I am with him on that. God is personal, but never private. Let's learn from Falwell's legacy – about how and how not to apply our faith to politics.

Jerry Falwell's death signalled both an end and a new beginning. Because he was the pioneer of the Religious Right and its most visible (if not its most influential) leader, his death is a milestone. We are now indeed in the post-Religious Right era. No, the Religious Right is not dead or gone, and it will still be a major factor in Republican party politics. But its era is over, its monologue is over, and the peak of its influence is now past. What will the next era of faith and politics bring?

The Nineteenth Century
Comes to the Twenty-First

At heart, I am a nineteenth-century evangelical, born in the wrong century. Nineteenth-century American religious revival was linked directly with the abolition of slavery and other movements for social reform. Christians helped lead the abolitionist struggle, efforts to end child labour, projects to aid working people and establish unions, and even the battle to obtain voting rights for women. Here were Christians fighting for social justice, precisely because of what God had done for them – an activity with which too many Christians, in the public perception, have not been associated in the era of the Religious Right.

Leaders such as evangelist Charles Finney did not shy away from identifying the gospel with something as specific as the antislavery cause. Finney was a revivalist and also an abolitionist, and for him the two were closely connected. Finney is called "the father of American evangelism", but he directly linked spiritual revival and social reform. That's the way it always is for revival – faith becomes life-changing, but rather than remaining restricted to personal issues and the inner life alone, it explodes into the world with a powerful force. For Finney and the other revivalists of his day, taking a weak or wrong position on social justice was literally a "hindrance to revival".

I first learned about Finney and our other revivalist forebears when I was in seminary, during the early years of the Sojourners community in Chicago. We, too, were struggling to define a socially engaged evangelicalism when we discovered this legion of kindred spirits from the past.

I believed that the evangelical faith I had learned as a child naturally led to social engagement, and that was the impulse that prompted the founding of Sojourners. But we were often estranged from mainstream evangelicalism, which focused almost exclusively on private piety. When we met the historical heroes from past revivals, we realized our concerns were not foreign to evangelicalism and, indeed, that others in earlier times and places had come to the same conclusions we had.

In 1974–75 we published a ten-part series on the nineteenth-century revival movement in the magazine that became *Sojourners.* The first article, in June 1974, began: "The current generation of evangelical Christians has been to a great extent deceived by a strange quirk of history… The last half century or so of evangelical apathy on social issues is assumed to be characteristic of the whole history of evangelicalism. The calls to Christian discipleship, social involvement, and political engagement… are assumed to be a new emphasis… This perspective is false to history and obscures a heritage that needs to be recovered." We then went on to tell the stories of Charles Finney, Jonathan Blanchard, Theodore Weld, and many others, including the role of the Grimke sisters and Lucy Stone in developing an evangelical feminism. The series was published in 1976 as the groundbreaking book *Discovering an Evangelical Heritage,* by its author, Donald Dayton, our teacher of the revivalist history.

Today, a new generation of Christians (young and old and with allies in other faith traditions) are coming of age – again. Their concerns are the slavery of poverty, the sexual trafficking of God's children, environmental "creation care", human rights and the image of God in genocidal places like Darfur, the sanctity of life and the health of families more broadly applied, and how the Prince of Peace might view our endless wars and conflicts. Whether they know it or not, they are really nineteenth-century American evangelicals for the twenty-first century. They are learning that the social mission of the church in the world will never be accomplished without the fire and passion that comes from personal faith. They have found that justice is absolutely integral to the gospel, but that a social gospel cannot be sustained without a personal experience of Jesus, who brings the gospel good news.

I strongly believe that faith matters and can make a difference, not only in our personal lives but also in our world. The church's historians tell us that spiritual activity cannot be called revival until it has changed something in a society. In other words, spiritual renewal does not necessarily become spiritual revival without some decidedly social consequences. I believe the time is ripe for the kind of spiritual revival that leads to clear social commitments and outcomes. This book has argued throughout that when politics cannot resolve problems, the role of social movements becomes more and more important, and the best social movements have spiritual foundations.

Revival is necessary, because just having a new and better political agenda will not be enough. Getting to the right issues isn't enough. Having the right message isn't enough. Finding the right programme isn't enough. The real question is what will motivate and mobilize the kind of constituencies that will move politics to change. I believe that will require the energy, power, and hope that faith can bring. People acting out of their best ideas and values is a good thing, but people acting out of their deepest wells of faith can be an even more powerful thing.

We have rediscovered our nineteenth-century revival roots; now we need to rediscover that message for the twenty-first century. On a more personal level, the revivalist history has helped me to find myself in my own evangelical tradition again. Reviving the connection between faith and social justice has helped me to find my way back home.

Something is happening, and I see it on the road every week. I meet the new evangelicals who are rejecting a partisan and parochial American religion and coming back to Jesus. I talk to Catholics who are rediscovering the rich tradition of Catholic social teaching and a more personal faith. I am in constant dialogue with many in the Protestant denominations who are also returning to the roots of their faith, wanting to restore the connection between evangelism and social justice. African American, Latino, and Asian Christians in the United States are helping us all to create a "post-white" American church.

I also am meeting a new generation of Jewish and Muslim believers who see the "revival" of their traditions, not their secularization, as the best response to the threat of fundamentalist extremism in all our great religions. The dialogue between those trying to revive the "prophetic" traditions in their own faith as an alternative to fundamentalism may prove to be one of the most exciting and productive interfaith conversations we have seen in many years.

Because religion has no monopoly on morality, those who are still wary of religion are joining the dialogue as well. "Spiritual but not religious" seekers should be welcomed – and it seems that Jesus always did that. Faith-inspired activists have always worked alongside those with no religious faith but motivated by deep moral and ethical commitments. "Religious" and "secular" progressives have a long and deep history of relationship. That must become true again. What will that take? As far as the religious partners are concerned, they must believe, as their secular counterparts do, in the separation of church and state. No religion should be established (or favoured) by the state – not one religion over the others, not any religion against those citizens with no religious faith. As the great leader of the Protestant Reformation, Martin Luther, once remarked, "I would rather be governed by a competent Turk than by an incompetent Christian."

The separation of church and state does not mean the segregation of moral values from public life, or the banishing of religious language from the public debate. Secular citizens must not require their religious neighbours to keep their faith silent in public life or confine it to private matters. In choosing not to establish any religion in American public life, the founders of our country were not seeking to diminish the influence of faith and its moral values, but rather to increase their influence on the social fabric and political morality – precisely by setting religion free from the shackles of the state and protecting the independence needed to keep faith healthy and strong. The attempt to strip the public square of religious values undermines the moral health of the nation, just as any attempt to impose theocratic visions of morality is a threat to democratic politics. In this dynamic religious and political environment with many shifting winds, a genuine spiritual revival could change everything.

Justice Revivals: Coming to a City Near You

A genuine spiritual revival may be coming to a city near you. Imagine something called Justice Revivals, in the powerful tradition of revivals past but focusing on the great moral issues of our time. Imagine powerful preaching and music at night with marches in the streets during the day. Imagine linking the tradition of Billy Graham with the tradition of Martin Luther King Jr. Imagine a new generation of young people catching fire and offering their gifts, talents, and lives in a new spiritual movement for social justice. Imagine such revivals taking place in our cities' great convention centres but resulting in thousands of small groups for ongoing discipleship, training, and action in every neighbourhood of those cities. Imagine disillusioned believers coming back to faith after many years of alienation, while other seekers discover the power of faith for the first time. Imagine a revival of faith that didn't result in sectarian warfare but rather respectful dialogue between our diverse religious communities and a new interfaith collaboration in overcoming the social crises that confront us all.

Imagine politics being unable to co-opt such a spiritual revival but being held accountable to its moral imperatives. Imagine social movements rising out of spiritual revival and actually changing the wind of both our culture and our politics. Imagine a fulfillment in our time of the words of the prophet Amos: "Let justice roll down like waters, and righteousness like an ever-flowing stream." Just imagine.

APPENDIX

Jim Wallis Sr.
Man of Faith

On the morning of November 8, the day after the 2006 midterm elections, my dad died, very suddenly. I left immediately for Detroit and exited all the post-election discussions. For the next week, I was deeply involved with my family back home, my four siblings and all their children, his many friends, and the two churches he helped to found. He had left behind an outline of the funeral service that he would like, which included my doing the eulogy. He had told my brother that he hoped by planning the service ahead of time it would be less of a burden on his family. Less burden... right – it would be the hardest sermon/talk I've ever had to give, and I wasn't at all sure that I would get through it. But I wanted the words to pay tribute to my father. He deserves to be grieved well, and I will be grieving him for some time – in ways, for the rest of my life. But with the grief, there is also profound gratitude for the legacy that his children, grandchildren, and the countless people whose lives he touched will be blessed with forever. I tried to capture some of that in this eulogy I offered for my father.

"I glorified you on earth by finishing the work that you gave me to do." These are the words of Jesus in the garden, but they also apply to his faithful servants – John 17:4.

On behalf of the family, I offer our deepest thanks to all of you who loved our dad. Thank you for coming. The size of this congregation [almost six hundred people] is a real tribute to him. And thank you especially for ministering to us these last few days by sharing the stories about how our dad and mom so influenced your lives. Those stories are precious treasures to us now.

Standing at Dad's casket, I heard the story of the little girl who would not come to the MOPS programme at his church (Mothers of Preschoolers, for moms and their toddlers, where my dad volunteered in his retirement years) unless "Grandpa Walrus" was there to hold her in his lap. From the most important to the little child, we were all special to him. Someone said, "When you look at all the influences in your life, your dad is right there." I heard that time and time again. He was there, for all of us.

The grandchildren really miss him. Several of them said, "He was our best cheerleader." Grandpa made sure he had a front-row seat to the lives of all his children and grandchildren. He never missed anything. So many people have used the word *encourager* when they talk about my dad. We had a president who was called The Great Communicator. Well, we could certainly call my father The Great Encourager. I heard Marcie's little son, Lucas, say, "When I came to his house, he always told me, 'Good-looking shirt, cool shoes.' When I came over last night, nobody told me how great I looked." My own son Luke had a weekly phone call with Grandpa after baseball games, to talk through the game and how he did. When he heard that Grandpa had died, Luke broke into tears and said, "Now who am I going to talk about baseball with?" Countless others have told us our dad was their mentor, partner, teacher, or like a father or grandfather to them or their kids – "He made me/us feel like a part of his family." So many of the cards we have received said how much they will miss "Grandpa".

Someone said to me, "Your family must have felt jealous – so many of us had a piece of your family, your mom and dad." No, they always had plenty of love for us, and amazed us with their love for others. They literally taught us how to love. I was amazed again, in these last two days, as hundreds came to the funeral home, at how my dad and mom touched so many people – and so deeply. Where did they find the time? What a legacy. What a blessing for our family and for all of you.

Jim Wallis Sr. was vital till the end. When I called him on Wednesday morning, November 8 (the day he died), he asked, "Do you think that we are going to win the Senate, too, and not just the House?" This will be a nonpartisan funeral, but it was no secret that the party in power was not popular with my dad. We agreed to talk later that day about the remaining Senate races, but his heart suddenly stopped about three hours later.

Even near the end of his life, he became a favourite friend to so many – about a young woman who worked at the coffee shop he liked, he would say, "We're really getting to know each other pretty well." Or the nurse, "She's so nice and really sharp." And the doctors, "How do they know so much?" When everybody thinks someone was his or her best friend, it says an awful lot about that person.

But what kind of man was Jim Wallis Sr., and how did he become the man we knew?

Actually, his family life was very difficult. His father was shell-shocked in World War I and never really had much left to share. His only sister was always sick, and his mother was distracted. His own home was a rather cold, uninspired, and very nonrelational environment. It's hard to believe that the most relational man I've ever known came from such a background – where nobody taught him how to love. Dr. Merrill, his and our early family doctor, once said that my dad had the kind of family background that made people juvenile delinquents. I always remembered that.

Yet Jim Wallis excelled in everything he ever did. He was very bright – a strong A student, always curious and learning – and an athlete – on the football team and all-city in track at Redford High School, and then also on the track team at the University of Michigan. From the beginning, he was a natural leader, the captain of his sports teams, and the student body president in both high school and college.

He was always quite humble about it all, though. He was quite a high school "hunk", but never a ladies' man. He hardly ever dated until he met the beautiful and feisty Phyllis Morrell, who became the love of his life. She was already a deep woman of faith who broke fundamentalist rules (as my parents always did) by dating an "unsaved" boy, and led him to Jesus Christ. Faith took hold deeply in him and changed his whole life. I believe it was first my mom, then God and Jesus, who were teaching him how to love. Faith taught him how to love.

On the same day, my father graduated from college, was commissioned in the U.S. Navy, and was married. A busy day! He liked busy days, and seems to have passed that on to his kids. Then he was off to the Navy and World War II in the Pacific. His life was changed as a naval officer who also volunteered as chaplain on his ship.

One day last spring, during one of his regular visits to Washington, D.C., it was Luke's personal sharing day at school (all the kids have one) and he brought his grandpa to "share". When Luke told his classmates that his grandpa had been in the Navy during World War II, one kid asked who won the war. When they heard that we did, the class started cheering, having no idea at their age what war was like. But my father did.

Later that week, he and I went to visit the World War II Memorial, and he told me a story about his visit to Hiroshima, right after the bomb fell. Six decades later, he cried as he told me about the little five-year-old girl he met there in the rubble of war. I wrote about that talk on the bench at the memorial and the story of the little girl in a column. My father's social conscience was instinctive and deep.

Then he came home to a successful career with Detroit Edison and was soon the youngest executive at his level in the company. But his first love was his family, and the new church he and Mom helped to start, Dunning Park

Bible Chapel, known to many of you. It was our home church, and literally our home away from home. Last night in the car, my little niece Kaylee was complaining that her family always was the last to leave church! I replied, "I know what you mean!" With her parents, my dad helped to plant yet another church in his eighties, Life Church.

People quickly and early recognized a "teaching gift" in this young man. He spoke clearly, deeply, and passionately – and he had a great impact on people. My father had a way with words; he was a teacher and a preacher everybody wanted to hear. Speaking was a big part of his lifelong work. He knew how to say things. And people responded. The young adult class, which he taught every Sunday morning, became the hottest thing at Dunning Park – hundreds came through it. It was one of the biggest reasons Dunning Park grew so fast.

But here's what we saw. Every morning at 5:00 a.m. my father got up to study the Bible, and then he and my mom would get all us up for school and work at 7:00 a.m. He always had his "study" in the houses where we lived, with lots of books and commentaries. My father never went to seminary, but I've never known anyone who knew the English Bible better. His Bible was full of coloured underlining and notes on almost every page – it's the one thing I want to take home with me.

The best teachers are also lifelong students, and he was. My dad was always eager to learn more, and he was never satisfied with easy answers. Others would say, in effect, "That's the way we all think around here." Well, not him. I pray that I will be as open to the thinking and ideas of my children as he was with his.

He became a man of great heart and compassion. As we read today in Matthew 25, Jesus cared about the "least of these", and my dad did, too. With my father, Jesus always won out in the end. It was Jesus who ultimately made him challenge the easy assumptions of most people around him. He passed his social conscience on to all of his kids. And it is a big part of our lives. Franciscan priest Richard Rohr, one of the best-known teachers of spirituality and one of my best friends, wrote to me from Australia, "I know, and you know, that your father was the foundation for your own deep faith." He was, and was for all of his children, who are all people of faith.

And he was a foundation for so many others. He taught us to love. He taught us to be people of faith. And that's the legacy he would have us pass on now – all of us. That would be his commission to us today. Teach everybody you meet how to love, how to have faith. In the bathroom of his guest room where my family is staying now, there is a little plaque that reads LOVE IS NOT A FEELING, IT'S A DECISION. I remember both my parents saying that. (I put it in my suitcase.)

I think my dad was ready to go, but none of us were ready for him to go. But it was a good way to go. One minute he was talking to somebody – a nurse, a new hospital roommate, just as he was always talking to somebody – and the next minute his weakened heart just stopped. He was done.

Now it's our turn. And his heart will never stop for us.

Our reading from John 14 says, "In my Father's house there are many mansions. I go to prepare a place for you." Seven years ago, my mom passed on and got her "mansion/house". If you knew her, you know that she started fixing it up, getting it ready for him and for us. And if you knew my dad, you know he was about half of himself these last seven years. To be honest, his family, especially his grandkids, kept him alive and smiling. But oh, how he missed her! He still signed his cards to us, "We love you."

Now they're together again. The grandkids all talked about that, saying, "He's with Grandma now," in the place she was getting ready for him and for his family – and, I think, for all of us.

Today we can imagine them together again, hugging and smiling at all of us. My wife, Joy Carroll, a good priest and preacher, isn't sure what I am about to say is good exegesis of John 14, But I can imagine the two of them getting a big "open house" together even now. You see, their house was always open, their table was always open, and it was always big enough to include a few more.

For my mom and dad, there was always an occasion for a party. And I think they would want me to invite you right now to the biggest and best party they ever threw. Jim and Phyllis would invite you to the "Wallis Heavenly Open House". Whenever you are ready, they'll be waiting – just for you. We'll all be welcome.

My dad and mom were servants in this life. I'll close with one of his favourite passages – what he might say now to all of us on the day of his memorial home-sending. It's Philippians 2:1–11. I can almost hear him say, "Let the same mind be in you that was in Christ Jesus."

My dad was always one to deflect attention away from himself and give the glory to God. But on this occasion, we also pay tribute to him. Let us rise and give a big standing ovation to one of God's most faithful servants.

James E. Wallis Sr.: a man of faith!

NOTES

I. REVIVAL TIME

1. Kathleen Kennedy Townsend, *Failing America's Faithful* (Warner Books, 2007), 13.
2. Garth Lean, *God's Politician* (Darton Longman and Todd, 2007).
3. Interview by author, Jan. 12, 2007.
4. Michael Kazin, *A Godly Hero* (Alfred A. Knopf, Borzoi Books, 2006), xiii–xiv.
5. Kazin, interview by author, Jan. 12, 2007.
6. Stewart Burns, *To the Mountaintop: Martin Luther King Jr.'s Sacred Mission to Save America, 1955–68* (HarperSanFrancisco, 2004), 38–39.
7. Nelson Mandela, inauguration statement, Pretoria, May 10, 1994, http://www.anc.org.za/ancdocs/history/mandela/1994/inaugpta.html.
8. Oscar Romero's last sermon, March 14, 1980, http://www.haverford.edu/relg/faculty/amcguire/romero.html.

2. CHANGES IN THE AIR

1. CNN commentary, http://www.cnn.com/2006/US/06/05/warren.aids/index.html; *Newsweek* interview, http://www.msnbc.msn.com/id/15993470/site/newsweek/.
2. Lisa Miller, "An Evangelical Identity Crisis", *Newsweek*, Nov. 13, 2006.
3. Shane Claiborne, *The Irresistible Revolution: Living as an Ordinary Radical* (Zondervan, 2006).
4. Rich Nathan, "Evangelical Engagement – Promise and Pitfalls", God's Politics blog, Nov. 7, 2006.
5. John Howard Yoder, *The Politics of Jesus* (Eerdmans, 1972), 23.
6. Sen. Barack Obama, June 28, 2006, http://www.sojo.net/index.cfm?action=news.display_article&mode=C&NewsID=5454.
7. Zogby International/Faith in Public Life, "Exit Poll Shows Shift in Religious Vote Driven by 'Kitchen Table' Moral Issues", Nov. 15, 2006.
8. Lauren Sandler, "Lost Faith in the GOP", *Salon,* Nov. 10, 2006, http://www.salon.com/news/feature/2006/11/10/evangelical_vote/.

3. HOW TO CHANGE THE WORLD, AND WHY

1. "Mere Mission", N. T. Wright interview by Tim Stafford, *Christianity Today,* Jan. 5, 2007, http://www.christianitytoday.com/39913.

2. N. T. Wright interview.

3. Yoder, *The Politics of Jesus*, 23, 132, 161, 238.

4. Those who have been especially influential for me include: Oscar Cullman, Hendrick Berkhof, C. H. Dodd, G.H.C. MacGregor, Krister Stendahl, James H. Cone, Gustavo Gutiérrez, Jon Sobrino, Andre Trocme, Jean Lasserre, Harvey Cox, William Stringfellow, Walter Wink, Ched Myers, and Bill Wylie-Kellermann.

5. John Howard Yoder, *The Christian Witness to the State* (Faith and Life Press, 1964), 5.

6. The sources that I have drawn on for many years to answer these questions are many, but the most important include: John Howard Yoder, Dietrich Bonhoeffer, Martin Luther King Jr., Dorothy Day, American theologian William Stringfellow and French theologian Jacques Ellul, John Wesley and William Wilberforce, Charles Finney, William Jennings Bryan, Billy Graham, John Stott, Reinhold Niebuhr, and Mohandas Gandhi.

7. Martin Luther King, *Testament of Hope*, edited by James Melvin Washington (Harper & Row, 1986), 346.

8. Dietrich Bonhoeffer, Sermon on 2 Corinthians 12:9.

9. Jacques Ellul, *The Presence of the Kingdom* (Seabury Press, 1967), 42–43, 48.

10. Donald B. Kraybill, *The Upside-Down Kingdom* (Mennonite Publishing House, 2003).

11. Ellul, *Presence of the Kingdom,* 50–51.

12. John Howard Yoder, "The Kingdom as Social Ethic", in *The Priestly Kingdom* (Univ. of Notre Dame Press, 1984), 92.

13. Yoder, "The Kingdom as Social Ethic", 95–99.

14. Martin Luther King Jr., "A Look to the Future", address delivered at Highlander Folk Schools, Sept. 2, 1957.

15. Martin Luther King Jr., *The Strength to Love* (Harper & Row, 1963), 27.

16. Yoder, *Christian Witness,* 32.

17. Yoder, "The Spirit of God and the Politics of Men", in *For the Nations* (Eerdmans, 1997), 221–23.

18. Yoder, "The Spirit of God", 228, 235.

19. King, *Testament of Hope,* 276.

20. Yoder, *Christian Witness,* 42.

21. King, *Testament of Hope,* 230.

22. U.S. Conference of Catholic Bishops, *Faithful Citizenship,* 2003.

4. THE MORAL CENTRE

1. David Waters, "Church Needs a Pulpit, Not a Stage", *Commercial Appeal* (Memphis, TN), Dec. 5, 2004.

2. Paul Wellstone, *The Conscience of a Liberal* (Univ. of Minnesota Press, 2001), xii.

3. Michael Gerson, "A New Social Gospel", *Newsweek,* Nov. 13, 2006, http://www.msnbc.msn.com/id/15566389/site/newsweek.

4. U.S. Conference of Catholic Bishops, *Faithful Citizenship,* Nov. 2003, 2.

5. Catechism of the Catholic Church.
6. Catechism of the Catholic Church.
7. Manuel Velasquez, Claire Andre, Thomas Shanks, S.J., and Michael J. Meyer, "The Common Good", Markkula Center for Applied Ethics, Santa Clara University, http://www.scu.edu/ethics/practicing/decision/common good.html.
8. Gerson, "New Social Gospel".
9. Robert Franklin, *Crisis in the Village* (Fortress Press, 2007).
10. Beliefnet interview with Desmond Tutu, http://www.beliefnet.com/story/143/story_14326_2.html.
11. Desmond Tutu, http://www.cyc-net.org/today2000/today000328.html.
12. John Lewis, *Walking with the Wind* (Simon & Schuster, 1998), 87, 467, 472.
13. King, *Testament of Hope,* 617.
14. The Shalom Center, www. shalomctr.org.
15. Reza Aslan, *No god but God* (Random House, 2005), 29.
16. Aslan, *No god but God,* 40–41.
17. Imam Feisal Abdul Rauf, e-mail to author, Feb. 14, 2007.
18. Center for American Progress, Common Good Conference held at Georgetown University, Oct. 18, 2006, http://www.americanprogress.org/events/2006/10/common_good.html.
19. Remarks made by former President Clinton at Common Good Conference, Georgetown University, Oct. 18, 2006, http://www.americanprogress.org/events/special_events/commongood_wjc.html.
20. Michael Tomasky, "Party in Search of a Nation", *The American Prospect,* May 2006, http://www.prospect.org/web/page.ww?section=root&name=ViewPrint&articleId=11400.
21. John Carr, "The Consistent Life Ethic", *University of St. Thomas Law Journal,* Spring 2005.
22. E. J. Dionne, interview by author, Jan. 12, 2007.
23. CNN News, "Christian Coalition President-elect Resigns", Nov. 28, 2006, http://www.cnn.com/2006/POLITICS/11/28/christian.coalition/.
24. Dionne interview, Jan. 12, 2007.
25. Dionne interview, Jan. 12, 2007.

5. INCLUSION AND OPPORTUNITY

1. Brian Williams, interview with Bono, *NBC Nightly News,* http://www.msnbc.msn.com/id/12940132/page/2/.
2. Nicholas Kristof, "Win a Trip, and See a Different World", *New York Times,* March 11, 2007.
3. Kristof, interview by author, Jan. 25, 2007.
4. Bono, keynote address at the 54th National Prayer Breakfast, Feb. 2, 2006, http://www.americanrhetoric.com/speeches/bononationalprayerbreakfast.htm.
5. David Brooks, "The Storm After the Storm", *New York Times,* Sept. 1, 2005.

6. *Meet the Press,* Sept. 11, 2005, http://www.msnbc.msn.com/id/9240461/.

7. John Edwards, "Restoring the American Dream: Combating Poverty and Building One America", September 19, 2005, Center for American Progress, http://www.americanprogress.org/atf/cf/%7BE9245FE4–9A2B–43C7-A521–5D6FF2E06E03%7D/edwards_speech.pdf .

8. Zogby International/Faith in Public Life, "Exit Poll Shows Shift in Religious Vote Driven by 'Kitchen Table' Moral Issues", Nov. 15, 2006.

9. Zogby International, "Majority Call Fighting Poverty a 'Top Priority'", www.zogby.com/news/ReadNews.dbm?ID=1320.

10. United Nations, *Millennium Development Goals Report 2007,* http://www.un.org/millenniumgoals/pdf/mdg2007.pdf.

11. Christian Churches Together, "Statement on Poverty", Feb. 9, 2007, http://www.christianchurchestogether.org/poverty/.

6. STEWARDSHIP AND RENEWAL

1. Ched Myers, "To Serve and Preserve", *Sojourners,* March 2004, 28–33.

2. Brian McLaren, "Consider the Turtles of the Field", *Sojourners,* March 2004, 14–20.

3. Richard Lowery, *Sabbath and Jubilee* (Chalice Press, 2000).

4. National Association of Evangelicals, "For the Health of the Nation", 2004, 24–25.

5. Laurie Goodstein, "Evangelical Leaders Swing Influence Behind Effort to Combat Global Warming", *New York Times,* March 10, 2005.

6. See www.christiansandclimate.org.

7. Letter to Dr. L. Roy Taylor, Chairman of the Board, National Association of Evangelicals, March 1, 2007, www.citizenlink.org/pdfs/NAELetterFinal.pdf.

8. John McCain and Joe Lieberman, "The Turning Point on Global Warming", *Boston Globe,* Feb. 13, 2007.

9. David Ignatius, "The Climate-change Precipice", *Washington Post,* March 2, 2007.

10. Lyndsay Moseley, "Jonah's Warning and Global Warming", God's Politics blog, March 8, 2007.

11. Brian McLaren, "Joseph, Noah, and Pre-emptive Preservation", God's Politics blog, March 12, 2007.

12. "For the Environment, Rallies Great and Small", *New York Times,* April 15, 2007.

13. Bill McKibben, "The Gospel Versus Global Warming", God's Politics blog, Feb. 27, 2007.

14. Bill McKibben, "Sins of Emission", *Sojourners,* March 2004, 8–12.

15. Ken Walker, "Churches Go 'Green', Say Care for Creation Is Biblical", *Church Central,* July 11, 2007, http://www.churchcentral.com/nw/s/template/Article.html/id/24564.

16. Jane Lampman, "Churches Go Green", *Christian Science Monitor,* Jan. 23, 2003.

17. Pew Center on Global Climate Change, http://www.pewclimate.org/companies_leading_the_way_belc/.

7. EQUALITY AND DIVERSITY

1. http://www.bbc.co.uk/worldservice/africa/features/storyofafrica/9chapter6.shtml.
2. Phillip Rawls, "State Apologizing for Slavery", *Decatur (AL) Daily,* May 25, 2007; "Senate Mulls Slavery Apology", *Montgomery Advertiser,* April 19, 2007.
3. "House Passes Slavery Apology Resolution", *Wilmington (NC) Morning Star,* April 12, 2007.
4. Larry O'Dell, "Virginia Apologizes for Role in Slavery", Associated Press/ *Washington Post,* Feb. 25, 2007.
5. "Christians Launch Ad, Grassroots Campaign Calling for Comprehensive Immigration Reform", May 7, 2007, http://www.sojo.net/index.cfm?action=news. display_article&mode=p&NewsID=5859.
6. Noel Castellanos, "We Can't Ignore Our Immigrant Neighbors", God's Politics blog, Feb. 2, 2007.
7. Heather Boushey, "Strengthening the Middle Class: Ensuring Equal Pay for Women", testimony before the House Committee on Education and Labor, April 24, 2007, http://www.cepr.net/index.php?option=com_content&task= view&id=1145&Itemid=193.
8. Elizabeth Palmberg, "Teach a Woman to Fish…", *Sojourners,* June 2005, 29–34.
9. "Beijing Declaration", Beijing, China, Sept. 1995, http://www.un.org/women watch/daw/beijing/beijingdeclaration.html.
10. Beijing Declaration and Platform for Action, http://www.un.org/esa/gopher-data/ conf/fwcw/off/a-20.en.
11. Palmberg, "Teach a Woman to Fish…," p. 31, 32.
12. Grameen Bank, http://www.grameen-info.org/bank/index.html.
13. Neela Banerjee, "Clergywomen Find Hard Path to Bigger Pulpit", *New York Times,* August 26, 2006.
14. Scott Garber, "The Opposite of Racism", sermon at Washington Community Fellowship.

8. LIFE AND DIGNITY

1. U.S. Conference of Catholic Bishops, *Faithful Citizenship,* 2004, 13.
2. "An Evangelical Declaration Against Torture", 2007, http://www.evangelicalsfor humanrights.org/pb/wp_abaf1d69/wp_abaf1d69.html?0.06002779595197 2496.
3. Naomi Wolf, "Our Bodies, Our Souls", *The New Republic,* Oct. 16, 1995.
4. http://clinton.senate.gov/news/statements/details.cfm?id=233748&&.
5. Chris Gacek, "Court Ruling Hints at New Abortion Stance", *The Politico,* July 19, 2007, http://www.politico.com/news/stories/0707/5021.html.
6. "Democrats in Congress Pass Abortion Reduction Initiative", http://www.house.gov/delauro/press/2007/July/Labor_HHS_07_19_07.html.
7. Stephanie Simon, "Democrats Shift Approach on Abortion", *Los Angeles Times,* July 26, 2007.

8. "State of the World, According to John Paul II" (2005), http://www.zenit.org/article–11941?l=english.
9. James Carroll, "The Pope's True Revolution", *Time,* April 3, 2005.
10. David Batstone, *Not for Sale* (HarperSan Francisco, 2007), 1.
11. "President Bush Addresses United Nations General Assembly", Sept. 19, 2006, http://www.whitehouse.gov/news/releases/2006/09/20060919–4.html.
12. Jasper Mortimer, "Experts See Arabs Taking Sudan Position", Associated Press/ *Washington Post,* Oct. 4, 2006.
13. Transcript of press conference by Secretary-General Kofi Annan, United Nations Headquarters, Dec. 19, 2006, http://www.un.org/News/Press/docs/2006/sgsm10809.doc.htm.
14. "An Evangelical Declaration Against Torture", http://www.evangelicalsforhumanrights.org/pb/wp_abaf1d69/wp_abaf1d69.html?0.060027795951972496.
15. Cardinal Theodore McCarrick, USCCB press conference, March 21, 2005, http://www.usccb.org/sdwp/national/deathpenalty/mccarrick.shtml.
16. Death Penalty Information Center, "Executions by Year", http://www.death penalty-info.org/article.php?scid=8&did=146.
17. http://www.usccb.org/sdwp/national/deathpenalty/launchinfo.shtml.
18. Bud Welch, USCCB press conference, March 21, 2005, http://www.usccb.org/sdwp/national/deathpenalty/welch.shtml.
19. www.jesuit.org.
20. Transcript of the Archbishop of Canterbury's interview on BBC Radio 4's *Today* programme, Dec. 29, 2006, http://www.archbishopofcanterbury.org/releases/061229.htm.
21. Helen Prejean, "The Greatest Indignity of All", God's Politics blog, Jan. 25, 2007.
22. Renato Martino, Interview with *La Republica,* December 28, 2006.
23. Alan Cooperman, "Second New Leader Resigns from the Christian Coalition", *Washington Post,* November 29, 2006.

9. FAMILY AND COMMUNITY

1. Danny and Polly Duncan Collum, "Taking Back Our Kids", *Sojourners,* Jan. 2006, 12–19.
2. Diana Butler Bass, "Sin is Neither Republican nor Democratic", God's Politics blog, Oct. 3, 2006.

10. NONVIOLENT REALISM

1. Rich Nathan, "Evangelical Engagement – Promise and Pitfalls", God's Politics blog, Nov. 7, 2006.
2. Celeste Zappala, "A Mother's Cry for Peace", God's Politics blog, March 20, 2007.

3. Raphael G. Warnock, "To Redeem the Soul of America", address given at the National Cathedral, March 16, 2007, http://www.bpfna.org/cpwi_warnock.
4. "Trends in Global Terrorism", National Intelligence Estimate, www. dni.gov/ press_releases/declassified_NIE_key_judgments.pdf.
5. "The Terrorist Threat to the US Homeland", National Intelligence Estimate, www. dni.gov/press_releases/20070717_release.pdf.
6. Jonathan Weisman, "House GOP Leaders Fight Wiretapping Limits", *Washington Post,* Sept. 13, 2006.
7. Rich Lowry, "The 'W' Is Not for 'Wobble'", *National Review,* Sept. 13, 2006.
8. Peter Baker, "Bush Tells Group He Sees a 'Third Awakening'", *Washington Post,* Sept. 13, 2006.
9. President's Address to the Nation, Sept. 11, 2006, http://www.whitehouse.gov/ news/releases/2006/09/20060911-3.html.
10. Lowry, "The 'W' Is Not for 'Wobble'".
11. Gordon Brown, speech given at the Confederation of Indian Industry, Bangalore, Jan. 17, 2007, http://www.hm-treasury.gov.uk/newsroom_and_speeches/press/ 2007/press_06_07.cfm.
12. Gordon Brown, acceptance speech to Labour Party, June 24, 2007, http://www.labour.org.uk/leadership/gordon_brown_s_leader_of_the_labour _party.
13. Tony Blair, speech to the World Economic Forum, Jan. 27, 2007, http://www.weforum.org/pdf/A.M._2007/blair.pdf.
14. Kofi A. Annan, "What I've Learned", *Washington Post,* Dec. 11, 2006.
15. See Glen Stassen, *Just Peacemaking* (Pilgrim Press, 1998) and Walter Wink, *The Powers That Be* (Doubleday/Galilee, 1998).
16. David Cortright, *Building Peace,* in press; used with permission.
17. Gerald Schlabach, *Just Policing, Not War* (Liturgical Press, 2007).
18. Aleksandr Solzhenitsyn, *The Gulag Archipelago* (1973).
19. http://jmm.aaa.net.au/articles/13389.htm.
20. Robert Wright, "An Easter Sermon", *New York Times,* April 7, 2007

II. INTEGRITY AND ACCOUNTABILITY

1. Associated Press, *Sydney Morning Herald,* "Dictionary Reveals Most Looked-Up Words", December 11, 2005.
2. Amy Fagan and Ralph Z. Hallow, "Conservatives Fear Scandals Impact On 'Value Voters'", *Washington Times,* October 4, 2006.
3. Diana Butler Bass, "Sin is Neither Republican nor Democratic", God's Politics blog, Oct. 3, 2006.
4. Ted Haggard, letter to New Life Church, Nov. 5, 2006, www.newlifechurch.org/ TedHaggardStatement.pdf.
5. Wesley Granberg-Michaelson, *Leadership from Inside Out* (Crossroad, 2004), 13–14.

6. Robert Parham, "Sex Scandals Rock Republicans, Washington Elites", *Ethics Daily,* May 2, 2007, http://www.ethicsdaily.com/article_detail.cfm?AID=8864; Richard J. Foster, *Money, Sex and Power: The Challenge of the Disciplined Life* (Harper & Row, 1985).

12. WHAT'S ACCEPTABLE, WHAT'S POSSIBLE

1. Desmond Tutu, *An African Prayer Book* (Doubleday, 1995).
2. Thomas Merton, *No Man is an Island* (Harcourt, Brace, 1995); Merton, *Contemplation in a World of Action* (Doubleday, 1971).
3. Nelson Mandela, speech given at his inauguration as president of the Democratic Republic of South Africa, May 10, 1994, http://www.anc.org.za/ancdocs/ speeches/inaugpta.html.

Epilogue: RED LETTER CHRISTIANS AND JUSTICE REVIVALS

1. "Red Letter Christians" includes: Randall Balmer, David Batstone, Michael Battle, Diana Butler Bass, Tony Campolo, Noel Castellanos, Shane Claiborne, Chap Clark, Rev. Robert Michael Franklin Jr., Dr. Frederick D. Haynes III, Obery Hendricks, Rev. Tony Jones, Alexia Kelley, Brian McLaren, Fr. Richard Rohr, Rev. Dr. Cheryl J. Sanders, Dr. Ron Sider, Adam Taylor, Barbara Brown Taylor, and Rev. Romal J. Tune
2. Alan Cooperman, "Evangelicals at a Crossroads as Falwell's Generation Fades", *Washington Post,* May 22, 2007.
3. Michael Luo and Laurie Goodstein, "Emphasis Shifts for New Breed of Evangelicals", *New York Times,* May 21, 2007.
4. David Kuo, "Jerry Falwell's Mixed Legacy", J-Walking blog, May 15, 2007.

INDEX